IMAGES
of America

ASSYRIANS OF NEW BRITAIN

On the cover: Please see page 92. (Courtesy of Doris Jones.)

IMAGES
of America

ASSYRIANS OF NEW BRITAIN

Maegan BetGivargis-McDaniel

ARCADIA
PUBLISHING

ISBN 978-0-7385-5012-1

Published by Arcadia Publishing
Charleston SC, Chicago IL, Portsmouth NH, San Francisco CA

Printed in the United States of America

Library of Congress Catalog Card Number: 2007922814

For all general information contact Arcadia Publishing at:
Telephone 843-853-2070
Fax 843-853-0044
E-mail sales@arcadiapublishing.com
For customer service and orders:
Toll-Free 1-888-313-2665

Visit us on the Internet at www.arcadiapublishing.com

To all individuals who make an effort to ensure that their history is well preserved and will continue to thrive and to the first member of my family to come to Connecticut, Abraham Zaya George. You are missed and cherished by us all.

Contents

ACKNOWLEDGMENTS

A large number of people have helped me throughout the process of researching and documenting for this book. First off, I would like to thank my grandmother Florence BetIshoo because of her endless help in contacting people and assistance in gathering photographs.

Thank you to Lucy Abraham, Bob Badal, Amy Badal, Margaret Capsalaros, Jane Carroll, John Eshia, Marsha Gallo, Margaret Hecht, Doris Jones, Agnes Sargis, Sam Sargis, the New Britain Public Library, and South Church of New Britain for providing me with the information and photographs needed for this book. Special thanks to my editor, Dawn Robertson, who helped guide me through the process by regularly checking up on me and being available to answer all of my questions. Thank you to Sargon and Ninos Donabed for showing me that this could be done; also, thank you to Sargon for checking up on and assisting me when I was having trouble with the documenting process.

Endless thanks to Helen BetGivargis, Akadeena BetGivargis-McDaniel, Benjamin BetGivargis-McDaniel, Sharokin Betgevargiz, and Michael McDaniel for keeping me organized and assisting in compiling my endless amounts of research. I have so much gratitude for Michael Sotak, for his unwavering support and love and for taking the time to read over what I had written.

Much thanks to the BetGivargis, George, and BetGeorge family, especially the cousins, Bianca, Monica, Ladimer, Rumsin, Jason, Alex, Max, Gabby, Hailey, and Olivia, most of whom were fellow Assyrian Kids Club members and have held on to their Assyrian heritage enough to ensure that Connecticut will continue to have a vibrant and lasting Assyrian community.

Although most of my information came from New Britain Assyrians, a good amount of the history also came from books and internet sites. Works such as the *One Hundredth Anniversary Booklet* put out by South Church of New Britain in 1942, Yonatan Bet Soleiman's newspaper *Atour*, Thea Halo's memoir *Not Even My Name*, the Assyrian International News Agency, and a number of local history Web sites provided me with the facts that helped me piece together my information about New Britain and Assyrians.

INTRODUCTION

Assyrians are the indigenous people of Iraq, more specifically the locations between the Northern Mesopotamia and Turkey, until the Euphrates River in Syria and as far east as Lake Urmi in Iran. The land between these four countries was known as Assyria, and the history of these ancient people reaches back over 5,000 years ago.

Two rivers, which this civilization relied on for the ongoing life of the Fertile Crescent, run through Assyria, the Tigris and the Euphrates. Surrounding the Tigris are the Assyrian cities of Nineveh, Ashur, and Nimrod.

Assyrians have spoken two languages throughout the course of their history, the first being ancient Assyrian, known as Akkadian, and the second being modern Assyrian, now known as Neo-Syriac. The ancient Assyrian language was used until about 750 B.C.E. Aramaic came into play during the time that the Akkadian language was fading, though many Aramaic words were derived from the latter; it was some time before the language that is spoken now, Neo-Syriac, was fully developed.

Throughout history Assyrians have been known to practice two religions; the religion of Ashur, Ashurism, and Christianity. Ashurism is the first religion believed by Assyrians, and it was practiced until 256 C.E.; the term Assyrian is derived from the word Ashur, who was the god that was worshipped by Assyrians. The first nation to begin practicing Christianity was that of the Assyrians, the Assyrian church was established in 33 C.E.

Over the past century, much of Assyrian history has stood on the brink of extinction, with repeated massacres and the constant threat of assimilation. A number of massacres occurred in the early 1900s, but between 1915 and 1923 is still remembered as one of the worst Assyrian massacres to this day; the Assyrian patriarch was brutally murdered and it is written that 1.5 million Armenians, 750,000 Assyrians, and 353,000 Pontic Greeks were killed in this time. The second widely known massacre occurred in 1933 and is known as the Simele massacre due to its location in the Simele area of northern Iraq. Due to false reports of Assyrians in northern Iraq attacking soldiers, the Iraqi government sent soldiers to quell what they feared could be the gathering of armed forces. This government led action ended in massacres, which lasted only a number of days, but because of Iraqi soldiers being on edge from false reports, they ended up attacking over 60 Assyrian villages resulting in the deaths of 3,000 Assyrian men, women, and children.

Though Assyrians are largely from the areas surrounding northern Iraq, the vast majority of the ones that came to the United States in the early 20th century were from Iran. It is because of the missions created in Iran that many Assyrians were able to provide education for their children. The individuals that took advantage of what the missions had to offer in terms of education and church services were largely the Assyrian, being as they are one of the larger groups of Christians in Iran.

Since the massacres, Assyrians have faced constant challenges with further religious intolerance within Iraq, Iran, and neighboring countries, sometimes resulting in the loss of jobs and at other times leading to the loss of their lives. They have also faced the same hardships that all Iraqi people have gone through with the Gulf War, ongoing sanctions of the 1990s, and the current United States war in Iraq. The Assyrian populations of Iraq, Iran, and neighboring Middle Eastern countries is diminishing with the constant stream of immigrants trying to find refuge from war and religious intolerance in the United States and Canada.

Currently New Britain has a number of attractions that draw visitors and locals to in see them. It has the New Britain Public Library, the New Britain Museum of American Art, and the New Britain Youth Museum among other educational attractions. It plays host to the large numbers of students that attend Central Connecticut State University, as well as sports fans that come to watch baseball played by the New Britain Rock Cats.

New Britain had its earliest settlers in 1687 and officially became a township in 1850, though it became a city soon afterwards in 1871. A number of factories were centered in New Britain, so it became known for the role it played in created hardware. Stanley Works was one of the factories.

The history of the wire coat hanger relies on New Britain as well; it was invented by a New Britain native in the year 1869.

The majority of New Britain Assyrians came from one of these three villages: Goytapa, Tek Ardishai, and Babari. And in the early years of Assyrians being in New Britain, people of these three villages held fund-raisers to send aid to women and children in their home villages in times of war.

A number of businesses have been owned by Assyrian individuals and households since their arrival in 1905. A few of these businesses are the Arch Street Deli, Jones Jewelers, Benjamin Brothers photography, Sargis Plumbing, Hudson Fur Shop, a grocery store, a candy store, and a number of stock brokers and realtors throughout New Britain.

According to the 2005 census, the population of New Britain is comprised of about 73,000 individuals. Of that population, Assyrians make up about 250 New Britain households.

One

The Beginning

The South Church of New Britain was established in 1847, and since the early 20th century it has devoted much time and effort to the cause of immigrants abroad, going so far as to establish an Assyrian mission. It was involved, both locally and abroad, in an Italian mission, and it later became involved in Armenian, Chinese, and German missions.

The South Church of New Britain's first two missions abroad were begun by Ozora Stearns Davis, a biblical scholar who was pastor of the South Church of New Britain until he left to become president of the Chicago Theological Seminary in 1909. The Assyrian mission began forming in the year 1904, when Davis invited the first English-speaking Assyrian settler, Baba Jones, to Connecticut. Jones was an Assyrian citizen from Iran, and he brought 70 Assyrian men with him to the South Church of New Britain service the first Sunday after his arrival in New Britain. Jones acted as interpreter and leader of this group of 70 men, and Daniel Minor Rogers acted as the president of what was soon called the Persian-Assyrian Brotherhood. For the first year that Assyrians were in New Britain, Davis would preach, and Jones would translate the sermons into Assyrian.

It was to aid these men in feeling more at home and gaining self-reliance that Davis organized a night school at the church for them, with eight different instructors. It is because of those 70 men that the brotherhood, later shortened to the Assyrian Brotherhood, thrived; and beginning in 1905, a separate Assyrian service led by an Assyrian pastor was also conducted.

Assyrian women and children were not brought over to New Britain until 1914, 10 years after the first men had arrived. Upon the arrival of families, an Assyrian program was created at the church, with further changes to the brotherhood, a woman's bible study class, young people's groups, and so on. After World War I, hundreds of families and remnants of families immigrated to this country, leading to a drastic increase in the amount of Assyrians attending the South Church of New Britain during that time.

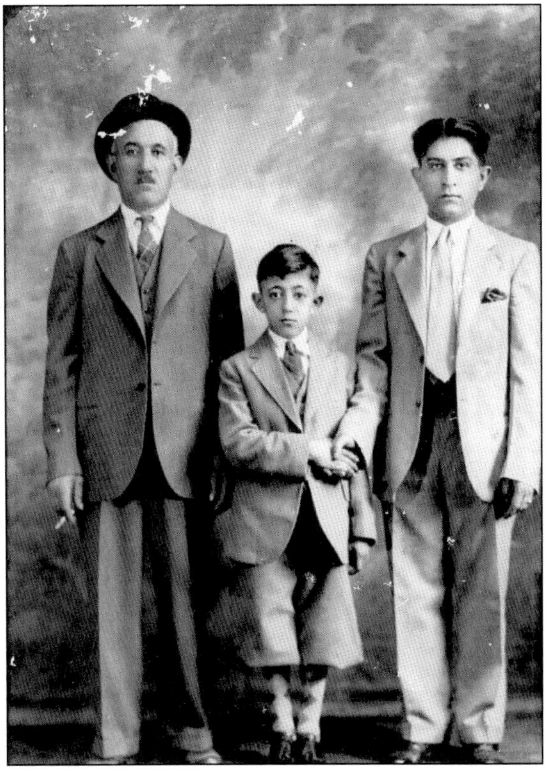

From left to right, John Ishoo, his son Peter, and his cousin Nick are featured in this photograph in 1932. This would be considered a family photograph of the time, and such photographs were taken to send home to Iran or Iraq to show to the rest of the family. (Courtesy of Lucy Abraham.)

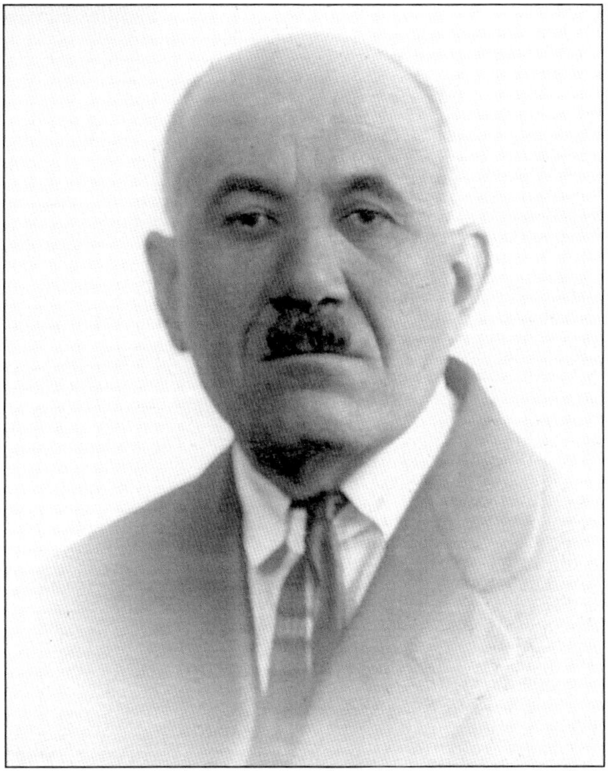

Many New Britain Assyrian families immigrated slowly. Often it was the men who would come to the United States to work and then send home for their families. Here is shown the citizenship photograph of John Ishoo, who moved to the United States after his daughter Dena Ishoo had already moved here.

Rebecca Ishoo, pictured in this citizenship photograph, came to the United States with her husband and two youngest daughters. Her oldest daughter had already come to the United States a number of years prior. This family followed the common trend of immigrants to send individual family members over first to get established and send for other family members later on.

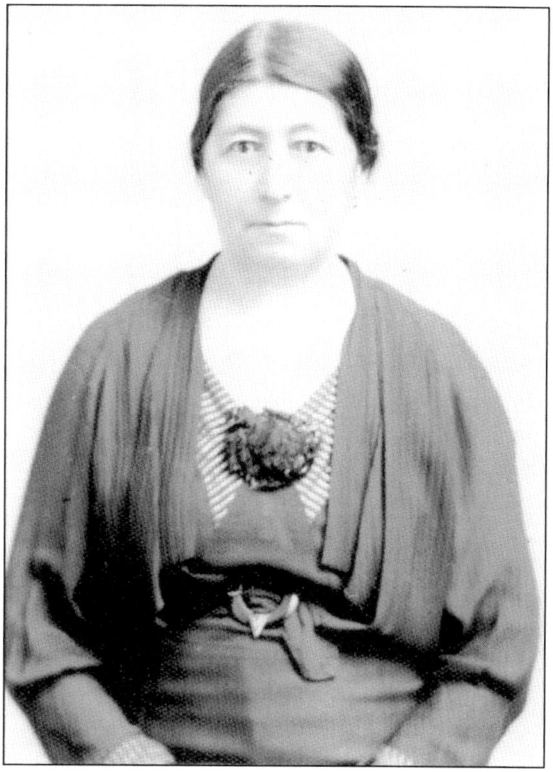

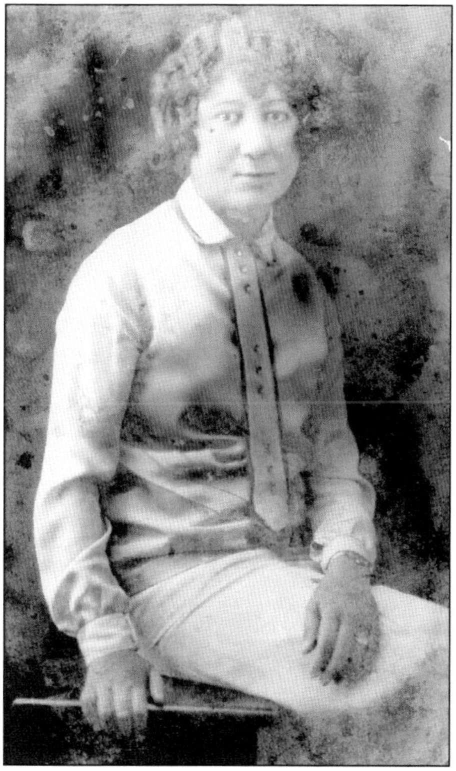

Dena Ishoo came over to the United States in 1922, prior to the rest of her family, and married Joe Alkhas in 1923. This is a photograph taken to send home to show to her immediate and extended family still living in Iran.

In this 1924 photograph stands Dena (Ishoo) Alkhas and her husband, Joe Alkhas, and between them sits his aunt Martha. Assyrians often came to the United States only after establishing family ties and friendships first, making it easier for them to get to know the culture and be around people they were familiar with.

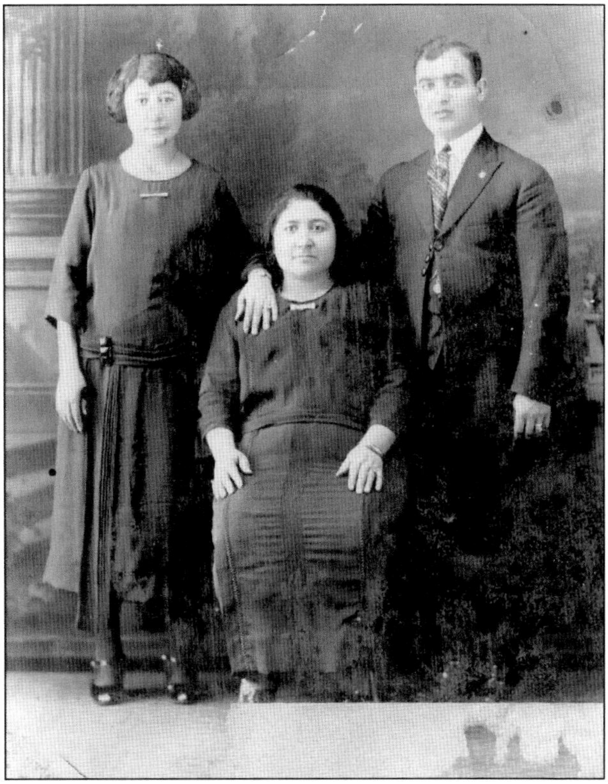

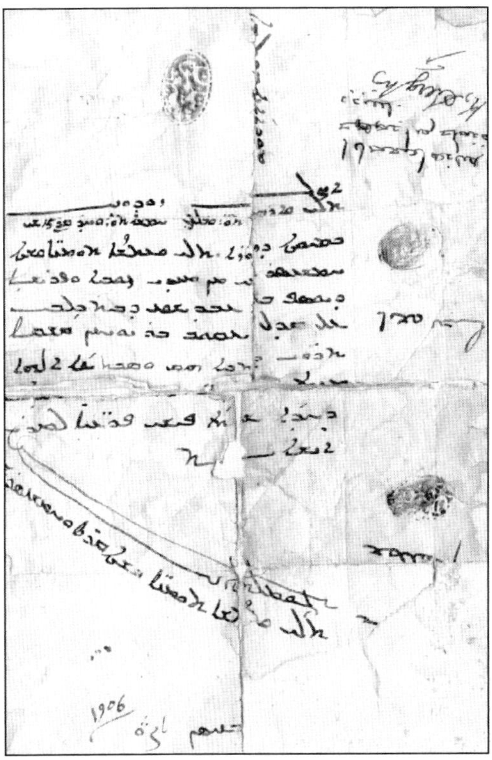

This letter, written in Assyrian, was to family members still living in Iran during the year 1906.

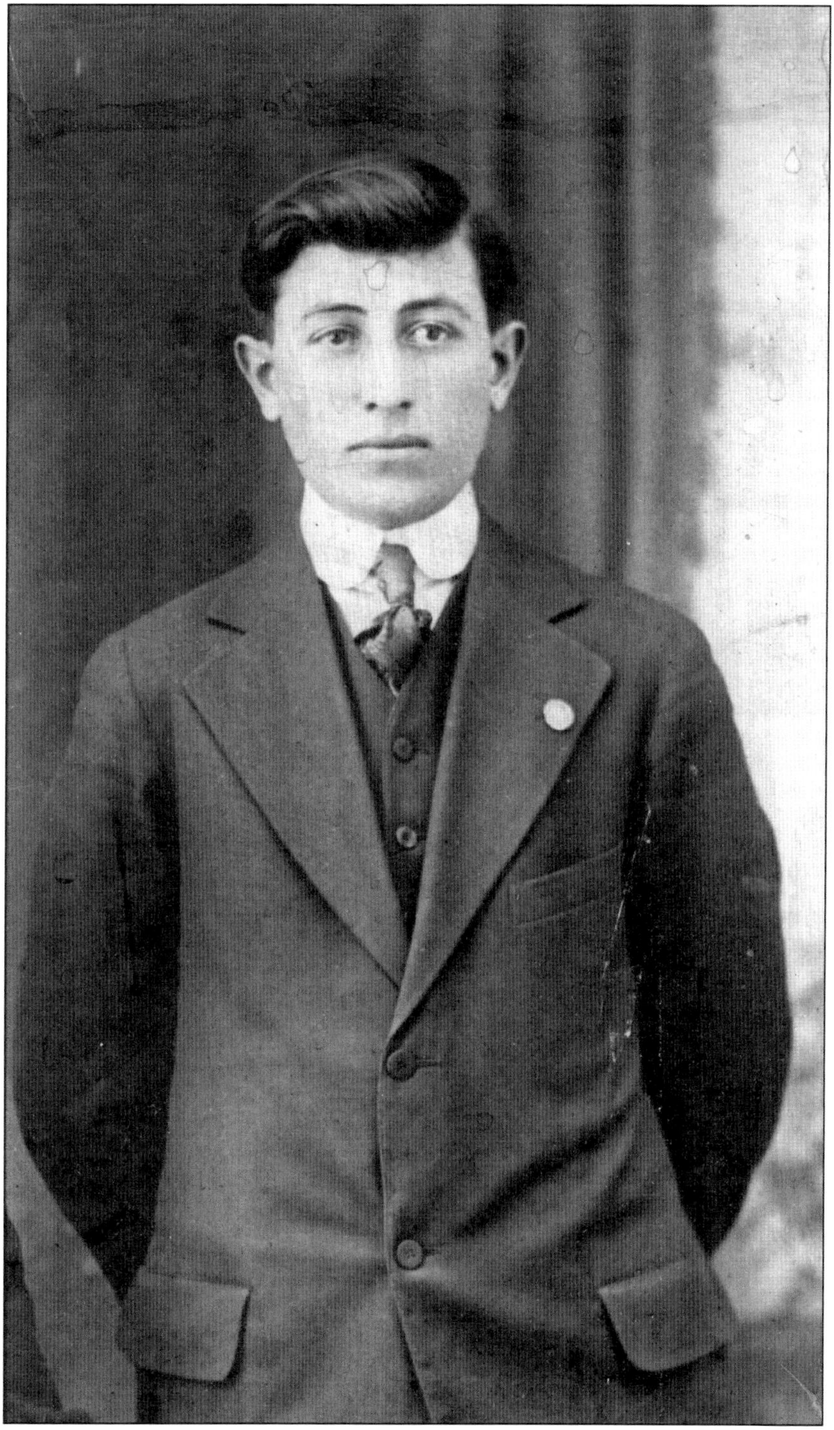

Young Assyrian men often left their homes in Iran around the age of 14 and began their journey to the United States. Upon their arrival in the United States, they would begin to work and establish friendships with other Assyrian locals, soon acquiring enough savings and knowledge of their surroundings to send for their families.

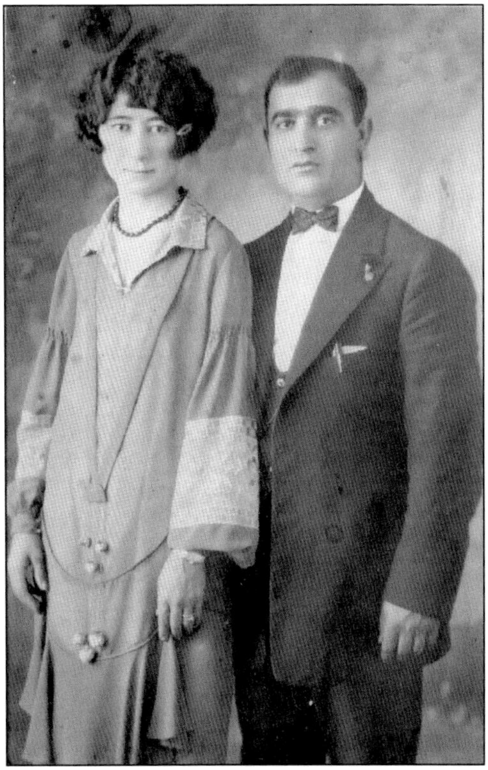

This photograph is of the newly married couple, Deena Ishoo and husband Joe Alkhas. This photograph would be taken with the intention of providing copies of the couple to various family members, both local and those who still resided in Iran.

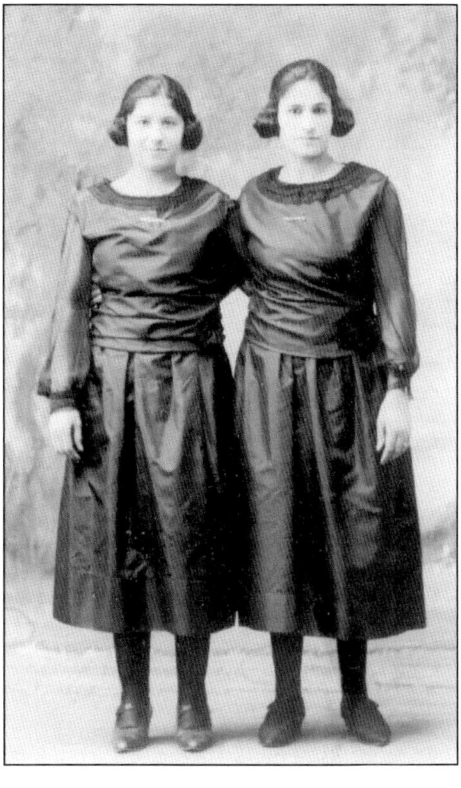

Martha Oshanna stands on the left of this early-20th-century photograph with her sister directly to her right.

Shown here is a professional photograph of a seated gentleman. This photograph was taken in New Britain.

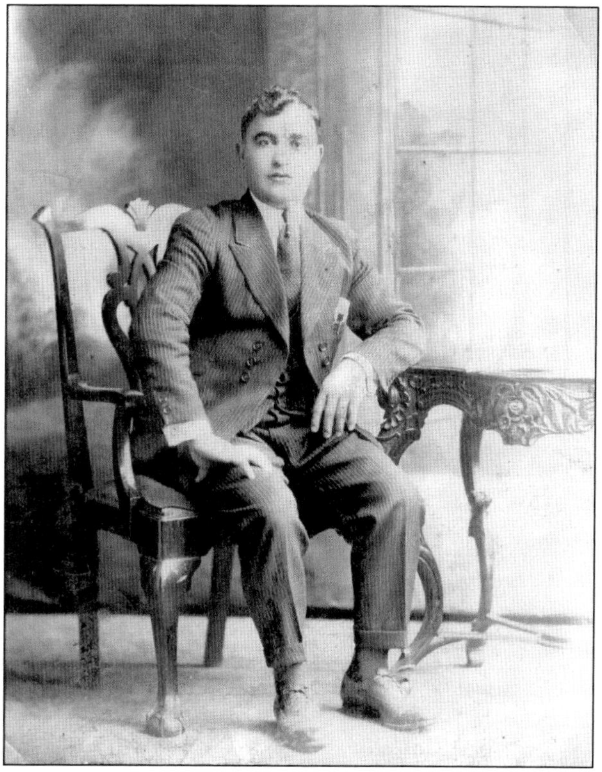

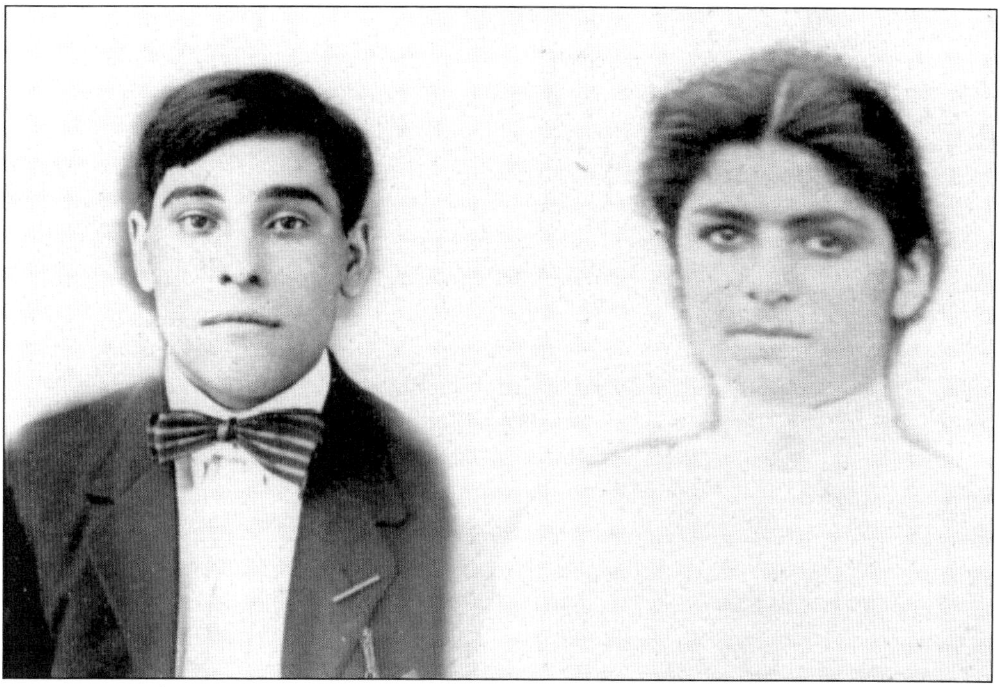

Yonatan BetSolieman, pictured as a young man, came to the United States at the age of 14 and used his love for the Assyrian language and culture to organize groups, a newspaper, and books to ensure that Assyrians continued to have knowledge about their history.

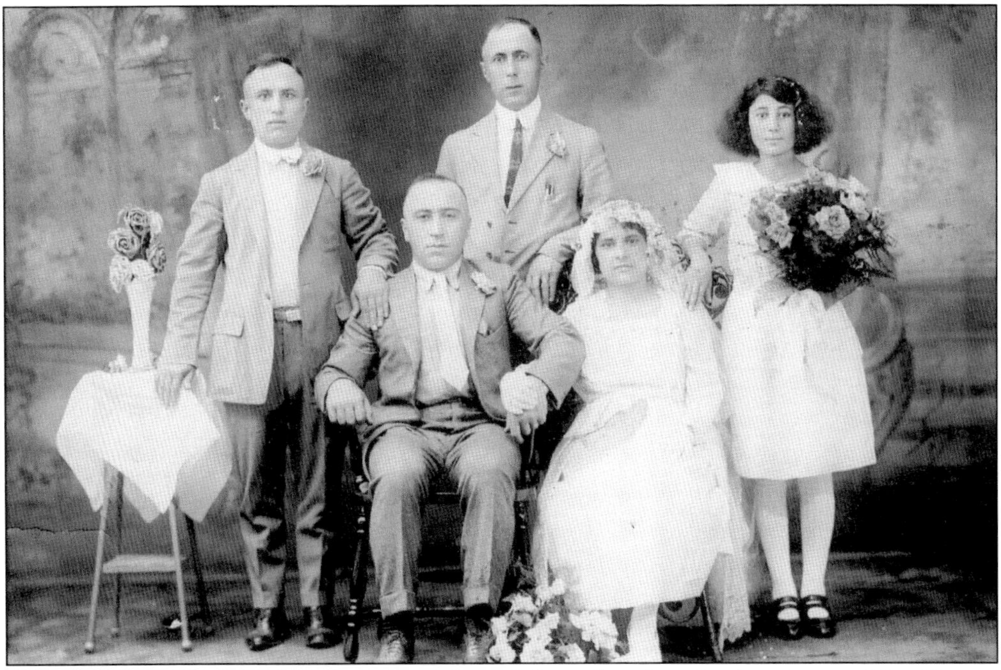

This photograph features a newlywed couple and their close friends. Assyrians in New Britain photographed a number of special occasions and important events on a regular basis, often with a small number of acquaintances. While the name of the married couple is unknown, the individuals in the background, from left to right, are Brahep Alkhas, Sepo Alkhas, and his wife, Dena Alkhas. The photograph was taken in 1922.

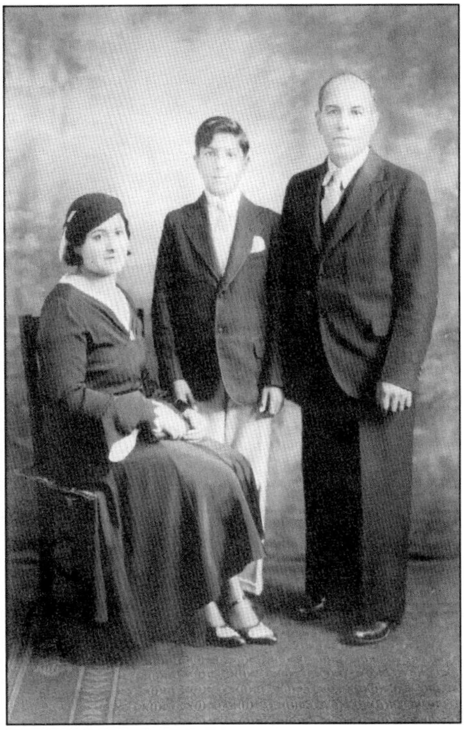

This family portrait was taken in the early 1920s upon the family's recent arrival to the United States with the intention of sending a copy home to Iran.

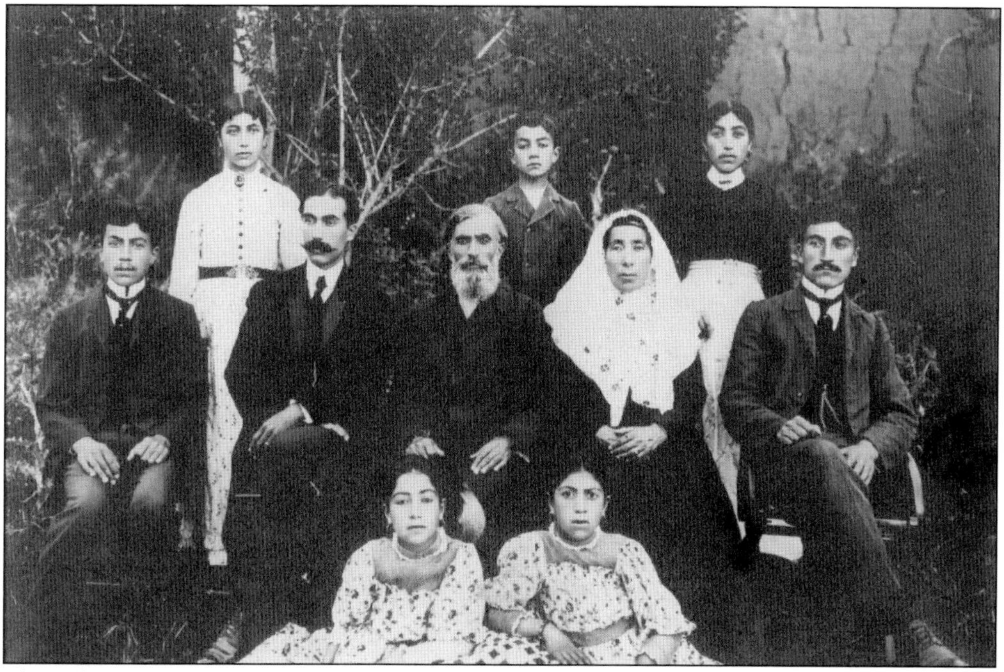

The Yohannan extended family is pictured as follows, from left to right: (first row) Shushan and Shalin; (second row) Issaac, David, Yukhena (Presbeterian minister), Miriam, and Shlemon; (third row) Rachael, Elishua, and Jacob. It was written on the photograph that one cousin, Hannah, was missing because she was married.

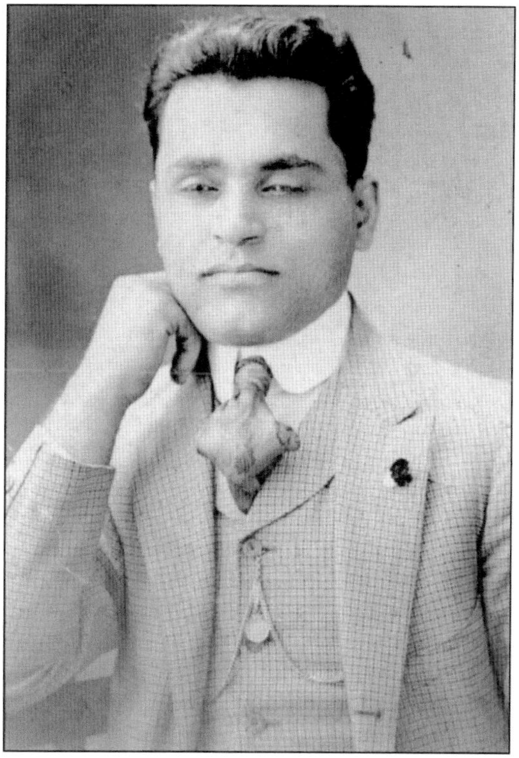

Yosep Niyas was an early New Britain Assyrian settler. He made his living as a musician and played in a number of small bands with other Assyrian-American individuals. (Courtesy of the BetGeorge family collection.)

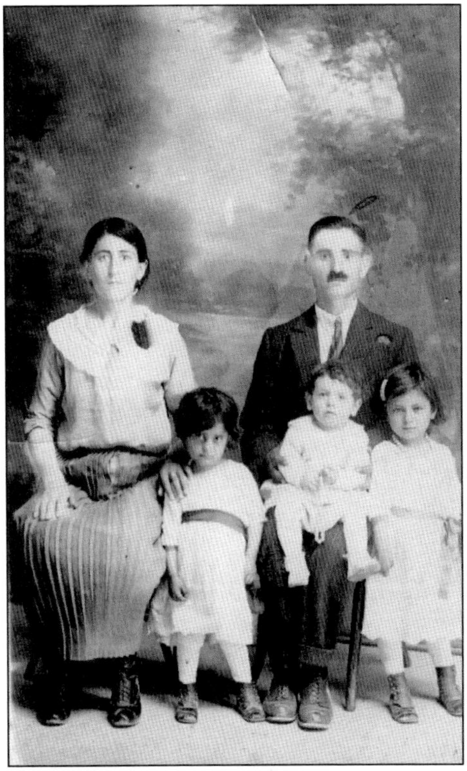

This family posed photograph was taken before they came to the United States, in the early 20th century.

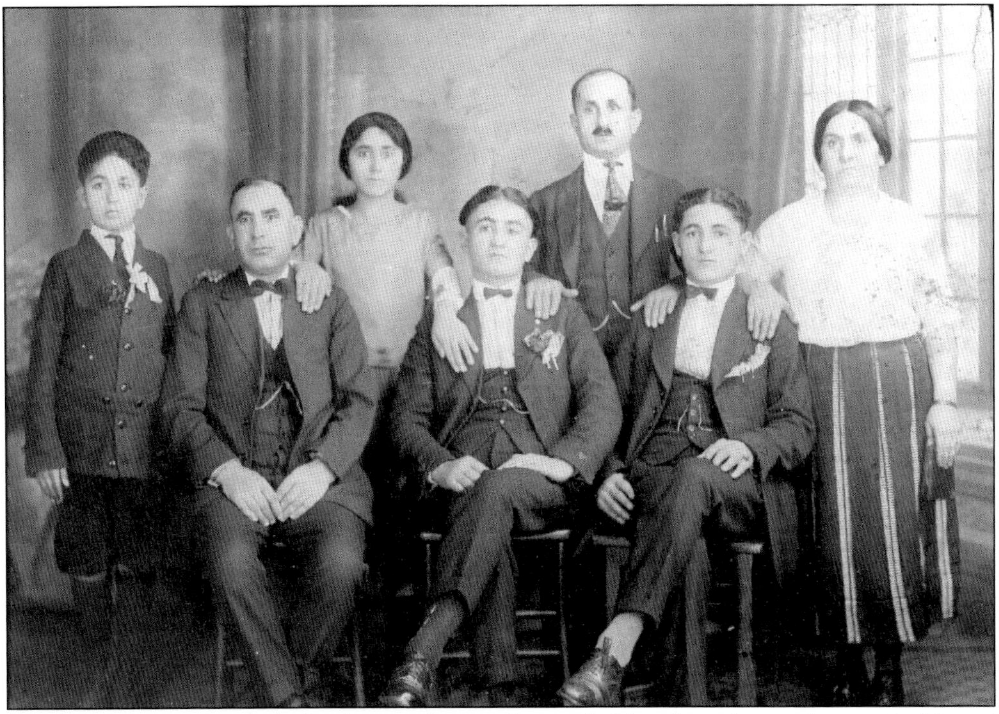

This family portrait includes both immediate and extended family and was taken in the United States. (Courtesy of the Badal family collection.)

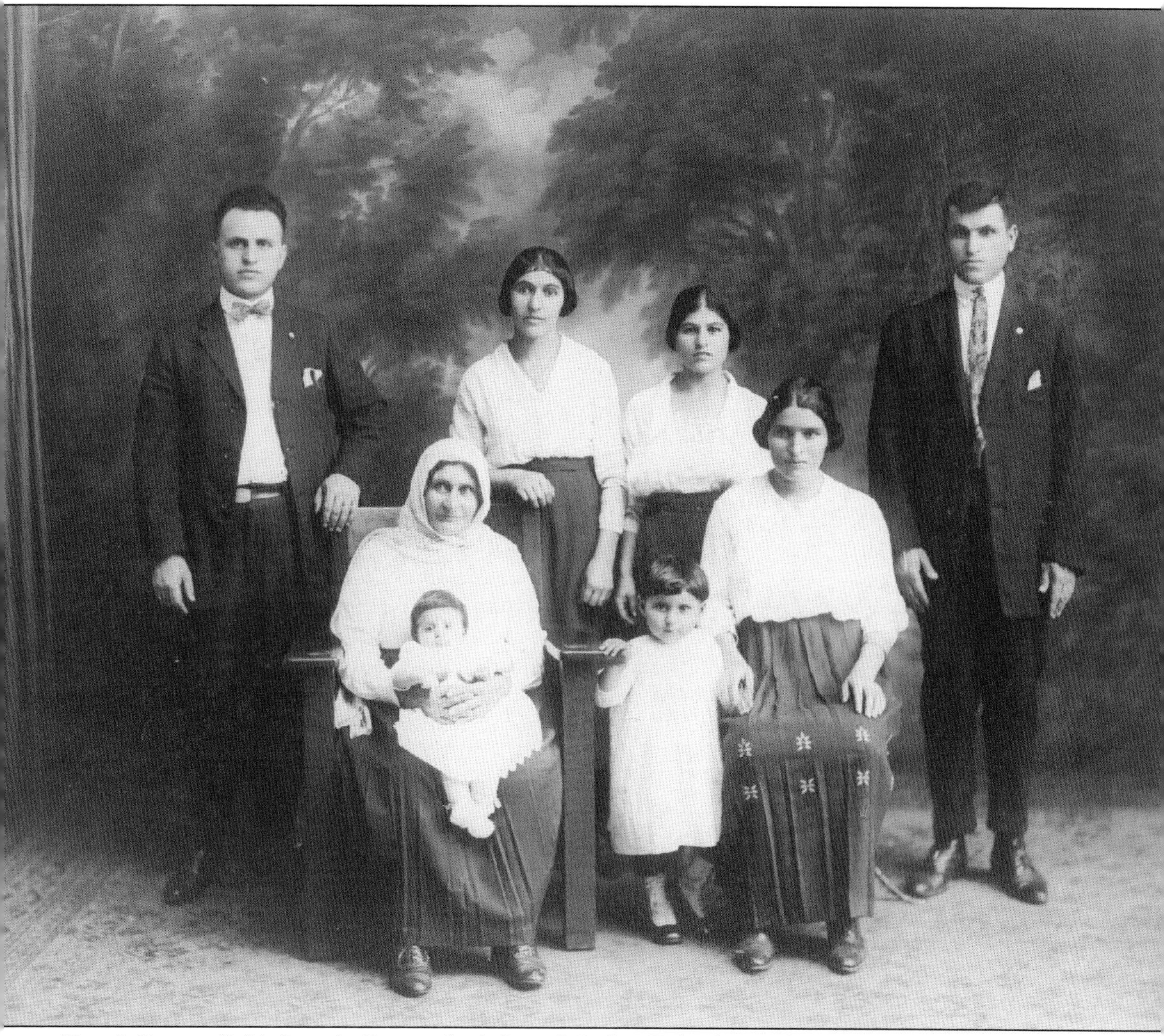

David George (left), Joseph George (right), and Gizbas Baba (second row, second from right), among others, pose for this family photograph taken in the United States.

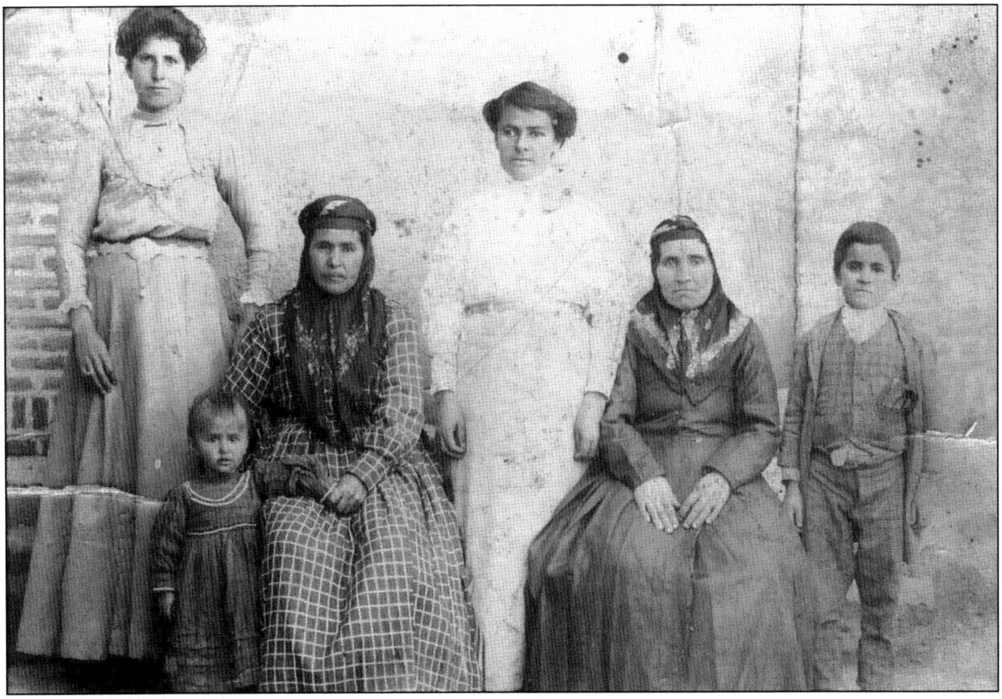

In this family photograph, the people are wearing clothing traditional to their native location. It was taken in Iran prior to the family making the trip to the United States.

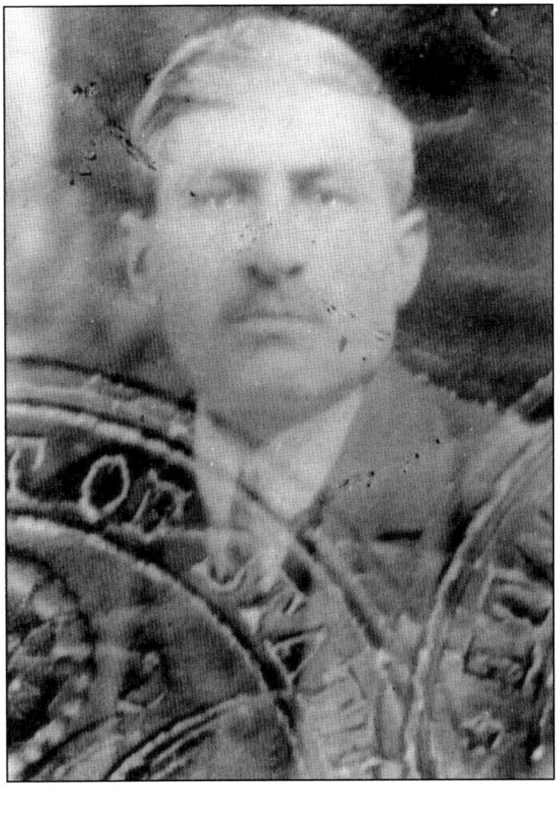

This is a copy of an official passport or naturalization photograph. (Courtesy of the Badal family collection.)

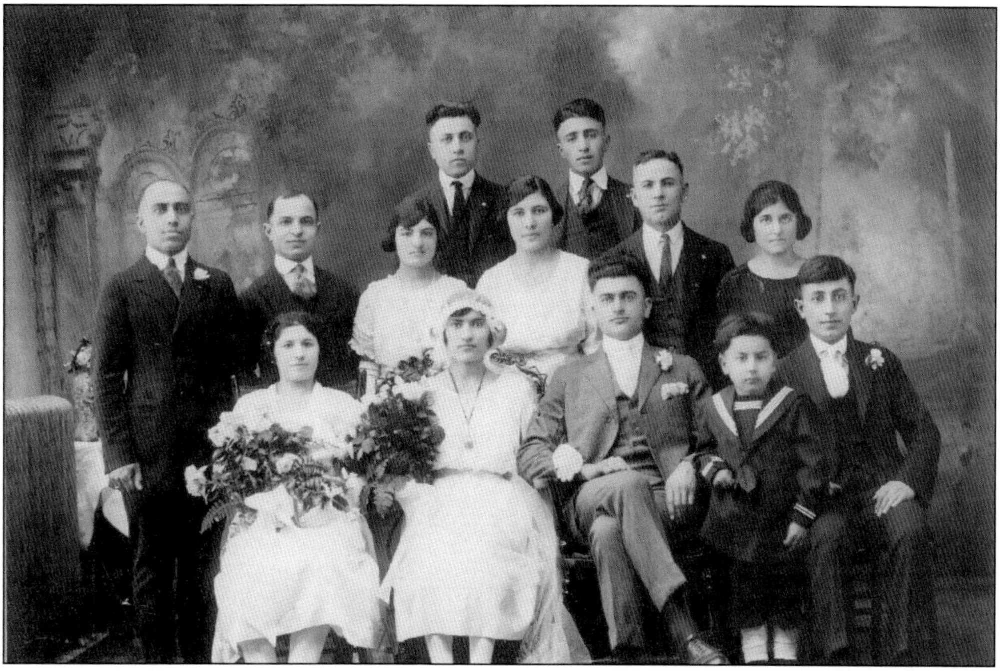

Pius Oshana, Martha Oshana, Avegal Aziz, and George Aziz pose in a wedding photograph. The bride and groom are unidentified.

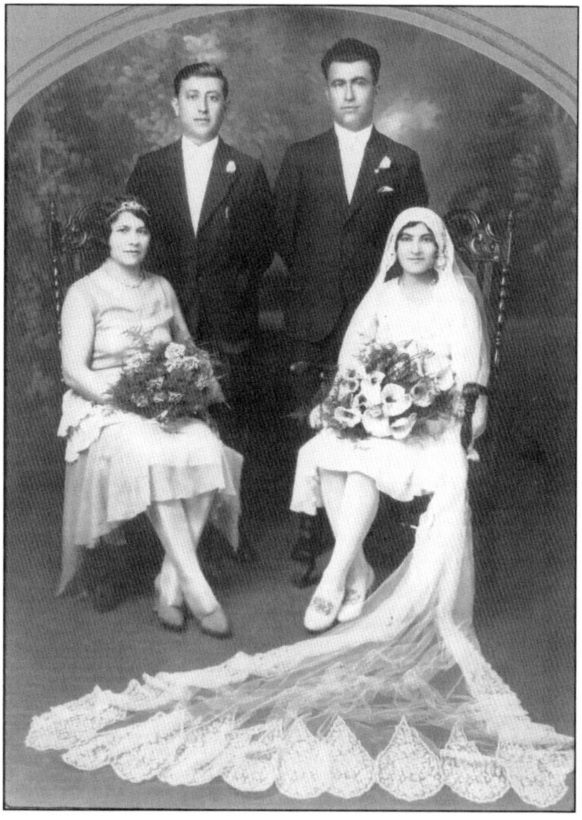

Pius Oshana and Martha Oshana are on the left of the photograph, posed beside the recently married Katharine Benjamin and Paul Aziz.

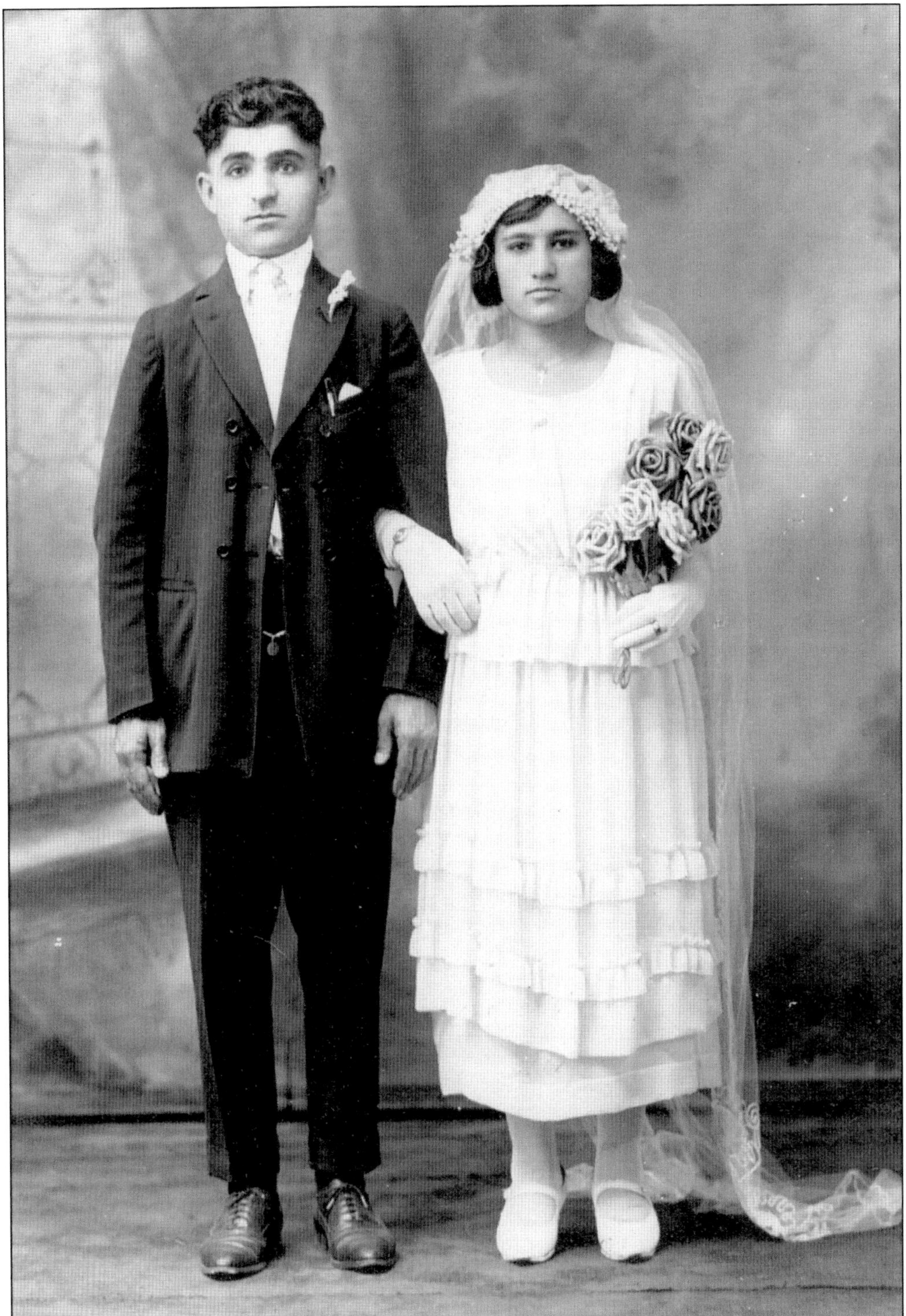

This professional wedding photograph of Rose and Israel Benjamin was taken in the early 20th century in the United States.

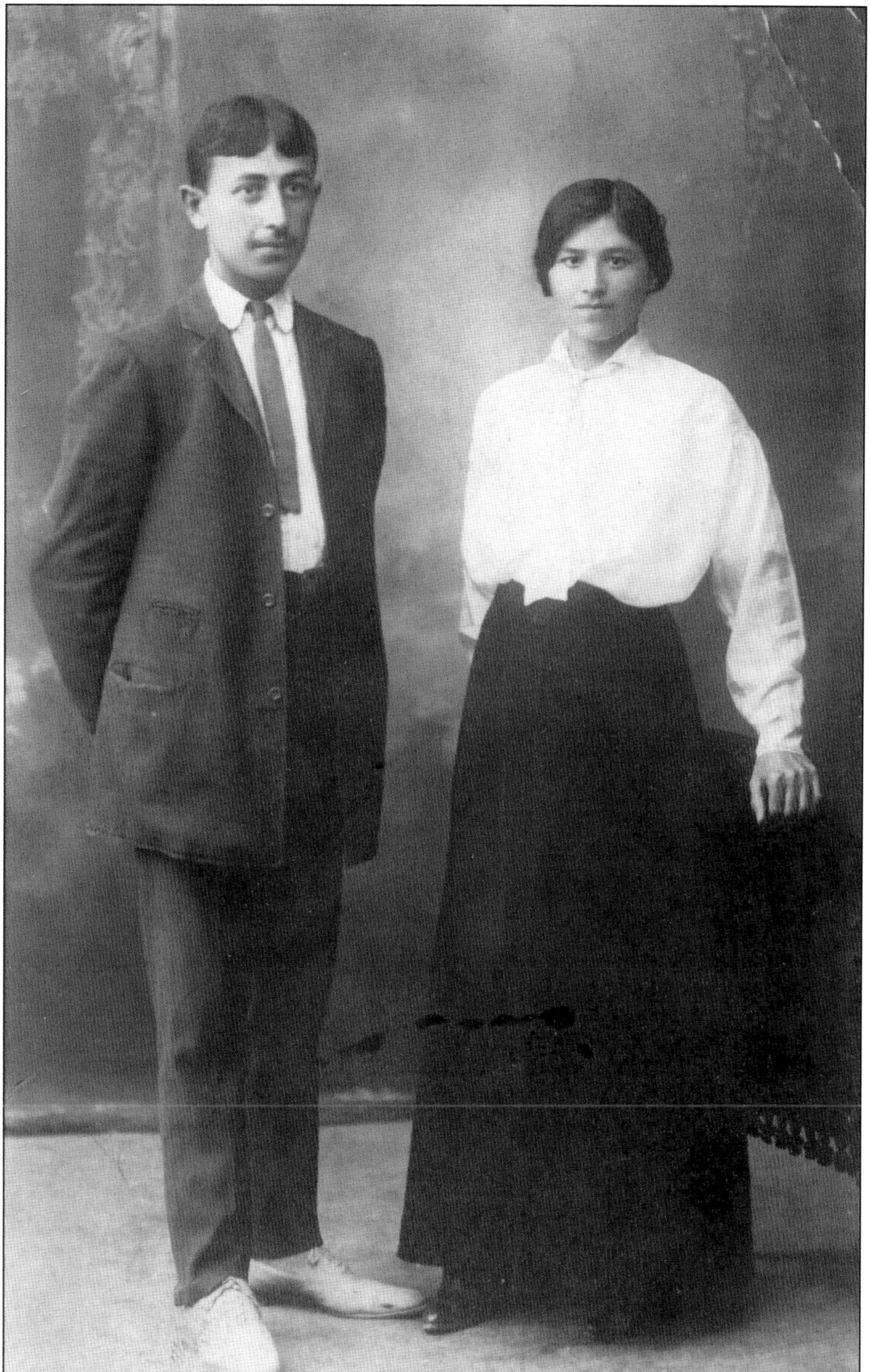

Pius Oshana migrated to the United States in 1916. His wife, Martha Oshana, arrived two years later with their 18-month-old son. This photograph was taken upon Martha's arrival.

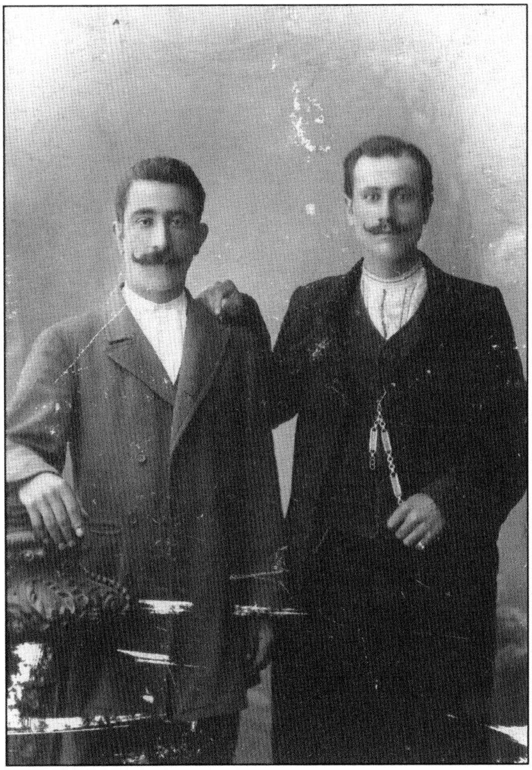

Two gentlemen from the Yohannan family are shown here. Unlike many photographs of that day, which were taken in studios, this casual photograph was taken either to send home to family or as a keepsake.

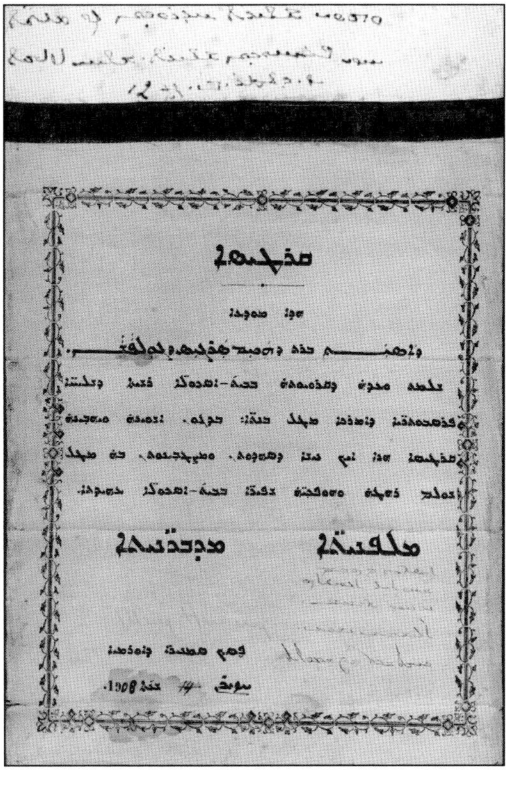

This diploma issued in Iran states that "Asyat, Daughter of Hakim Sargis from Goolpashan successfully completed the required educational studies at the School of the American Presbyterian Missionary for Girls in Urmieh Semenary 6.14.1908."

Two

DAILY LIFE

With the families and further groups of Assyrians packing up their lives in Iran and Iraq and coming to New Britain, the community was seeing rapid growth. St. Mark's Episcopal Church of New Britain was being used by the congregation of St. Thomas Church of the East for their Assyrian service and other events. The original community of Assyrians at South Church of New Britain was still going strong with new individuals arriving from Iran every year. The Assyrian National Association had been created in 1915 by a group of New Britain Assyrians and had elected officials and held annual conventions. Assyrians were beginning to move from New Britain to other locations throughout the United States, though more were coming from Iran to join relatives and acquaintances.

Assyrians originally held picnics and other such outdoor events at a number of locations within Connecticut, one location being on Farmington Avenue in New Britain; on the property that is now Pulaski Middle School. Other locations were Batterson Park, Walnut Hill Park, and a number of parks in nearby towns.

One major event that is still remembered of the history of New Britain Assyrians is the April 1926 visit of Surme MarShumun, sister of the recently killed Assyrian Patriarch. Her visit was written about in local Assyrian newspapers as being comparable to the visit of a queen. A banquet was held for her and she greeted all that had come to see her in both Assyrian and English. The first thing she spoke about was her visit with Pres. Calvin Coolidge, whom she had met with in Washington, D.C., prior to coming to Connecticut.

Fairview Cemetery in New Britain has a separate section in which the graves of Assyrians can be found to this day. Assyrians used Fairview Cemetery prior to the establishment of the current cemetery owned and operated by St. Thomas Church of the East.

Many job opportunities presented themselves to Assyrian immigrants upon arriving to the United States, as there were a number of factories in downtown New Britain that employed them. Some Assyrians continuously worked at the factories while others used the money made at the factories towards opening their own businesses.

New Britain also served as a starting point for many Assyrians; they would establish their livelihood in Connecticut and after becoming acquainted enough with America, they would move to a new location, often to Turlock, California.

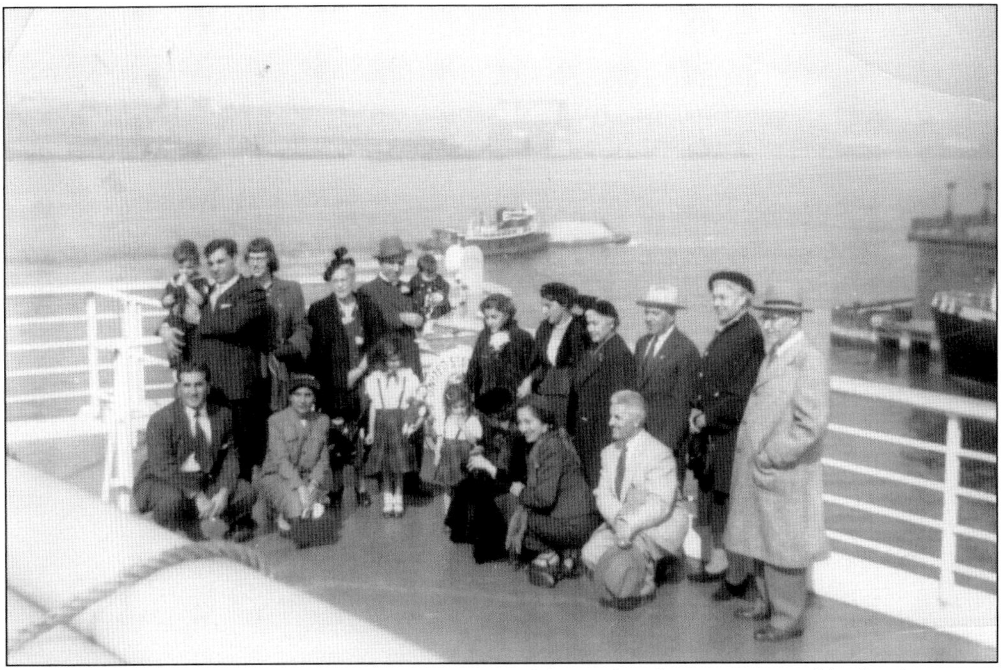

Day trips were not limited simply to Connecticut. Often a family or group would take short trips to nearby cities, which is the case in this photograph of a trip to New York City, where a group of adults and children pose aboard a ship.

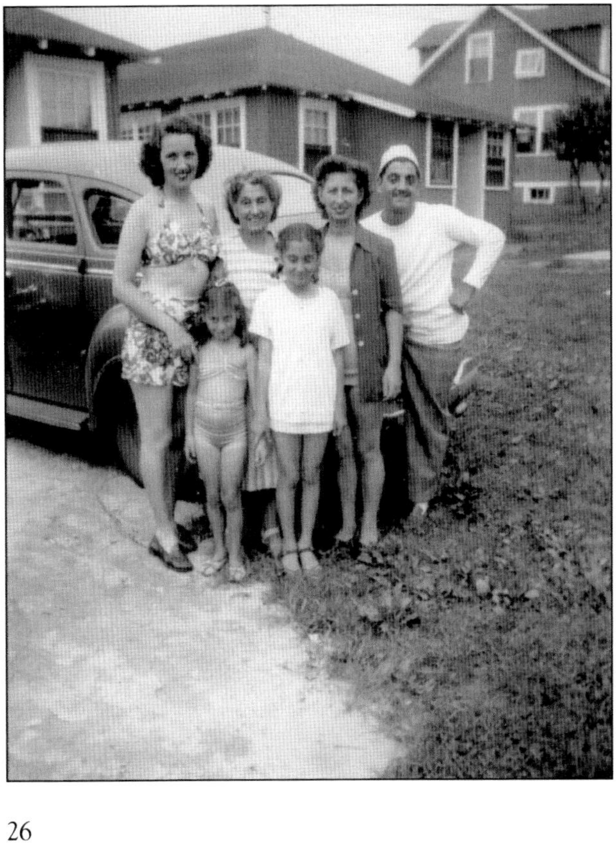

An Assyrian family is shown here during a trip to Sound View, where they would spend weekend and day trips. (Courtesy of the Badal family collection.)

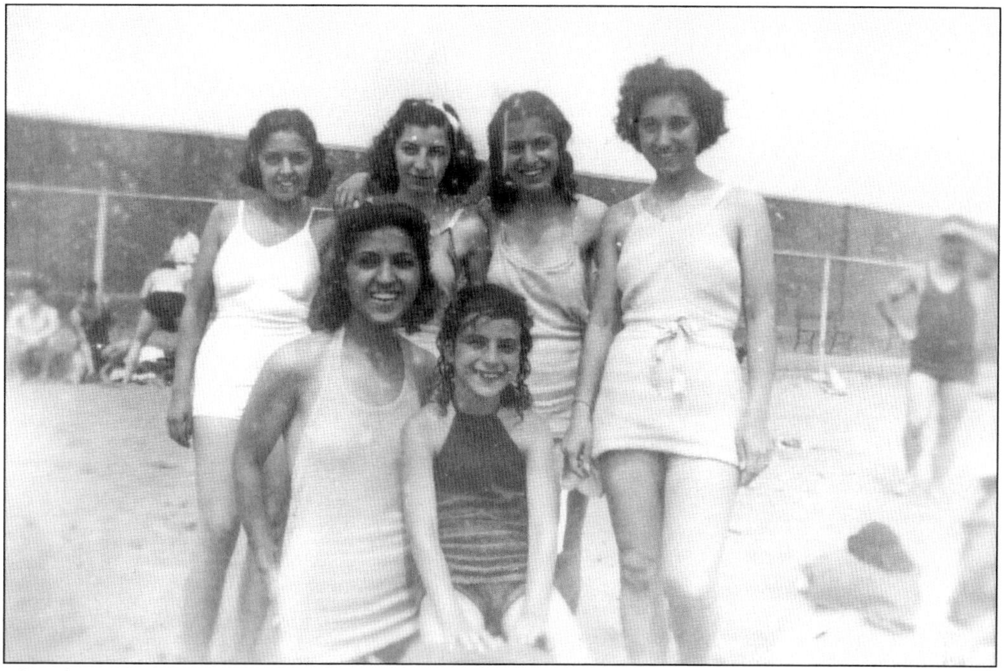

The shores of Connecticut and neighboring New England beaches were another location in which Assyrian families and groups of young people would go for day trips. In this photograph are a group of women on the beach, Mary Moses and Doris Jones among them.

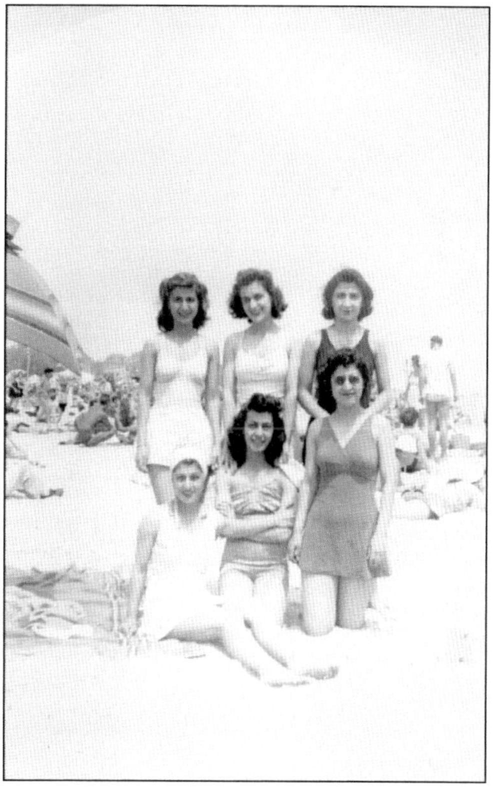

Hot summer days provided good reason to escape to the shore. In this beach photograph, from left to right, Rose Ernesto, Gladys Dooman, and Mary Bayram are seated amidst other young woman who were also New Britain locals.

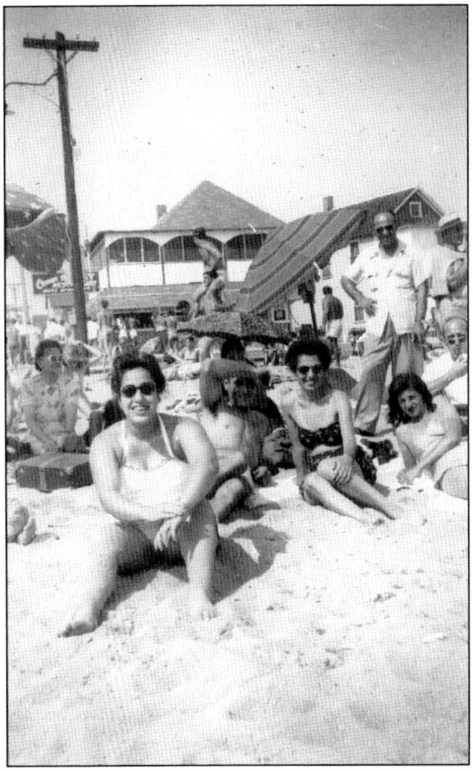

Most New Britain Assyrians migrated from Iran, which borders both the Caspian and Arabian Seas. This made beach trips a familiar and much-pursued pastime. (Courtesy of the Eshia family collection.)

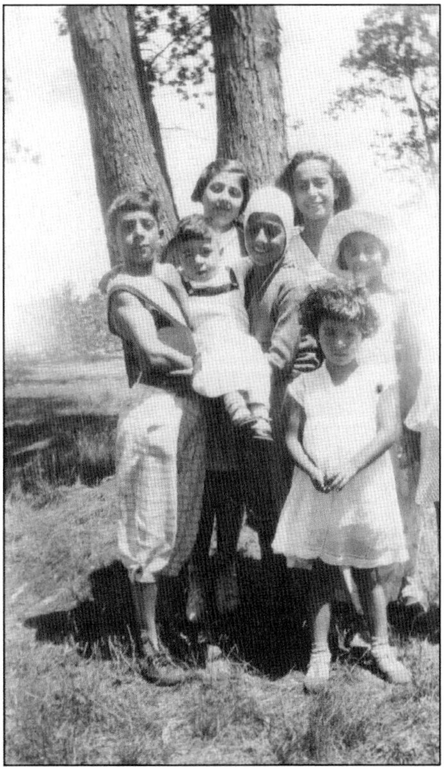

A group of Assyrian children is shown in 1932 during a swimming trip to a local lake.

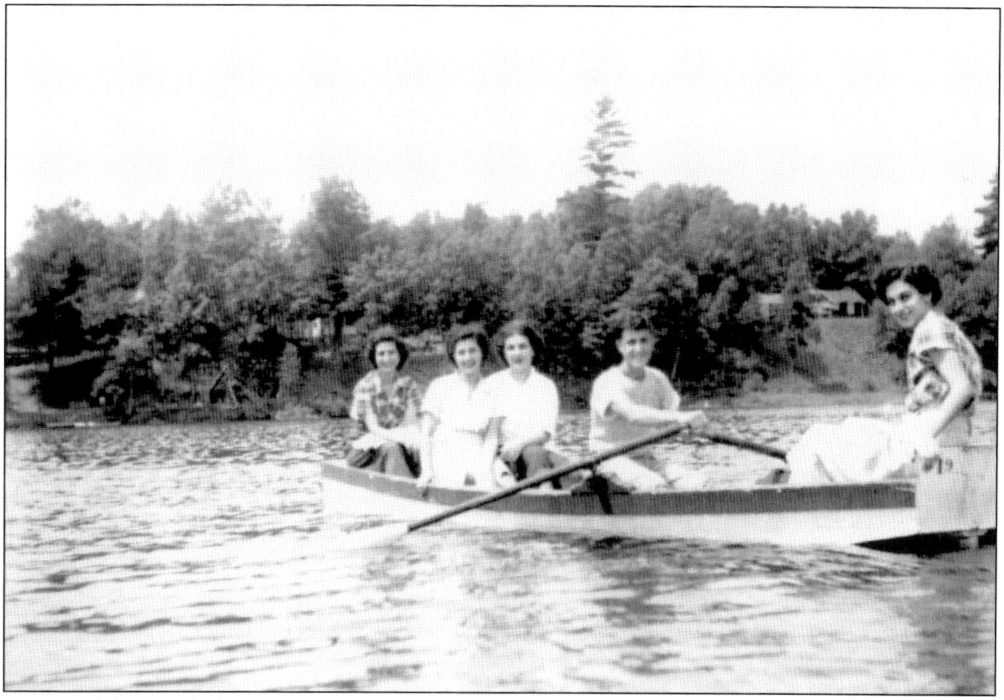

Young adults regularly took day trips to the Mohawk Trail region, which is located in western Massachusetts. In this photograph, a group is shown boating.

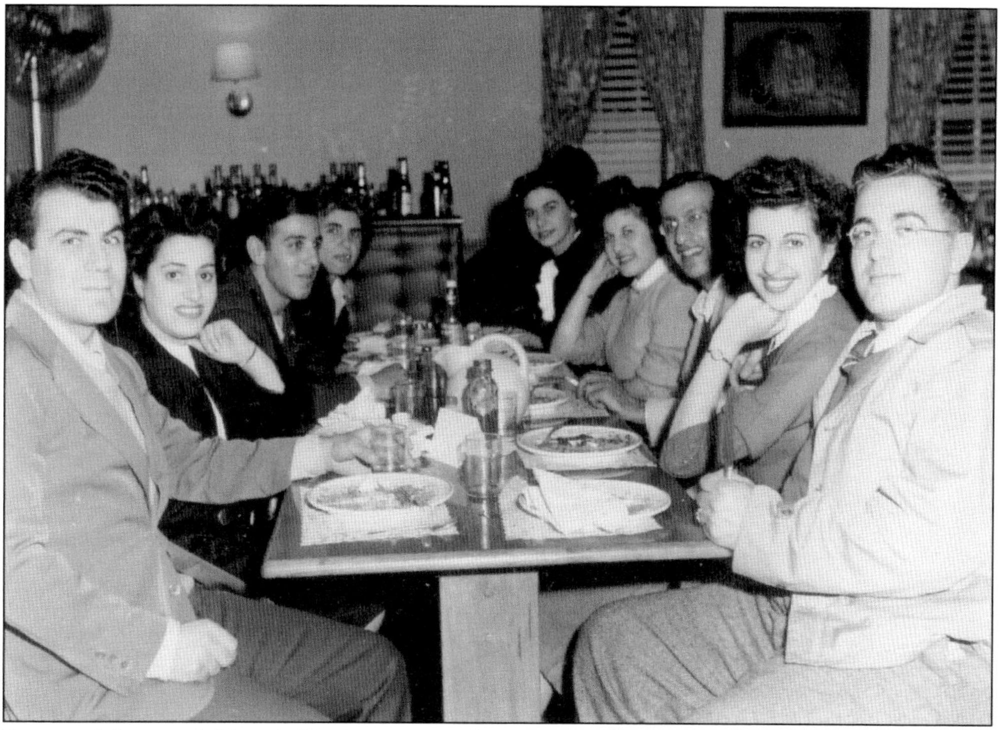

Young adults on a Mohawk Trail trip enjoy their lunch. Charlie Warda (left), Viola Baba, and Julie Bayram sit here, among others.

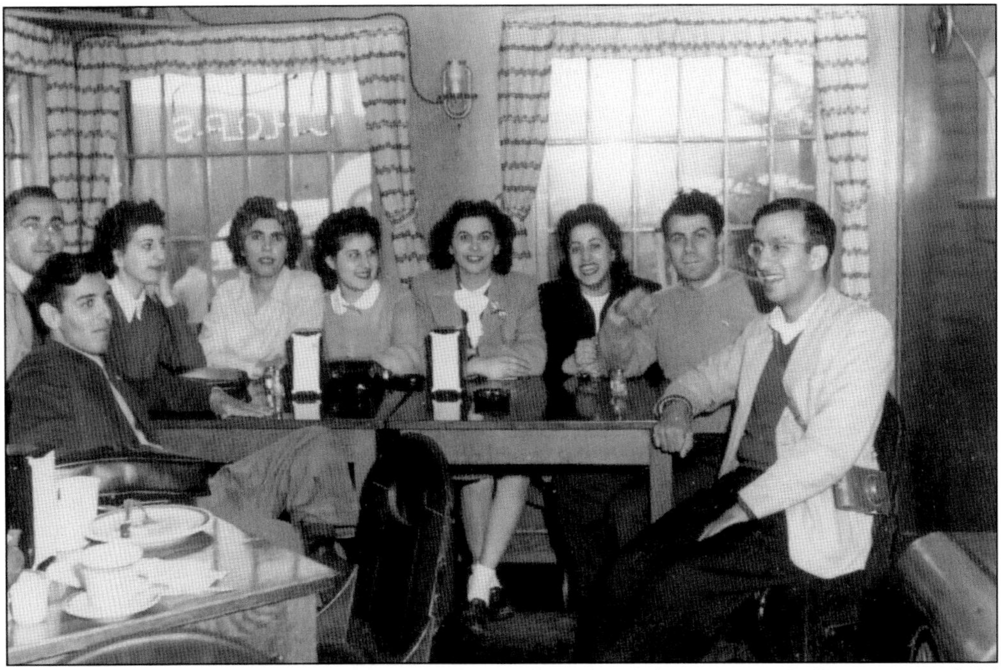

These young adults include Charlie Warda, Viola Baba, Julie Bayram, Bill Merza, and Al Abraham during the group's trip to the Mohawk Trail region.

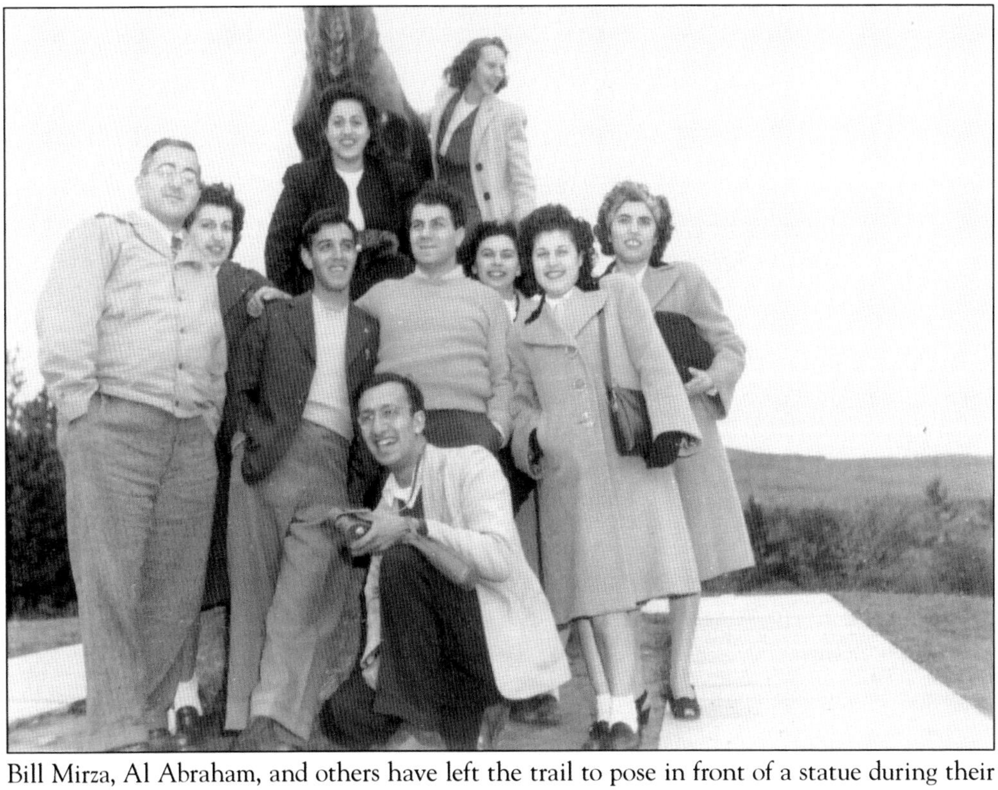

Bill Mirza, Al Abraham, and others have left the trail to pose in front of a statue during their trip to the Mohawk Trail area.

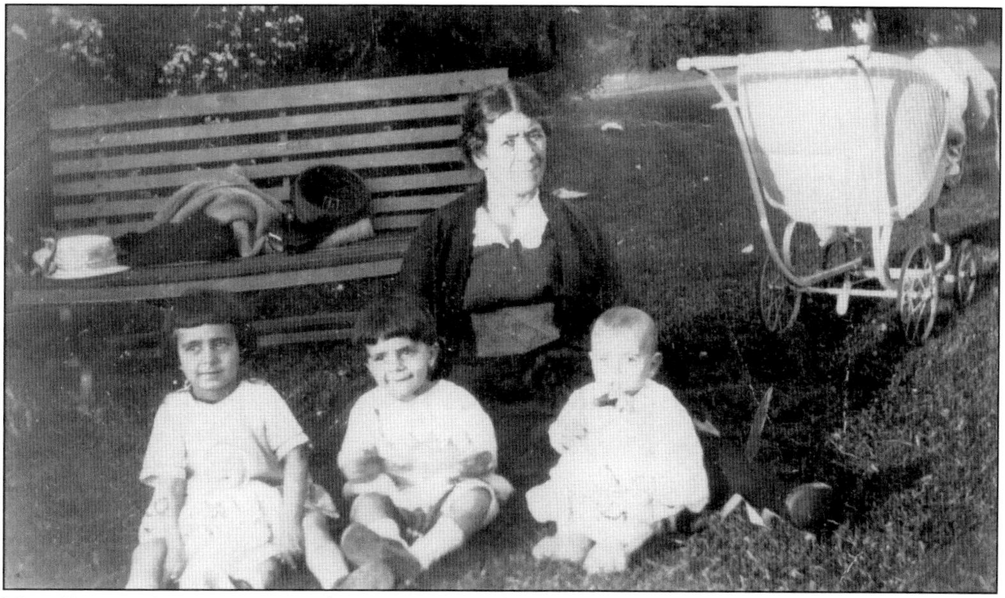

New Britain Assyrians come from a variety of backgrounds. Some were born in the United States, some came here as children, and others still continue to migrate to Connecticut. Featured in this 1922 photograph, from left to right, are children Gladys, Jain, and Eugene with their grandmother.

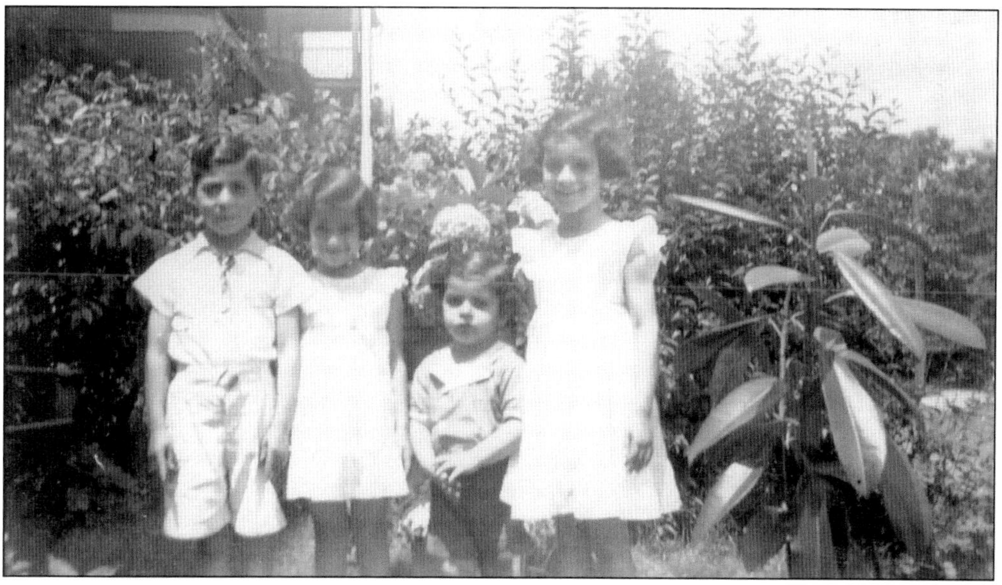

Shown in the yard of the Dooman family are children Barbara (second from left) and Doris (right) with two other youth. (Courtesy of the Dooman family collection.)

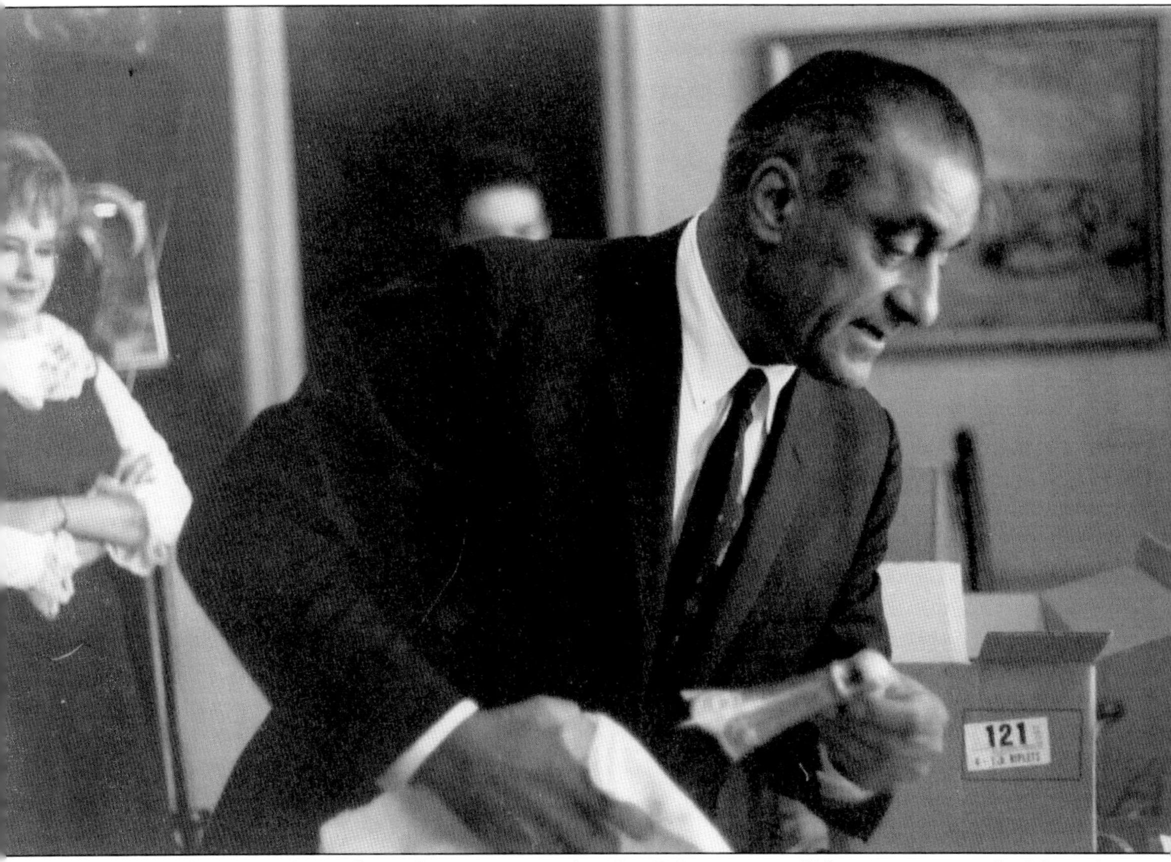

Yogi Yohanan is shown here about to open a bottle of champagne. Yohanan came to the United States with the initial hopes of joining the navy, but after spending a number of years in New Britain, he became a chef. He left New Britain to go to Georgia, where he opened up a restaurant named after himself.

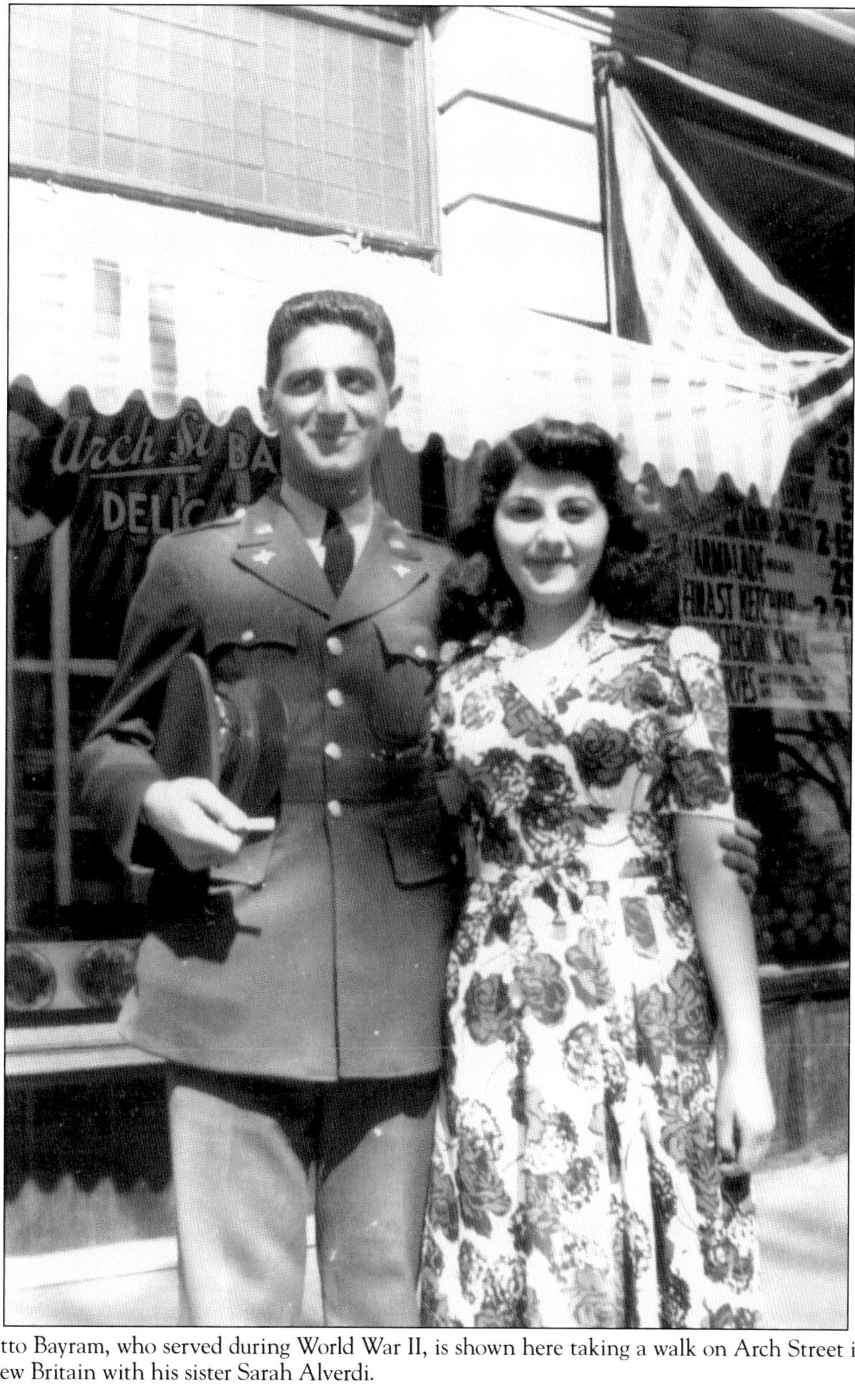

Otto Bayram, who served during World War II, is shown here taking a walk on Arch Street in New Britain with his sister Sarah Alverdi.

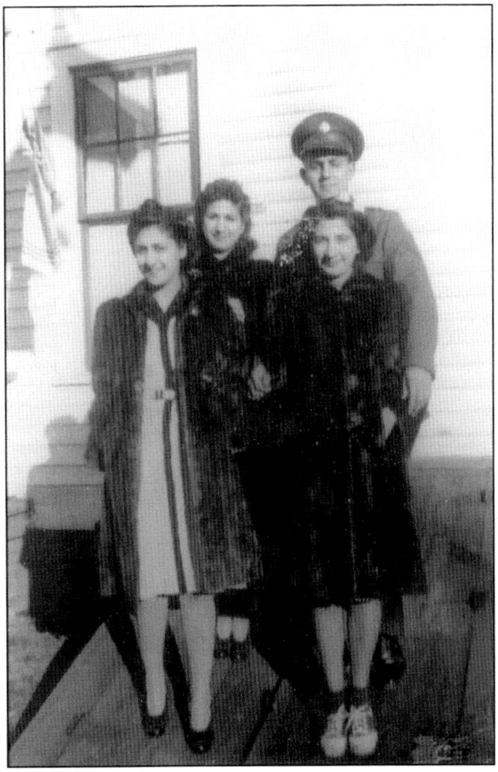

This group of young adults includes Mary Bayram, on the left, and Johnny Jones in the back.

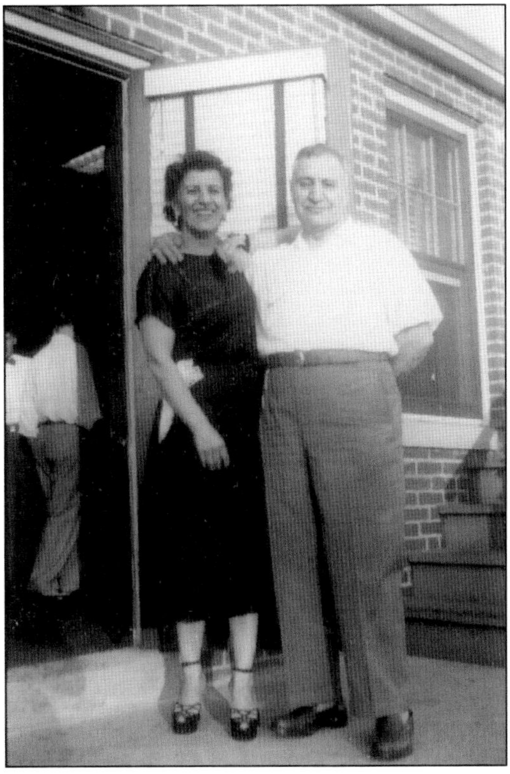

This couple poses in front of their home in this photograph that was taken in 1935. (Courtesy of Dooman family collection.)

George Isaac made a living as a painter. Many paint jobs on Assyrian and American houses were the work of Isaac.

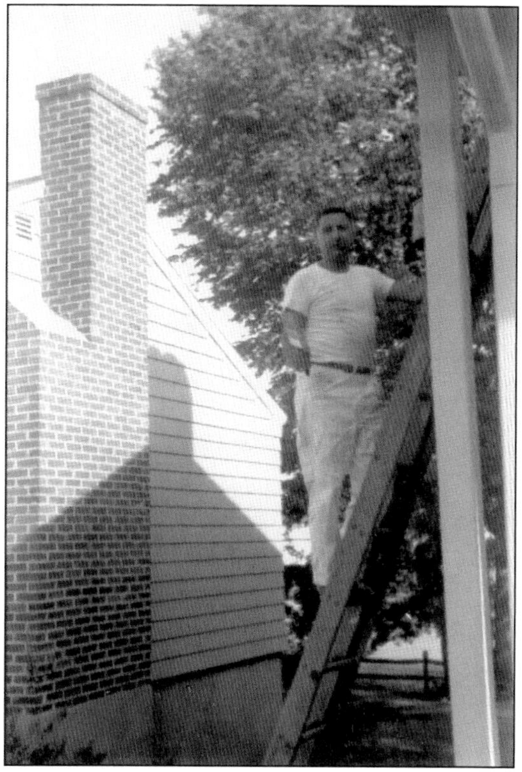

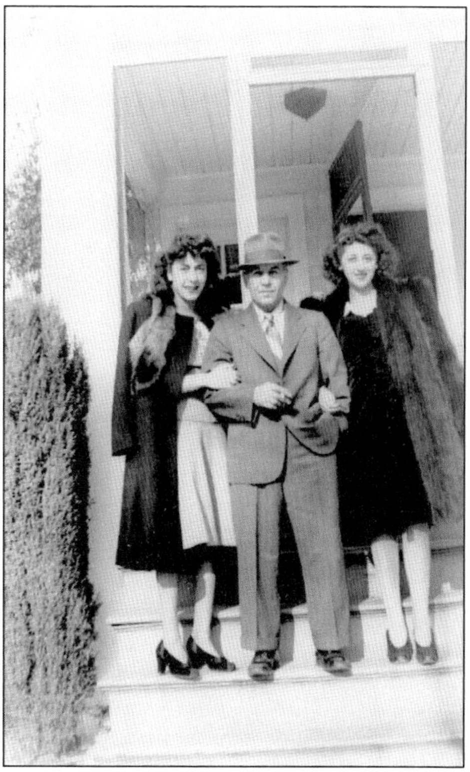

From left to right, Gladys Dooman, Joe Yonan, and Julie Bayram pose in front of a home as they prepare to leave on an outing. (Courtesy of the Dooman family collection.)

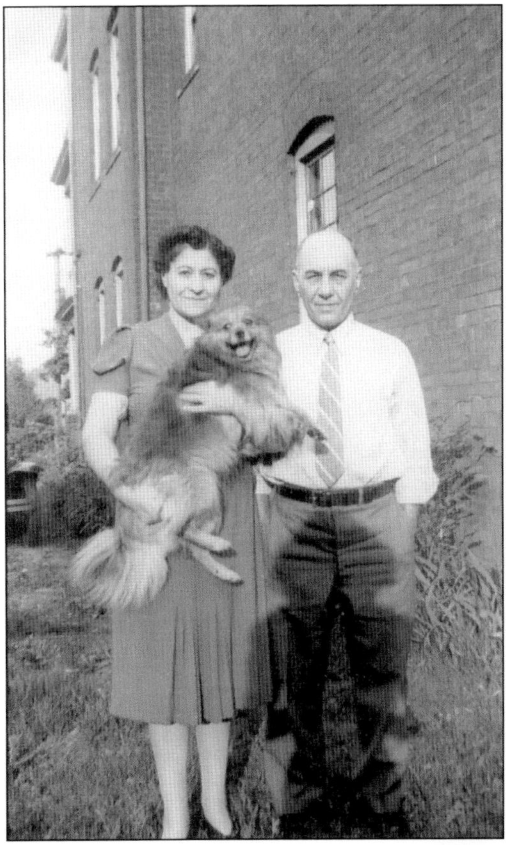

Anna and Joe Yonan are shown here in front of their New Britain home with their dog. Joe Yonan made his living as an electrician and provided his services to many homes in the central Connecticut area.

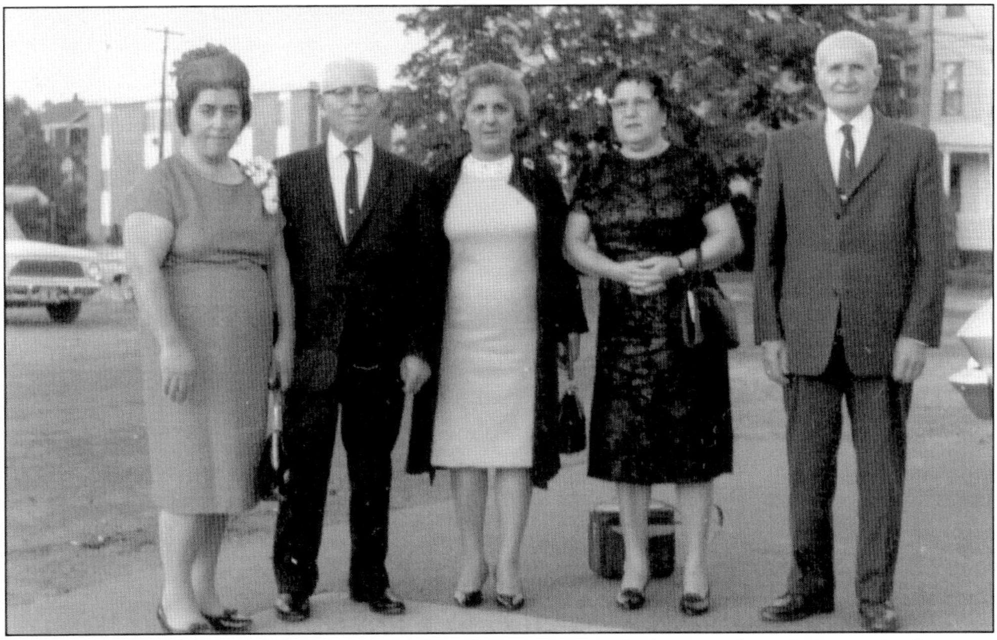

Kando Eshia is shown in the center of this photograph with four unidentified people during a Sunday afternoon after church. (Courtesy of the Eshia family collection.)

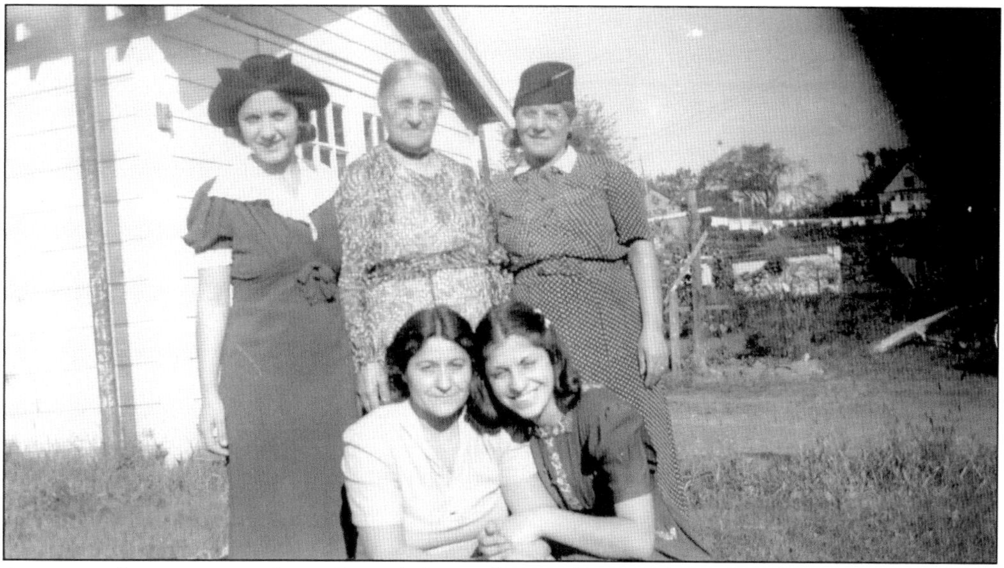

A group of women pose here. From left to ight are (first row) unidentified and Betty Eshia; (second row) Kando Eshia, Anna Yonan, and Nina Solomon.

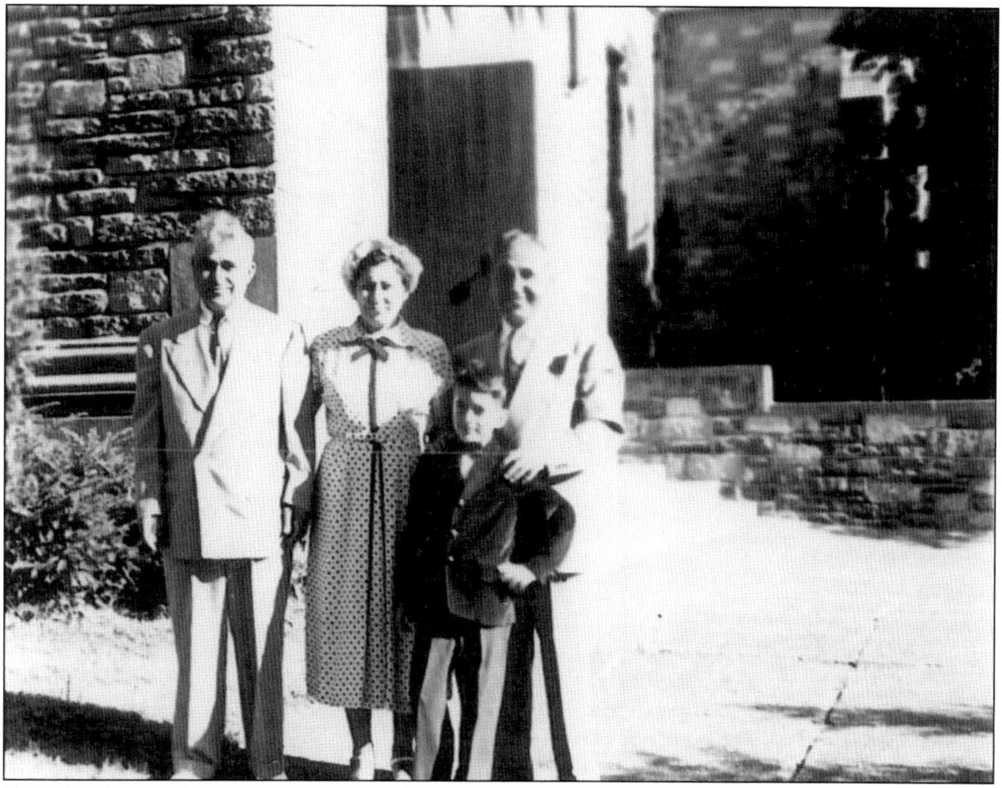

Four family members are shown posed in front of a church in this photograph. The adults are Nonu Benjamin, Katharine Benjamin, and Gabriel Benjamin.

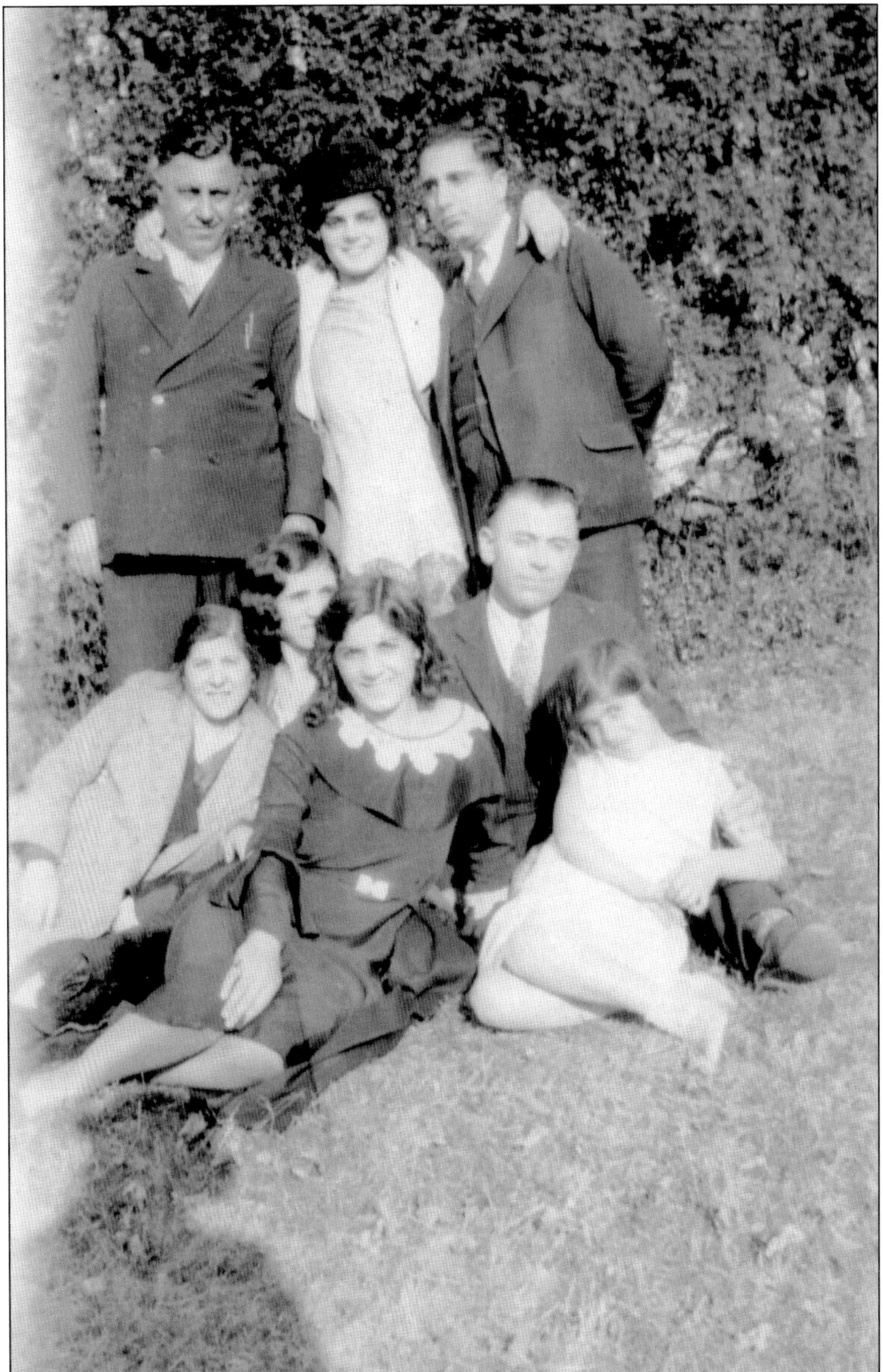

Seated in the photograph is the father of John and Betty Eshia. The rest of the photograph features family members and friends. (Courtesy of the Eshia family collection.)

John Eshia is shown here with his mother, Kando, and his sister, Betty. The photograph was taken on August 25, 1936.

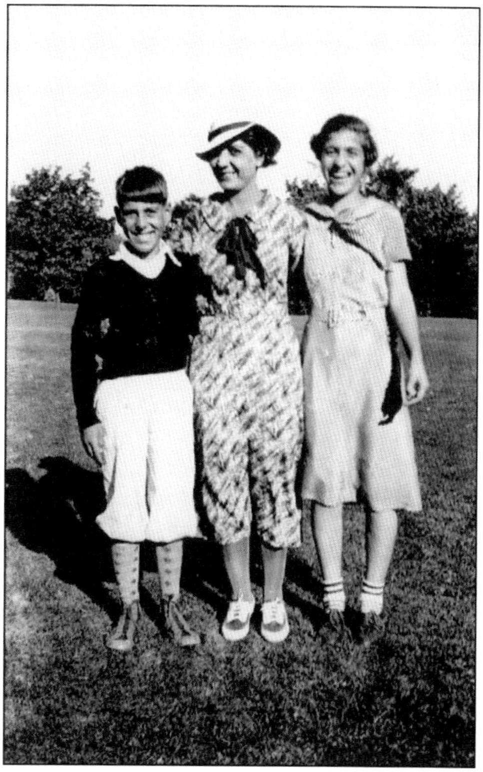

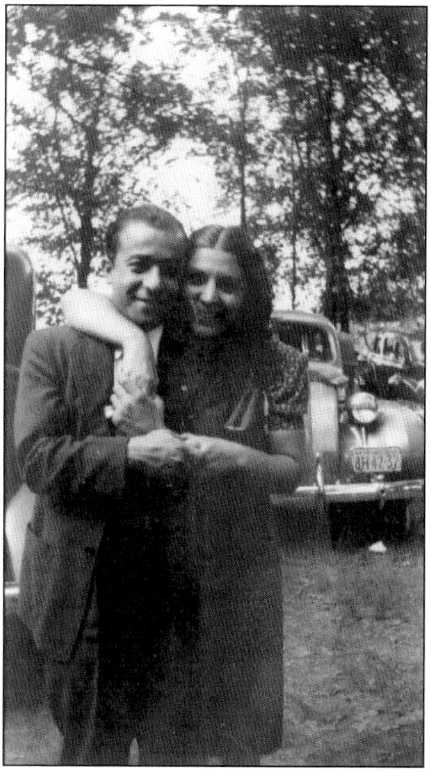

Kando Eshia is shown in this 1926 photograph hugging Izzy Yonan, a friend from Yonkers, New York.

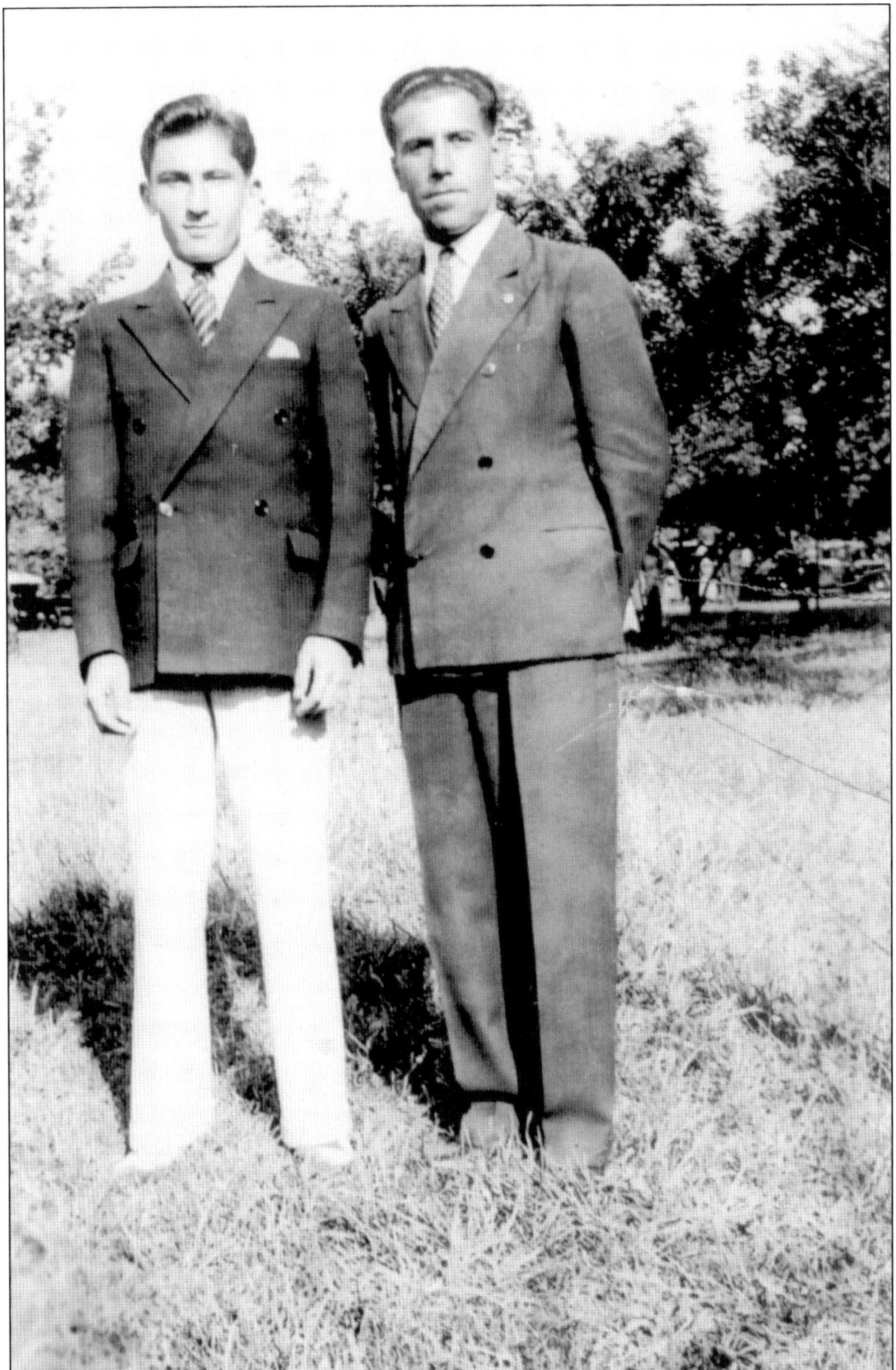

Mooshie "Jack" Badal (left) is shown in this photograph with a close friend. (Courtesy of the Badal family collection.)

The Dooman family is shown during an outing in the 1920s. The individuals in the photograph are Michel, Gladys, Jimmy, and their father, Sam. (Courtesy of the Dooman family collection.)

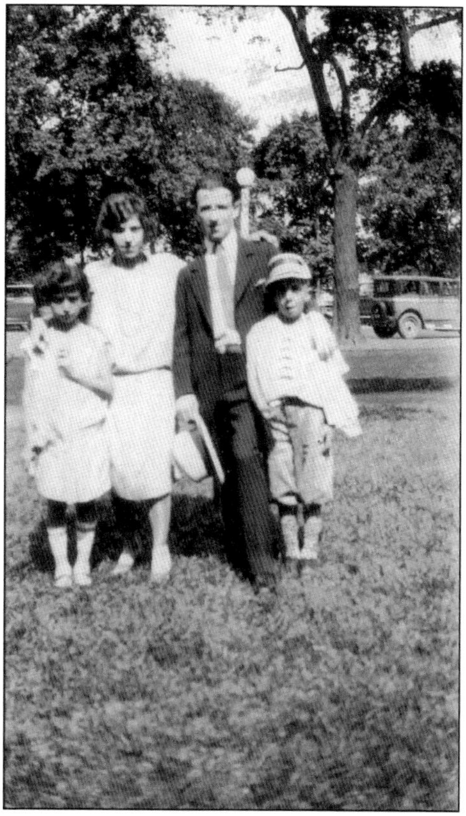

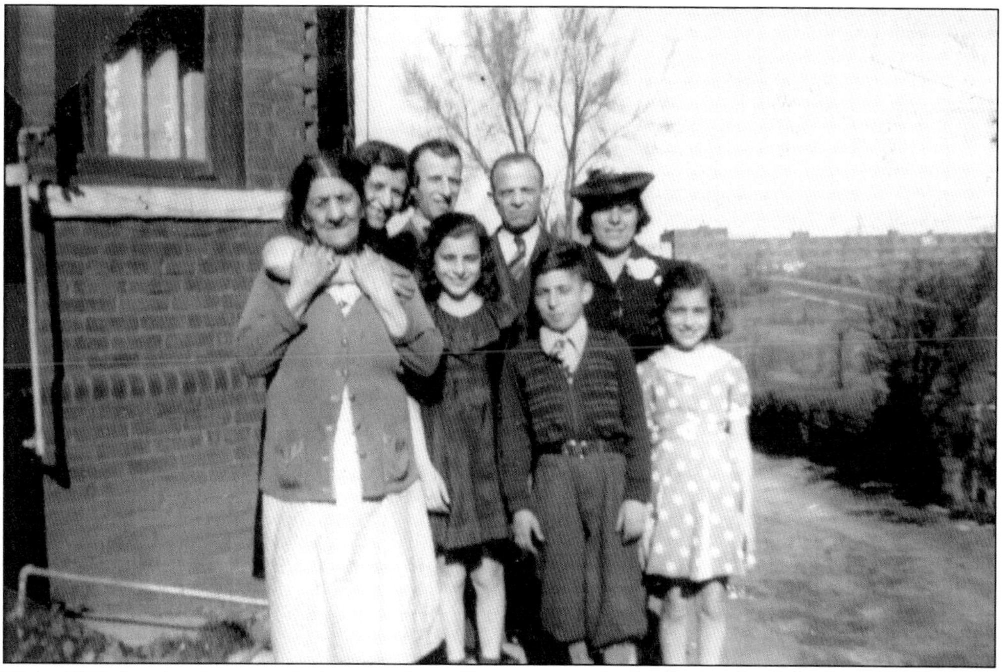

This 1935 family photograph features Sam Dooman in the back, on the left. (Courtesy of the Dooman family collection.)

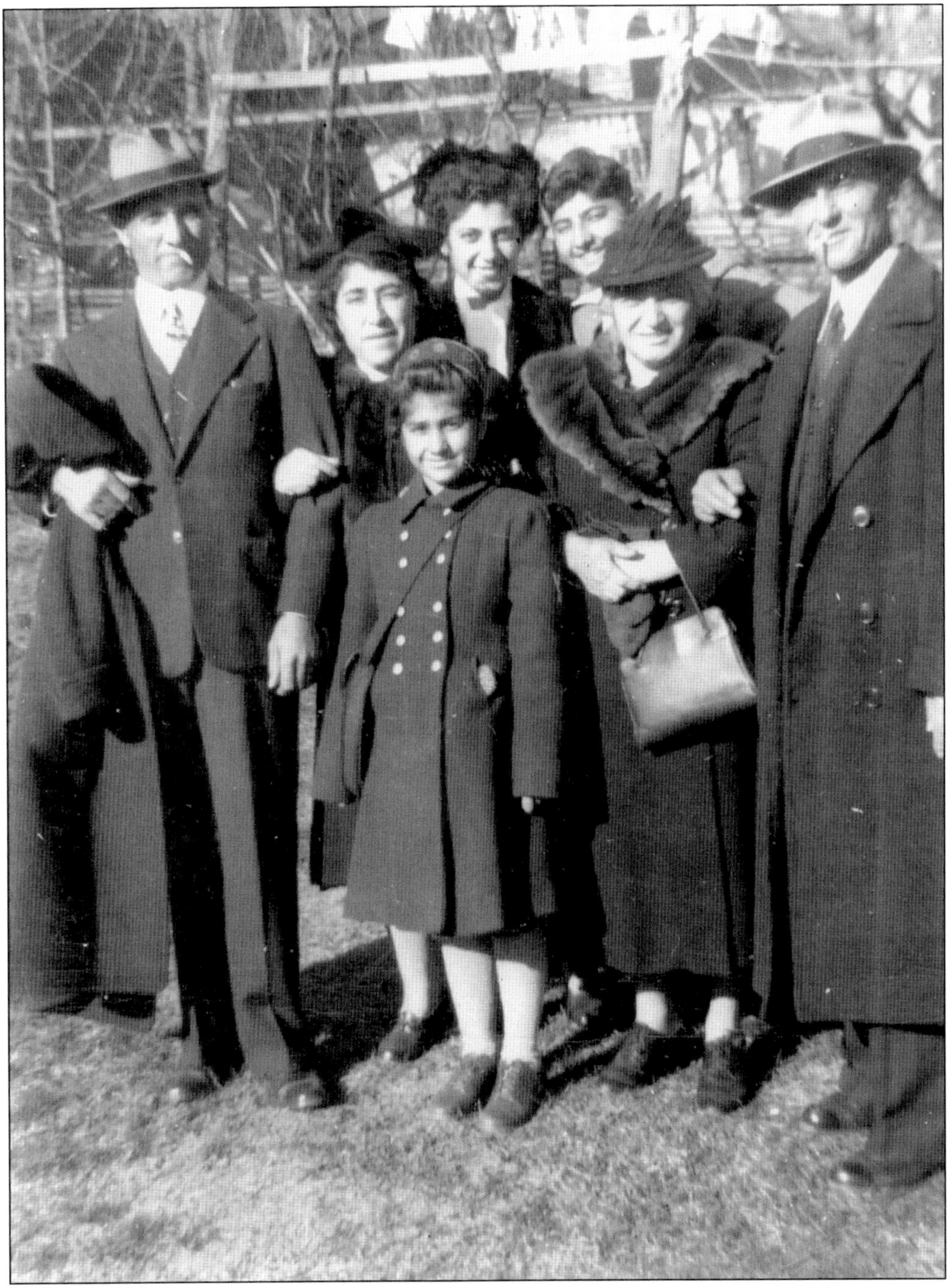

Displayed here is a Sargis family outing featuring, from left to right, David, Shushan, Agnes, Edward, Mariam, and Joseph, with young Annette standing in the front.

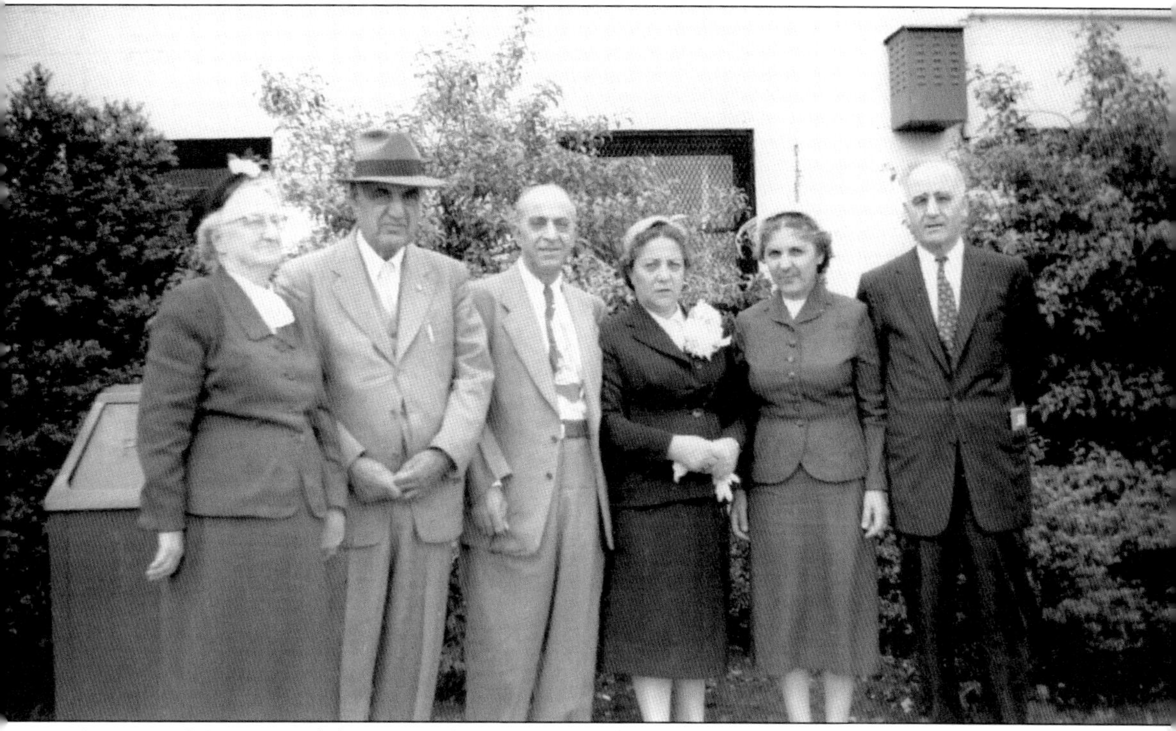

A group of Assyrian adults poses after church. Included in the photograph are May Shlemon and Mooshie Solomon, among others.

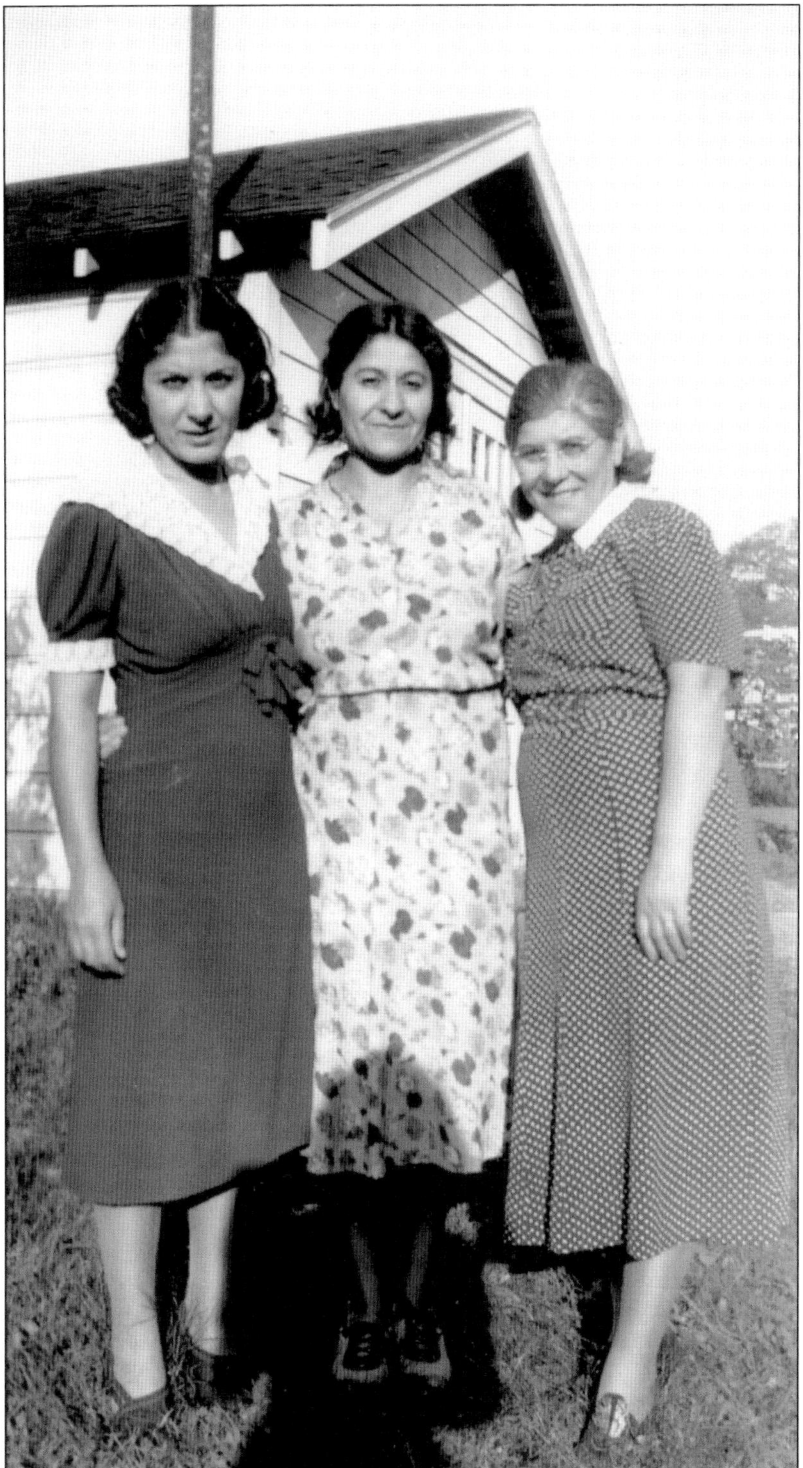

From left to right, Kando Eshia, Nina Solomon, and one other woman pose in this photograph. (Courtesy of the Eshia family collection.)

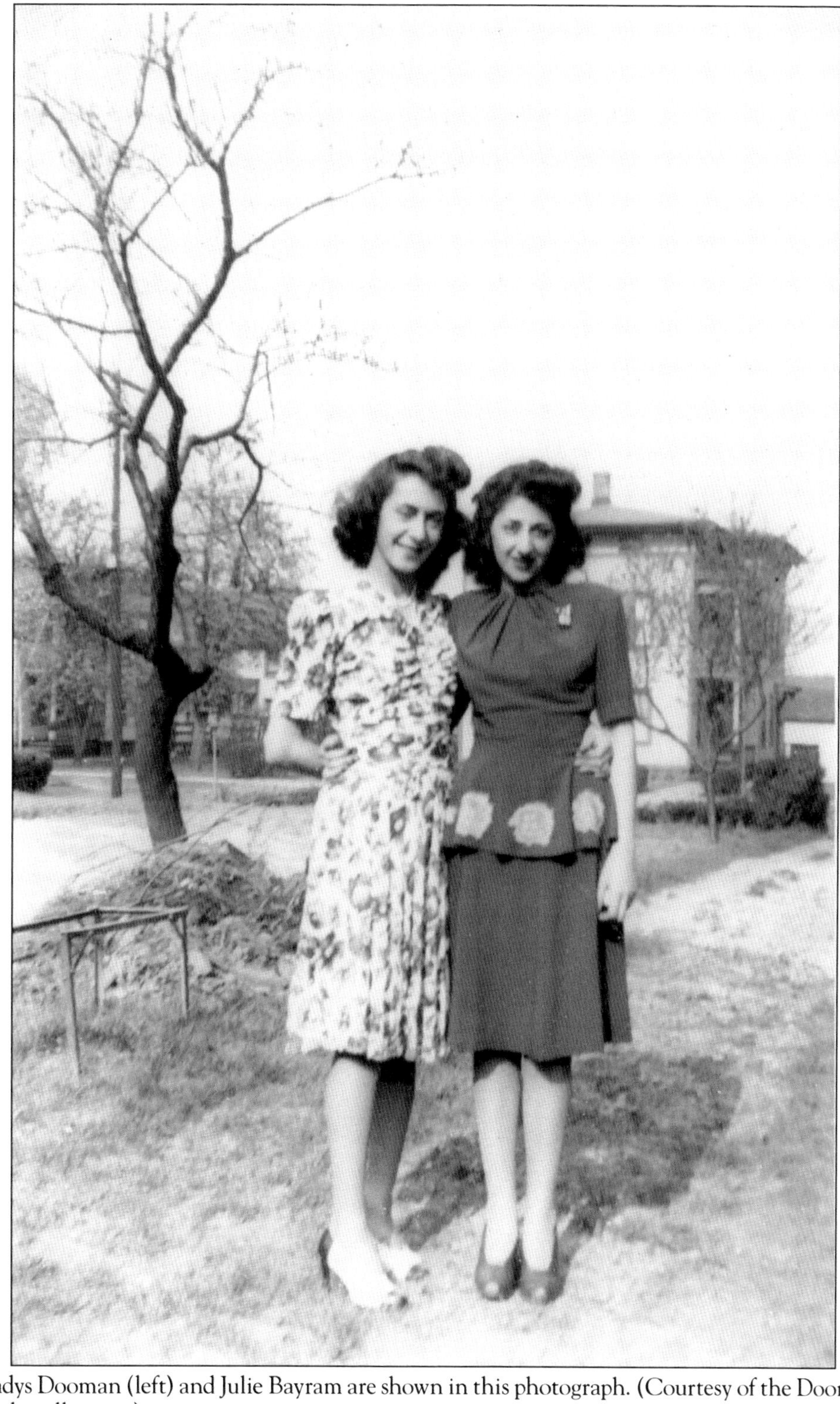

Gladys Dooman (left) and Julie Bayram are shown in this photograph. (Courtesy of the Dooman family collection.)

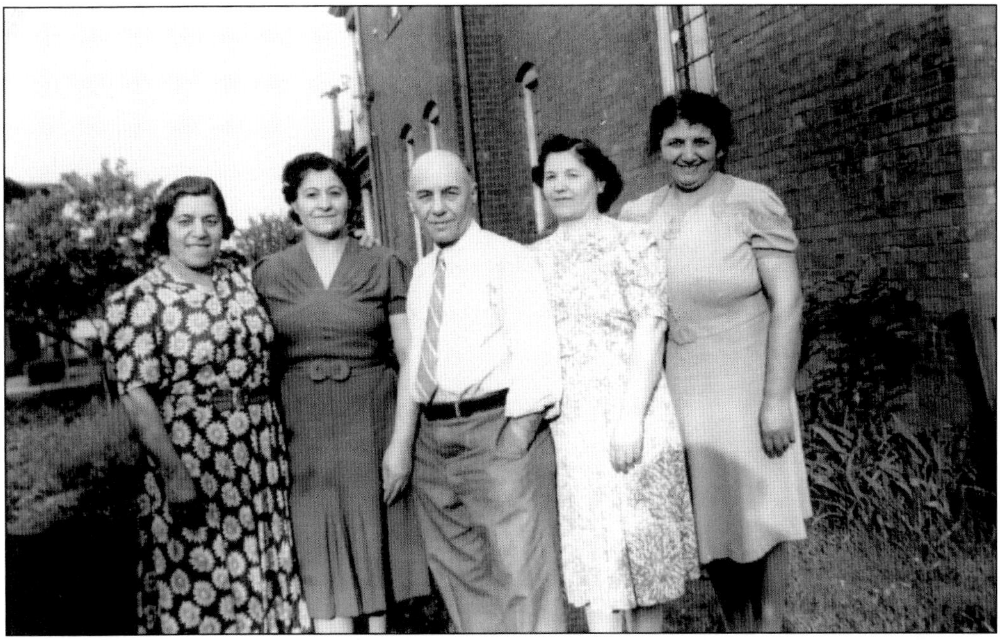

From left to right, Mikal Dooman, Anna and Joe Yohana, Martha Oshanna, and Sheerin Bayram are seen in this photograph on a Sunday afternoon after church. (Courtesy of the Dooman family collection.)

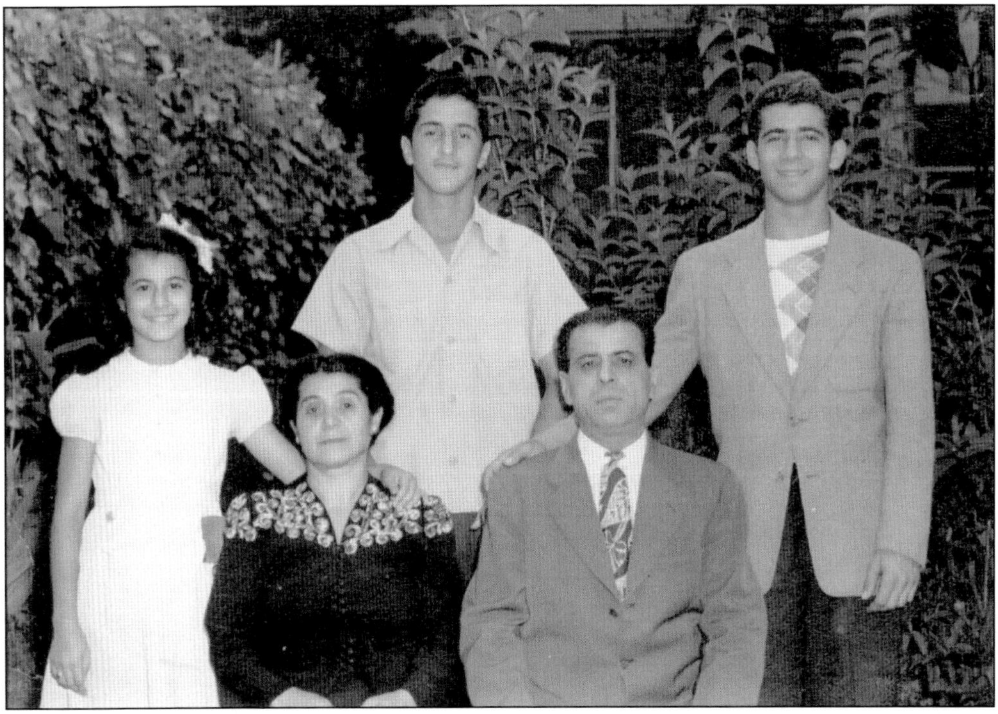

This family photograph, taken in 1946, includes Margaret Capsalaros, who is seen in with her parents and two brothers. (Courtesy of Margaret Capsalaros.)

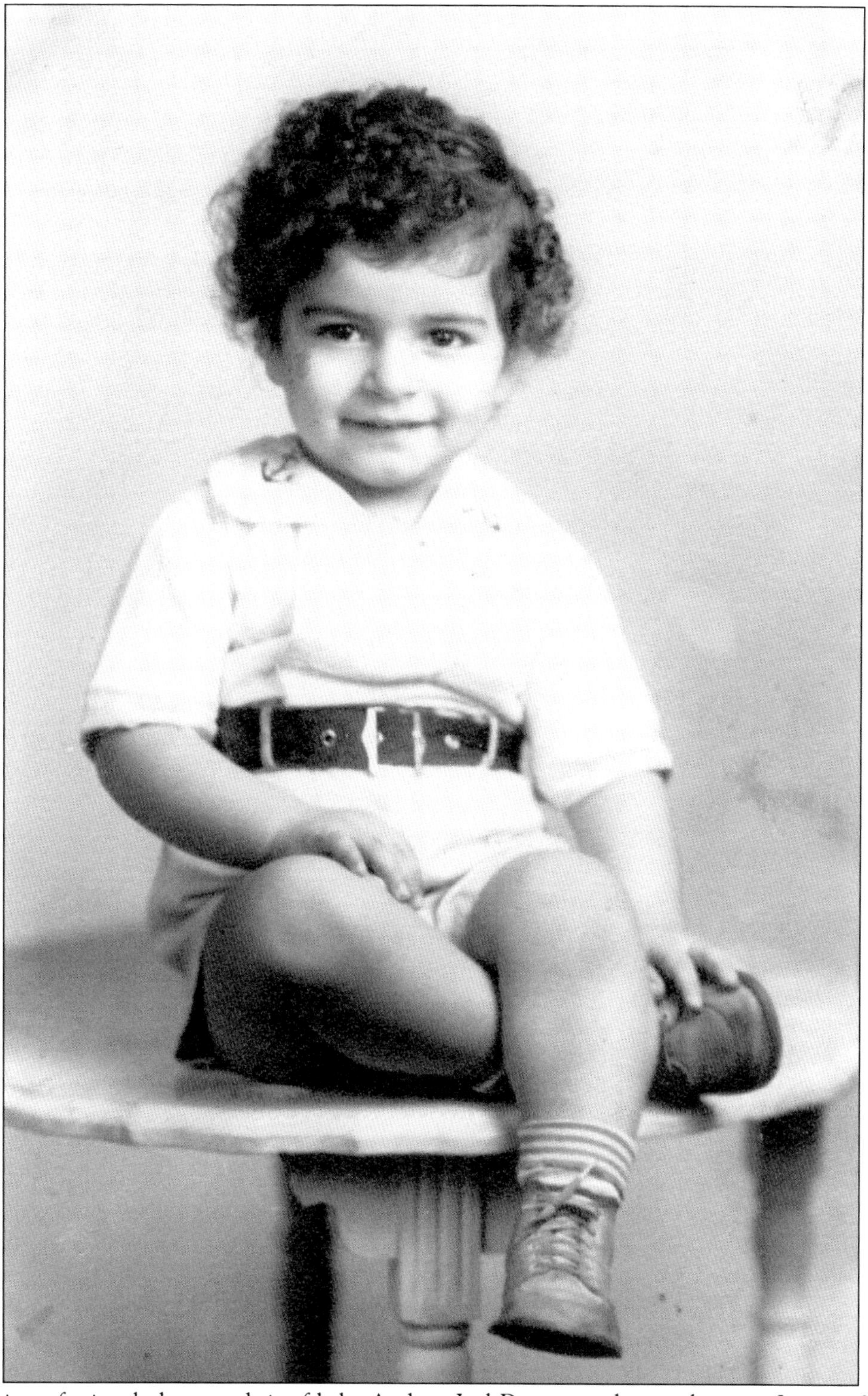

This professional photograph is of baby Andrew Joel Dooman, who was born on January 30, 1935, and passed away at the age of six. (Courtesy of the Dooman family collection.)

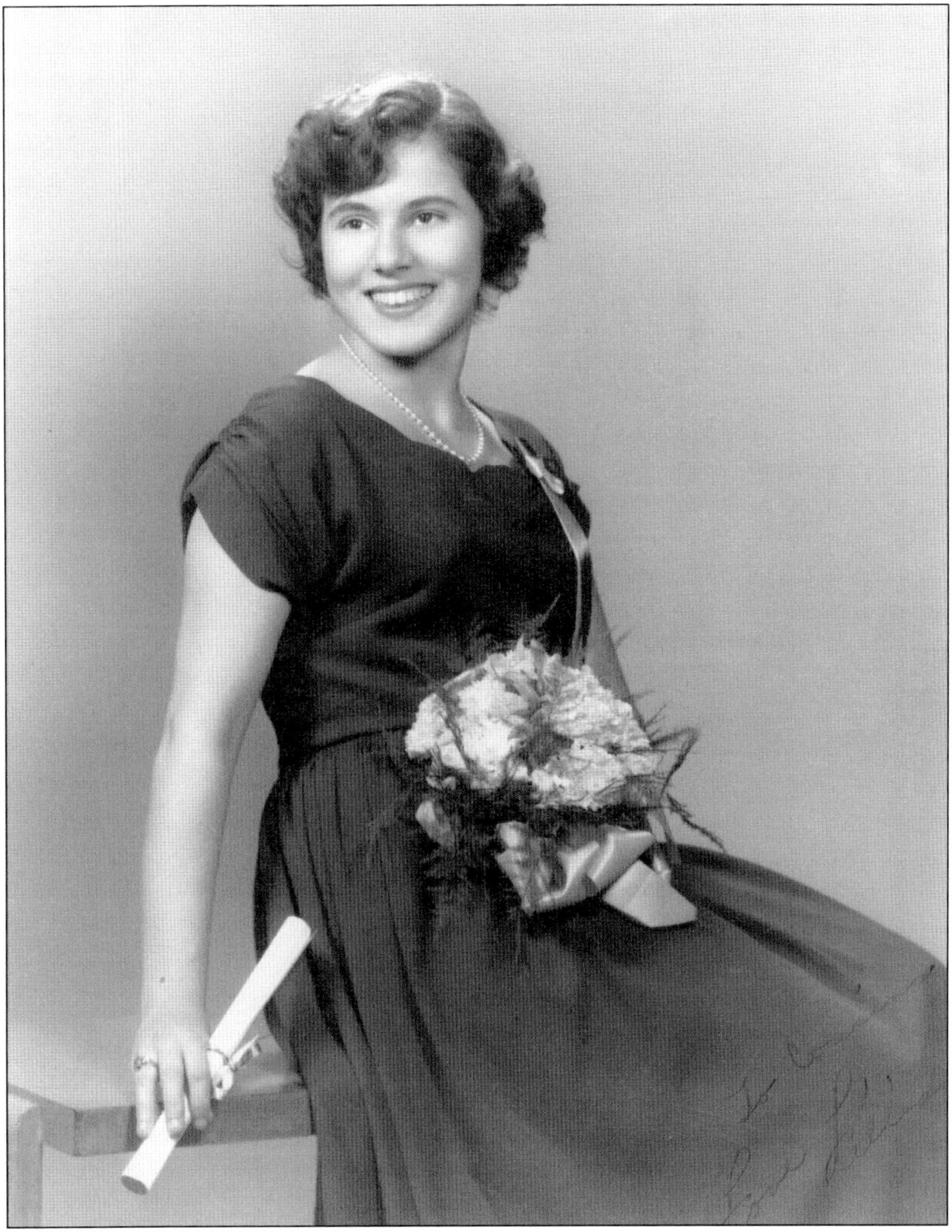

This high school graduation photograph was sent out to relatives upon the graduation of Lillian Ishoo. She is shown here holding her diploma. (Courtesy of the Abraham family collection.)

This photograph was taken on July 10, 1951. It was used as an official passport photograph.

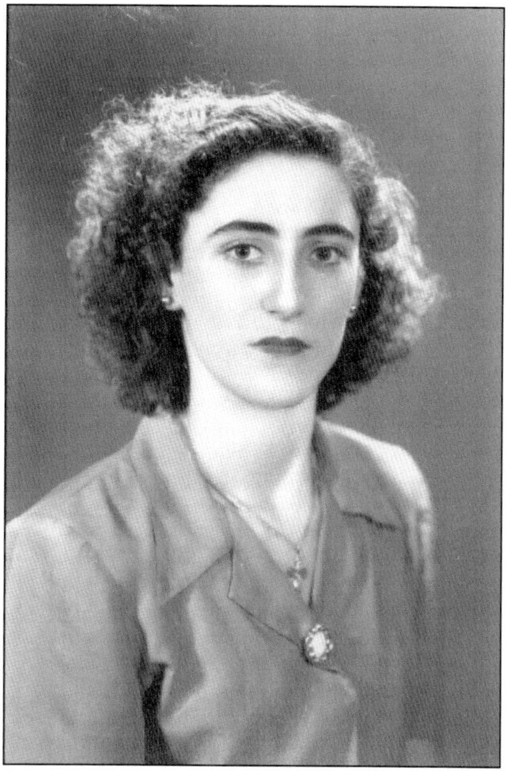

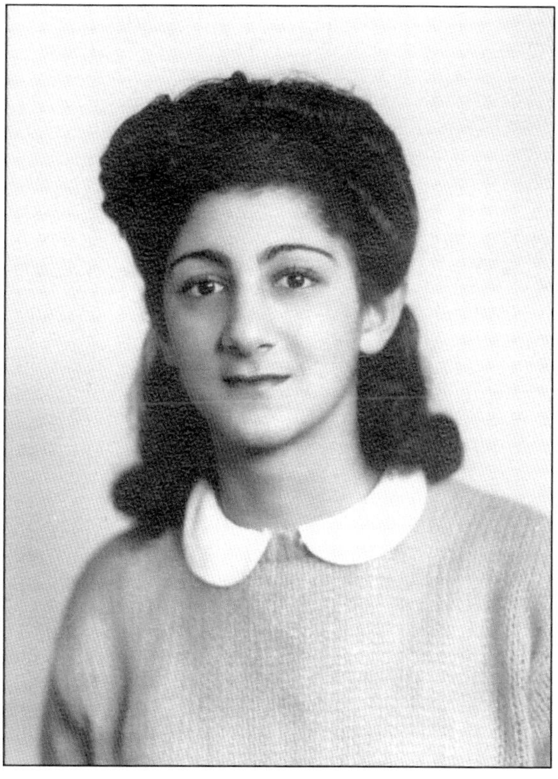

This is a portrait of Lucy Abraham. (Courtesy of the Abraham and Ishoo family collections.)

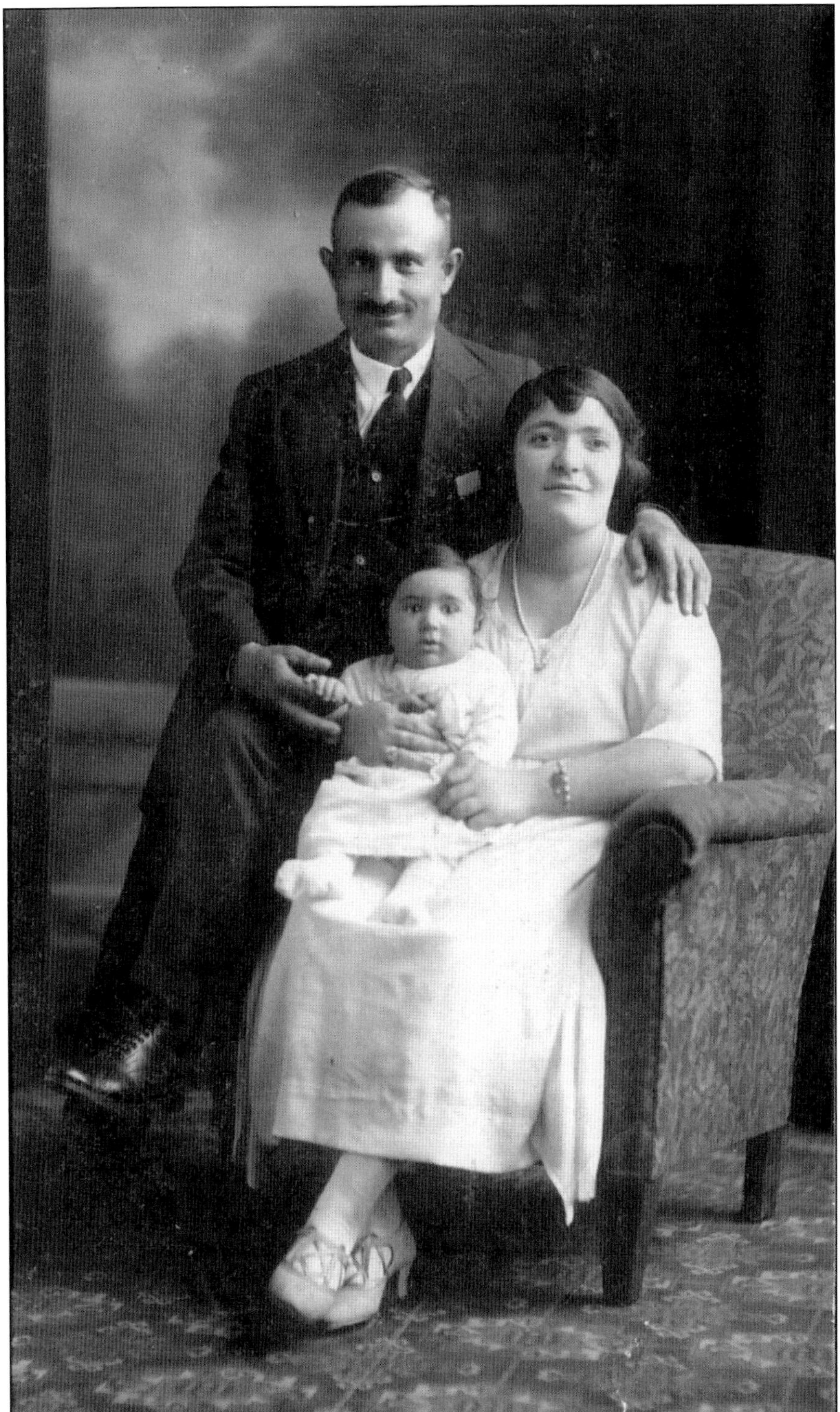

This photograph was taken in early 1920s of this newly arrived Assyrian family. The photograph was held on to and has been passed along New Britain family generations since then.

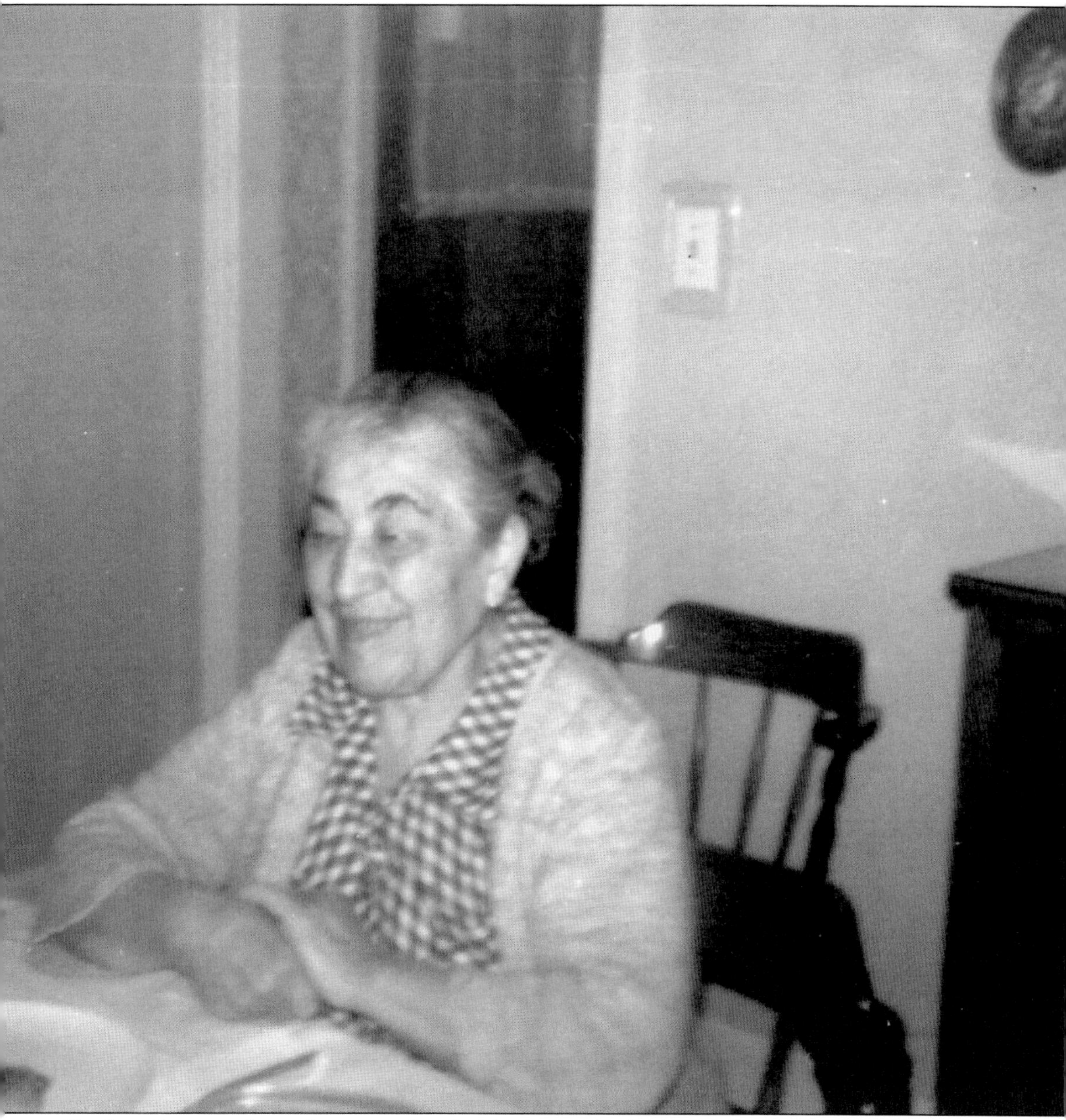

Shoshan Sargis is shown here seated in her home, at the kitchen table. She is the mother of Annette Sargis Baba.

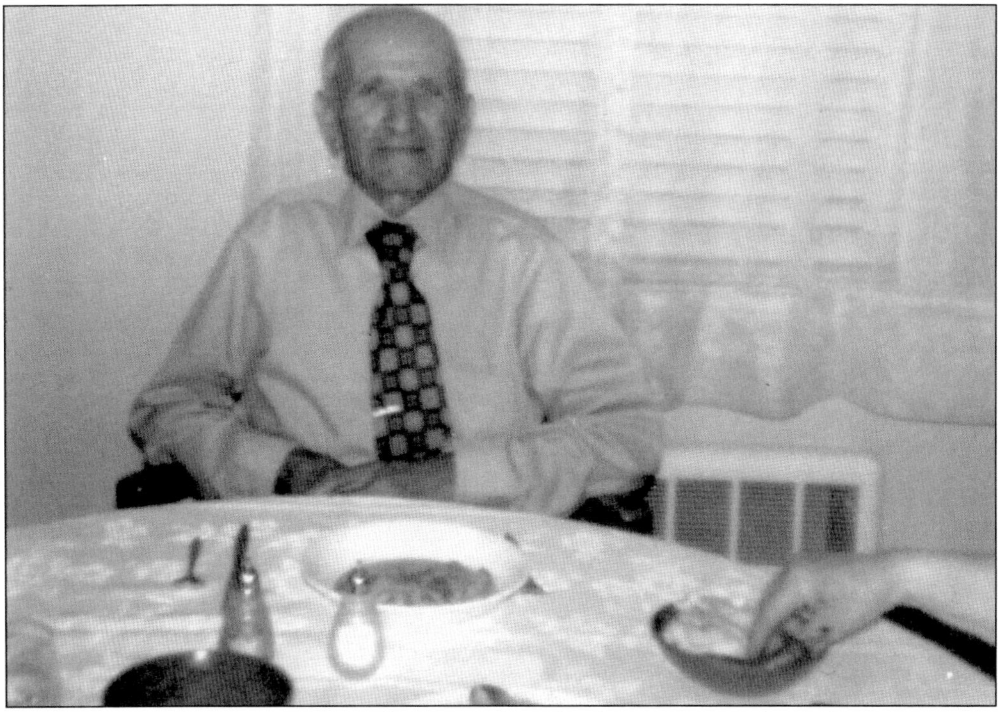

Shamasha David Sargis is shown here seated at his home. He is the father of Annette Sargis Baba.

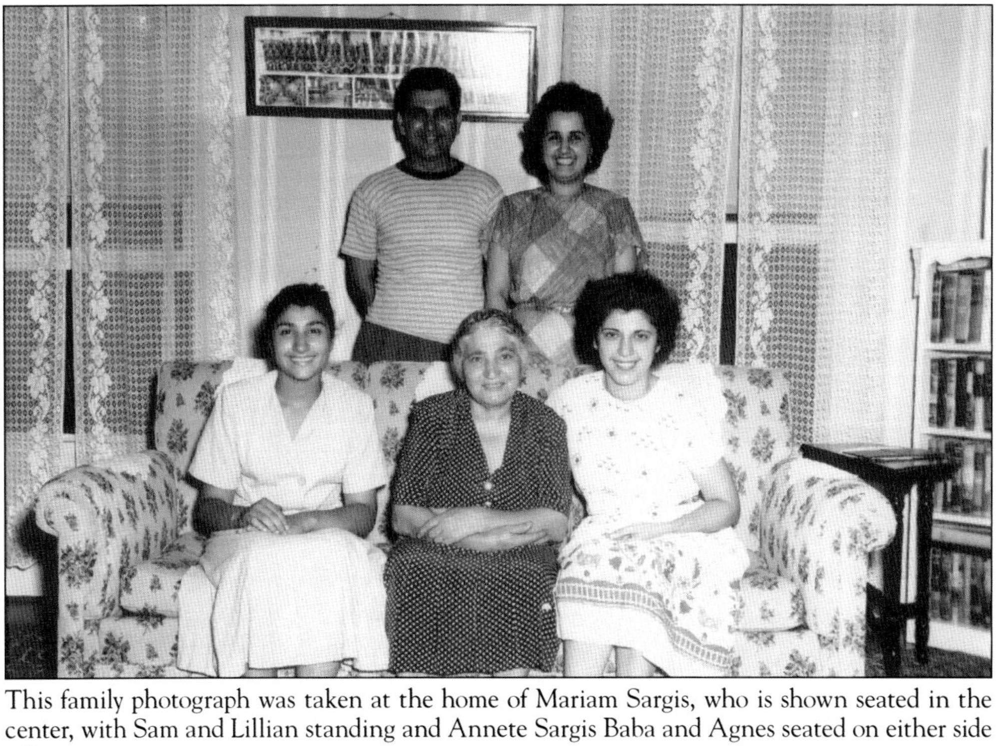

This family photograph was taken at the home of Mariam Sargis, who is shown seated in the center, with Sam and Lillian standing and Annete Sargis Baba and Agnes seated on either side of her.

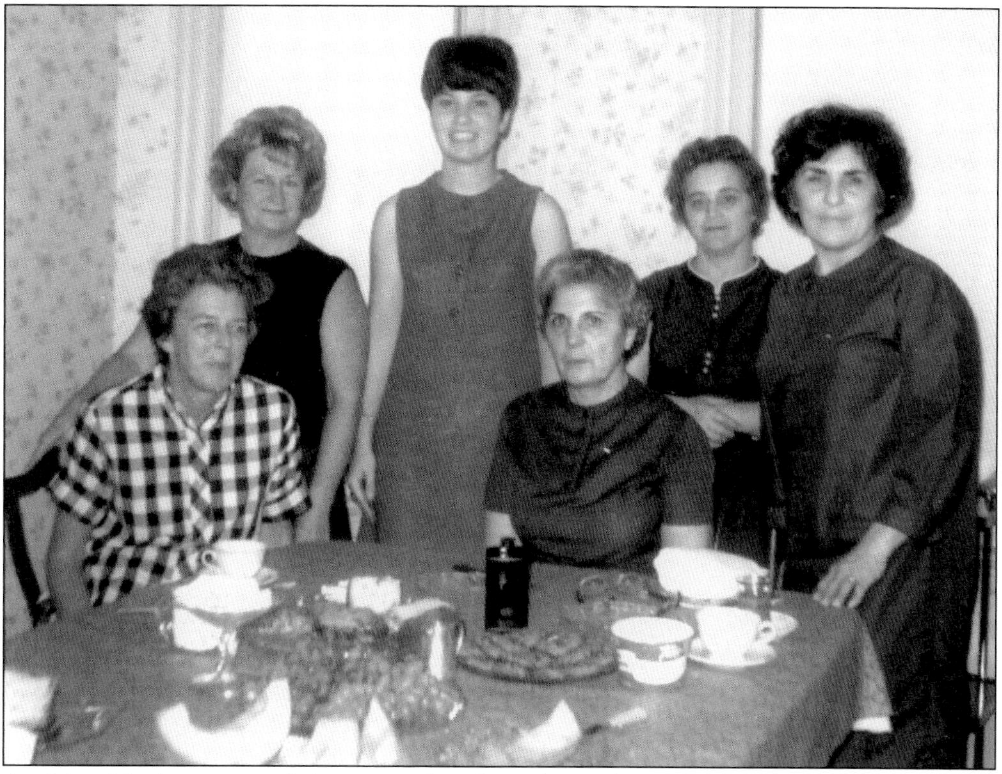

A visit with Assyrian and American friends is shown here. In the photograph are Karen Nathan, Hannah Lazar, standing in the center is Marsha Gallo, with Kando Eshia seated on the bottom right.

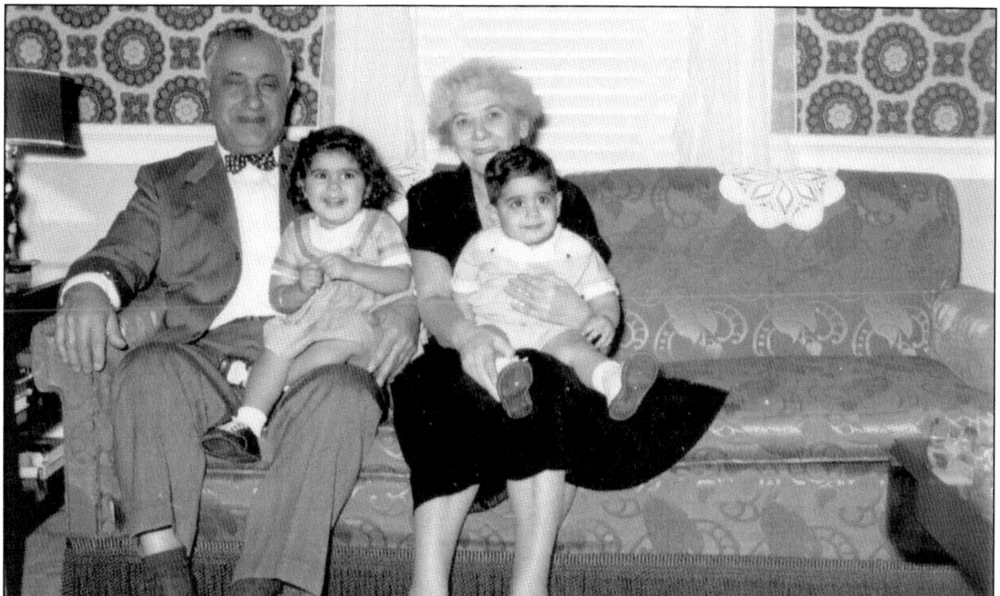

Wife and husband, Nina and Ohle Solomon, are shown here with their young grandchildren. The photograph was taken in the mid-20th century.

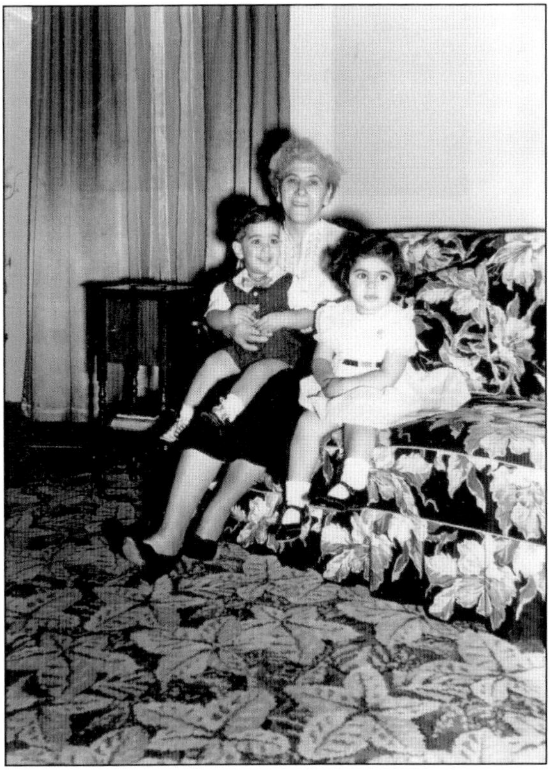

Nina Solomon is shown here holding her young grandchildren during one of their visits to her home.

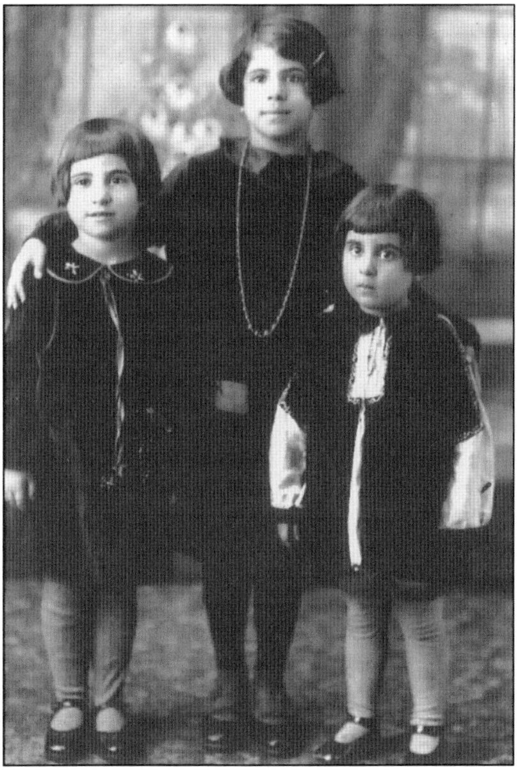

Shown here from left to right in 1925 are sisters Jenny, Nellie, and Julia Ives. They are the daughters of Ephraim and Margaret Ives of New Britain.

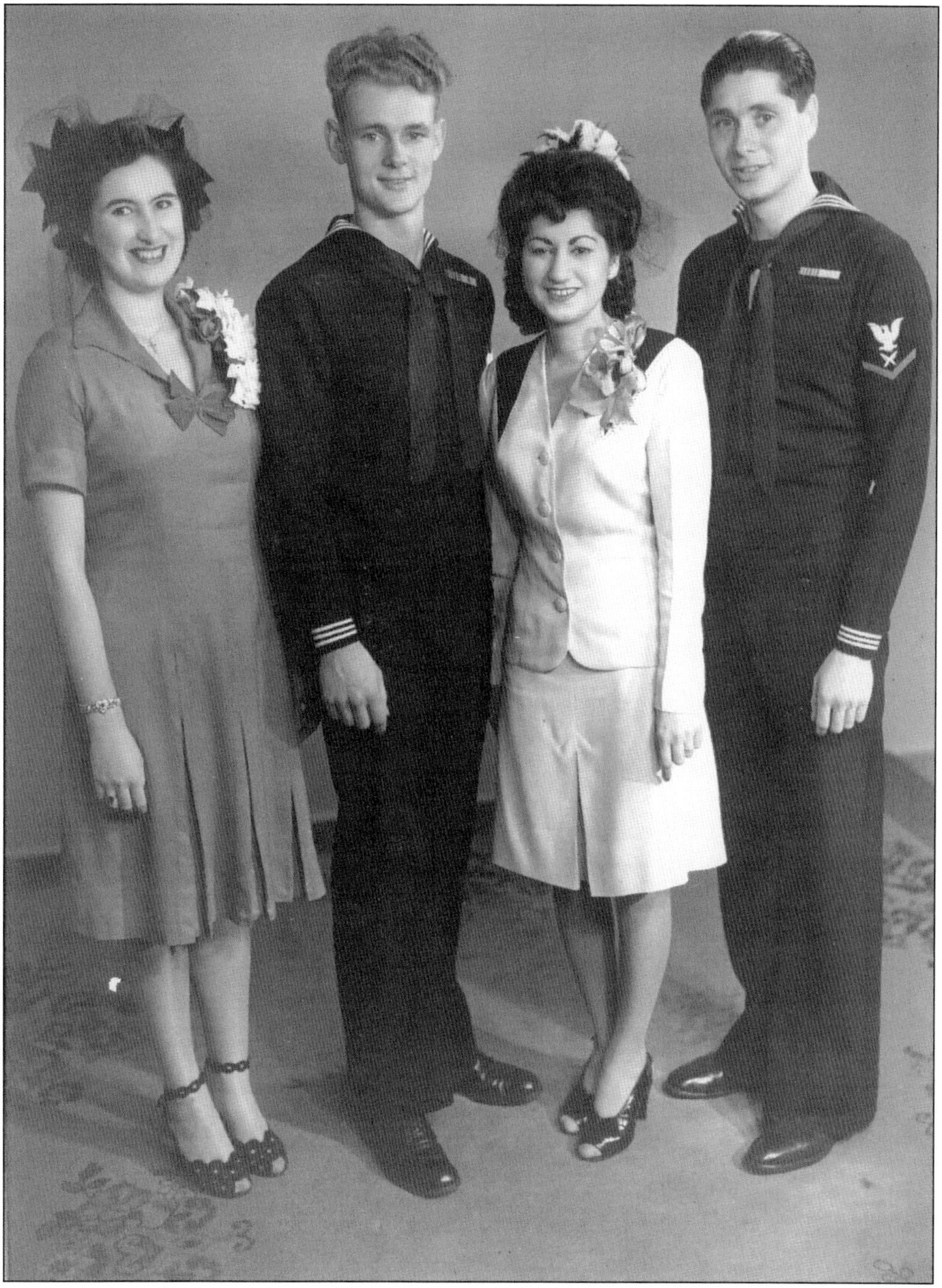

Veteran Leonard Simon, who graduated from Ohio State University, and his wife, Diane Emma Simon, a New Britain native, are the newly married couple shown here in October 1944. He served on the USS *Republic*, Division A.

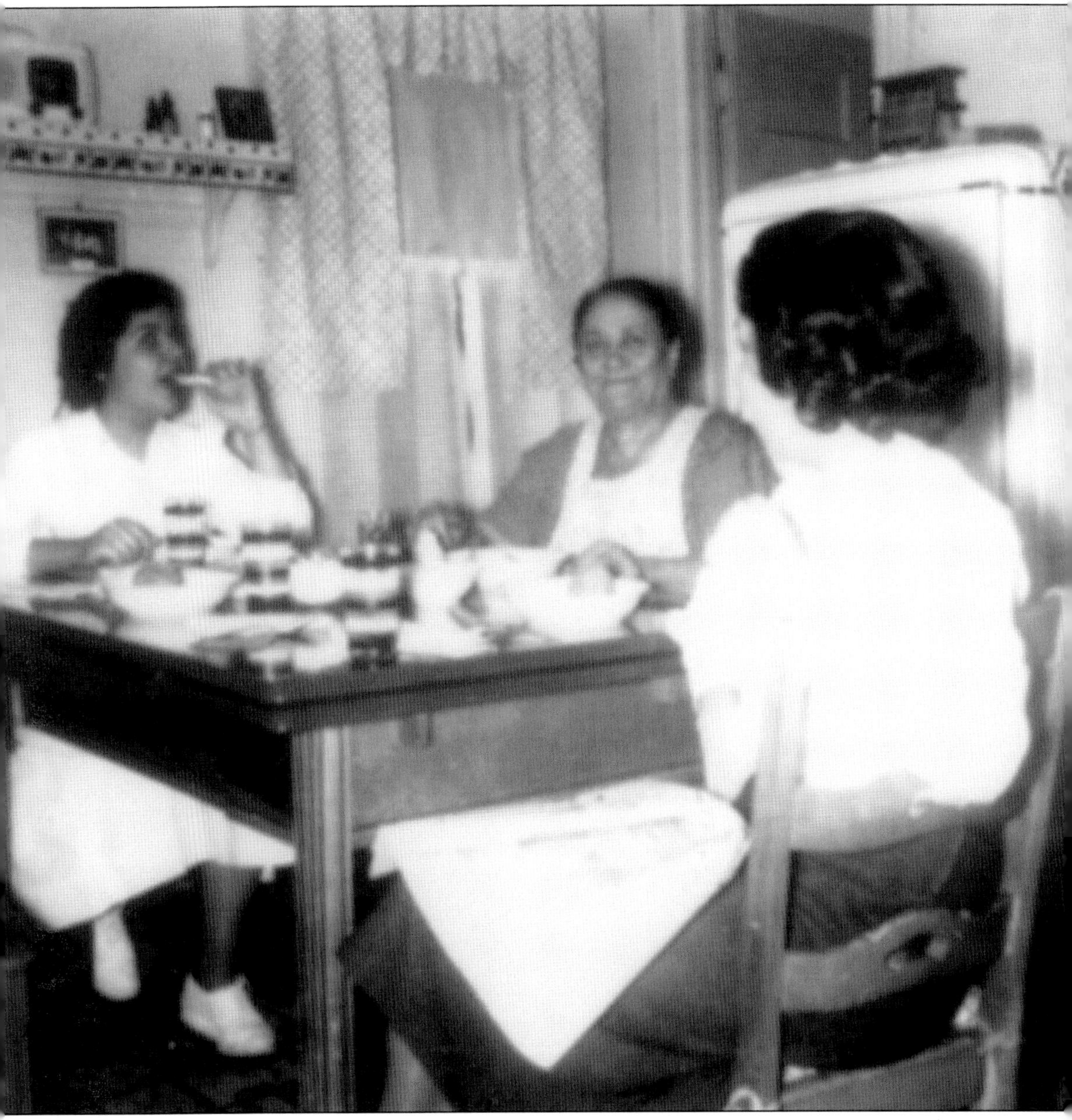

This photograph of an afternoon visit for tea and traditional Assyrian pastries was taken on Roberts Street in New Britain. Claire Sargis (left), who was a nurse, is seated in the kitchen of her friend Connie (center). (Courtesy of the Badal family collection.)

Siblings Bobbie and Connie Abraham are seated in this photograph.

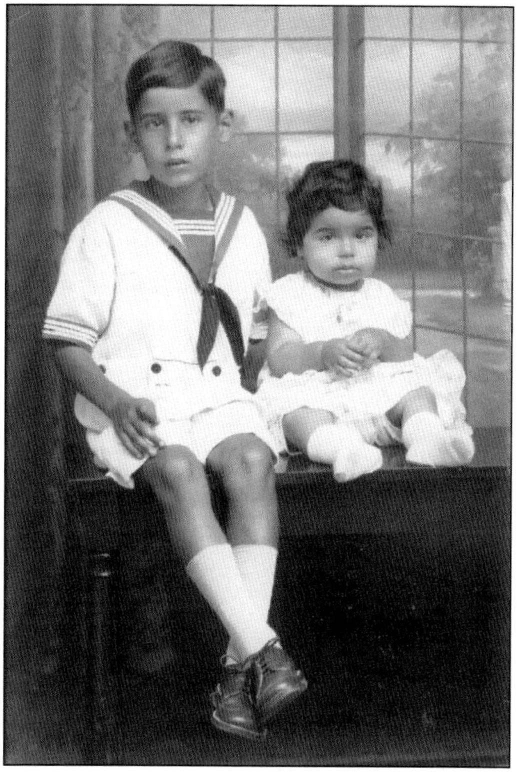

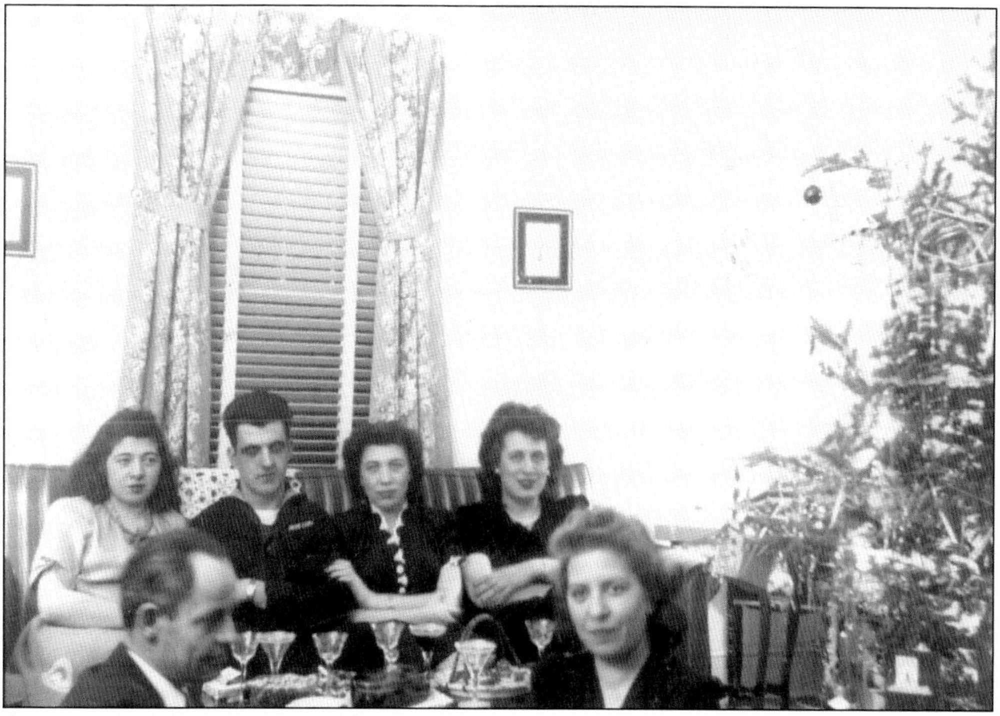

A group of adults is seen posed here in this photograph during Christmas. The man in the center had recently arrived home from serving in the armed forces.

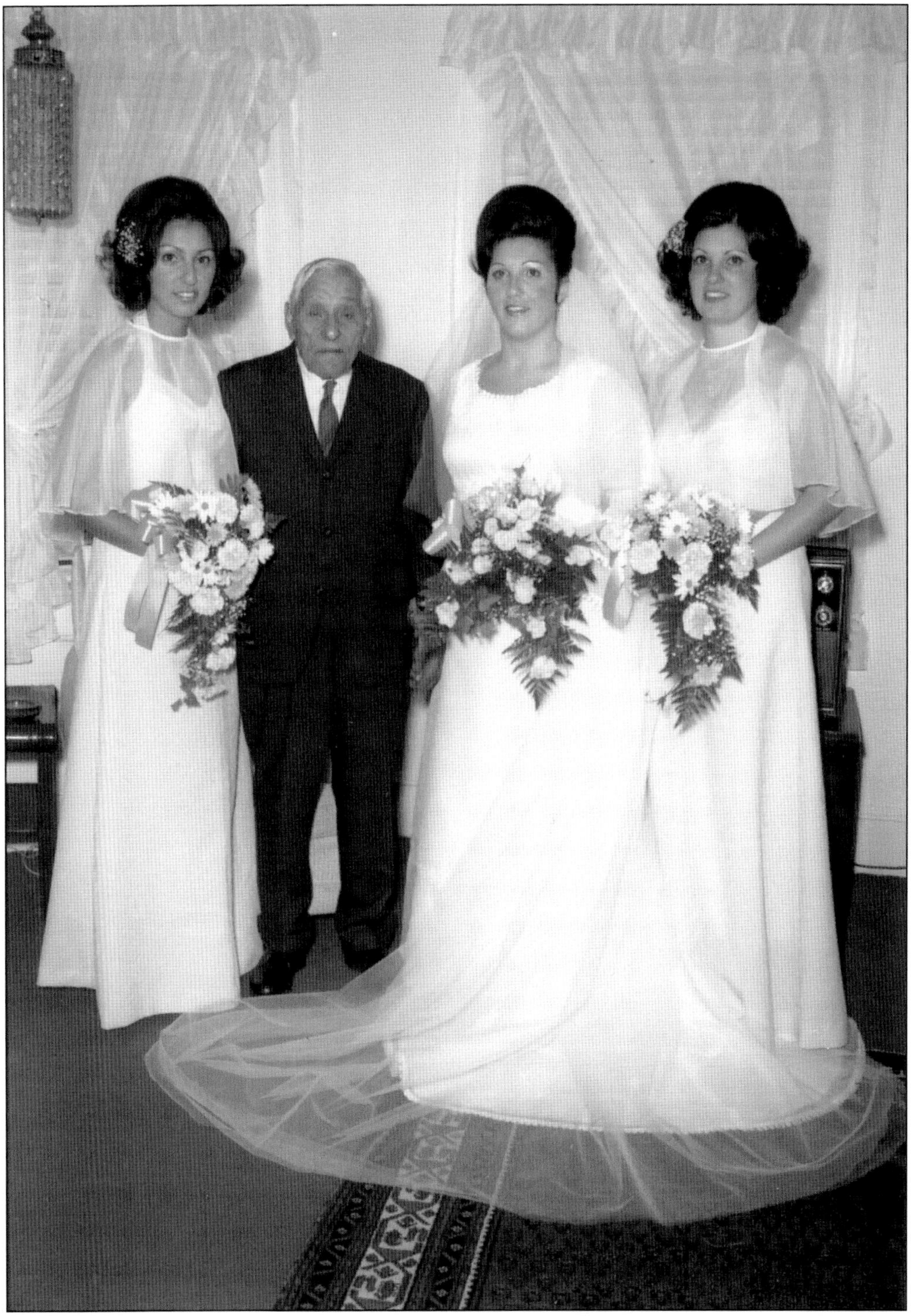

Shown in this photograph is Yonatan BetSolieman, posed with his three granddaughters, Marsha Gallo (left), Kathy Nelson (second from right), and Sandra.

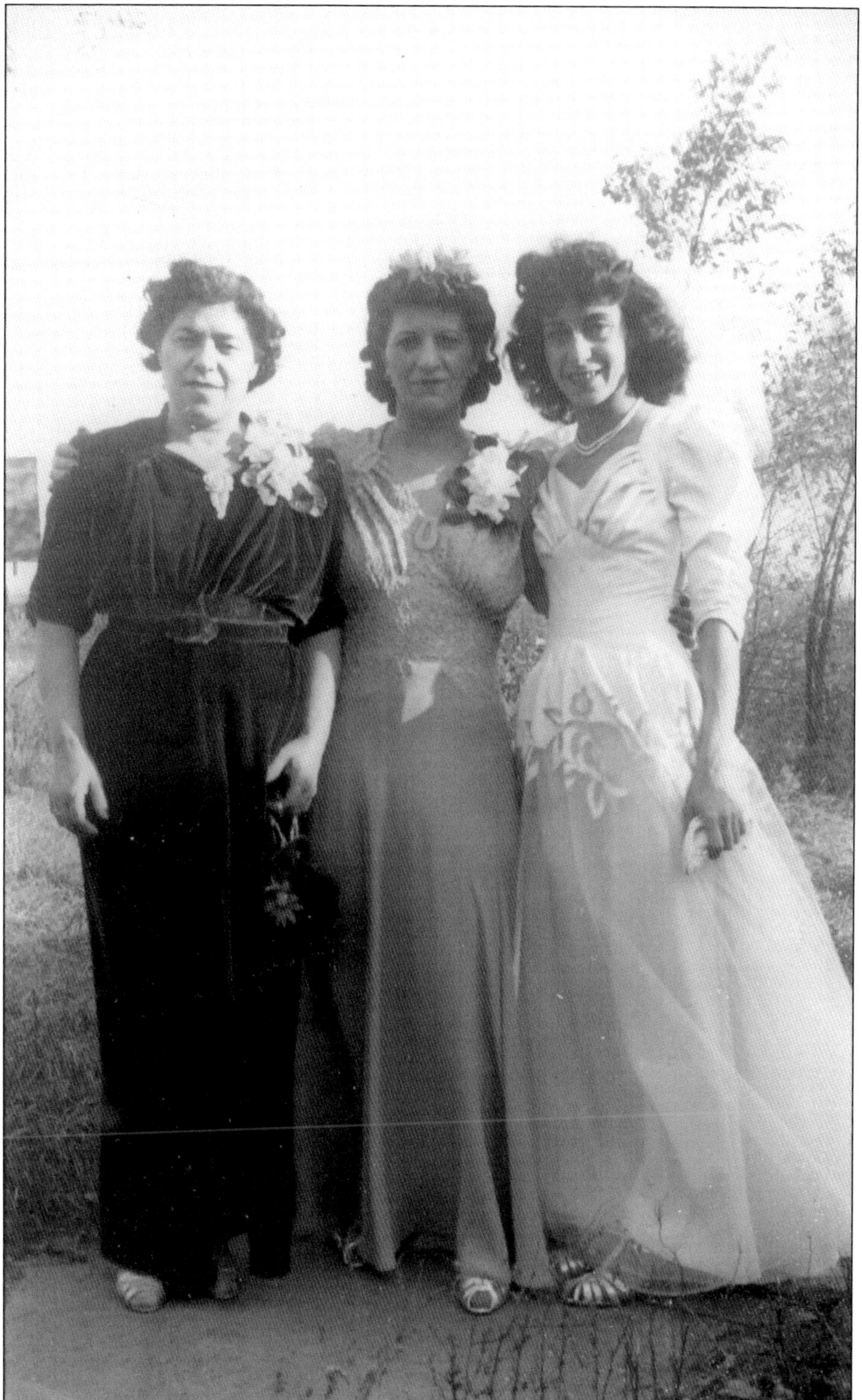

Mikal Dooman (center) and Gladys Dooman (left) are shown with an unidentified woman. (Courtesy of the Dooman family collection.)

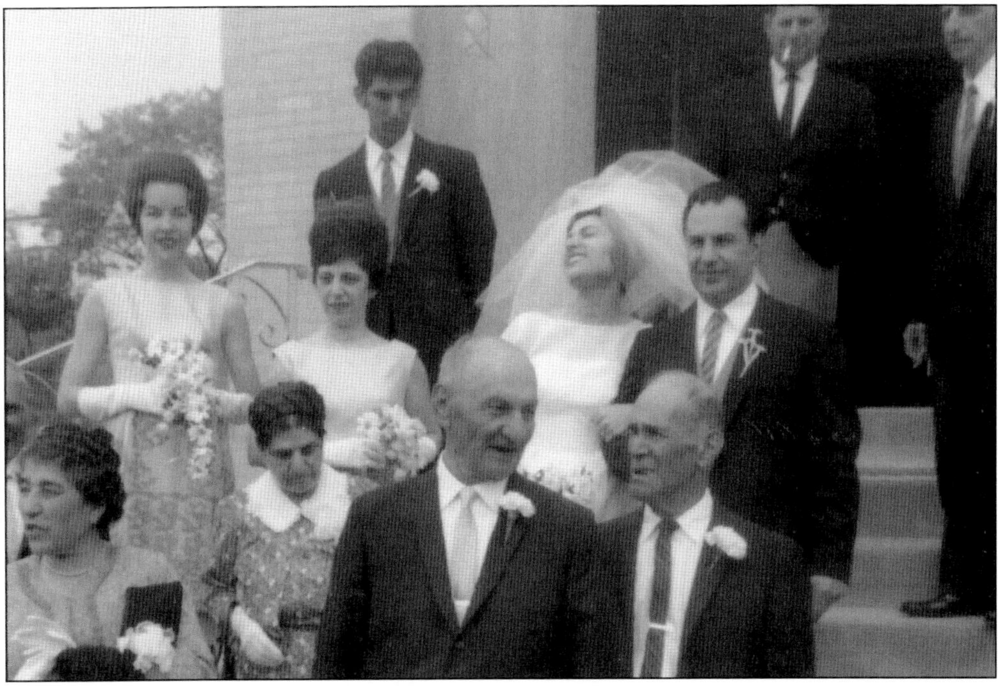

This photograph, taken in May 1963, includes the following, from left to right: (first row) Samasha David Sargis, Gizbas Baba, Joseph Sargis, and Absalam (Pasha) Baba; (second row) Cynthia Coolidge, Agnes Sargis, and Annette and Sam Baba; (third row) Shushan Sargis, Fred Pera, and unidentified.

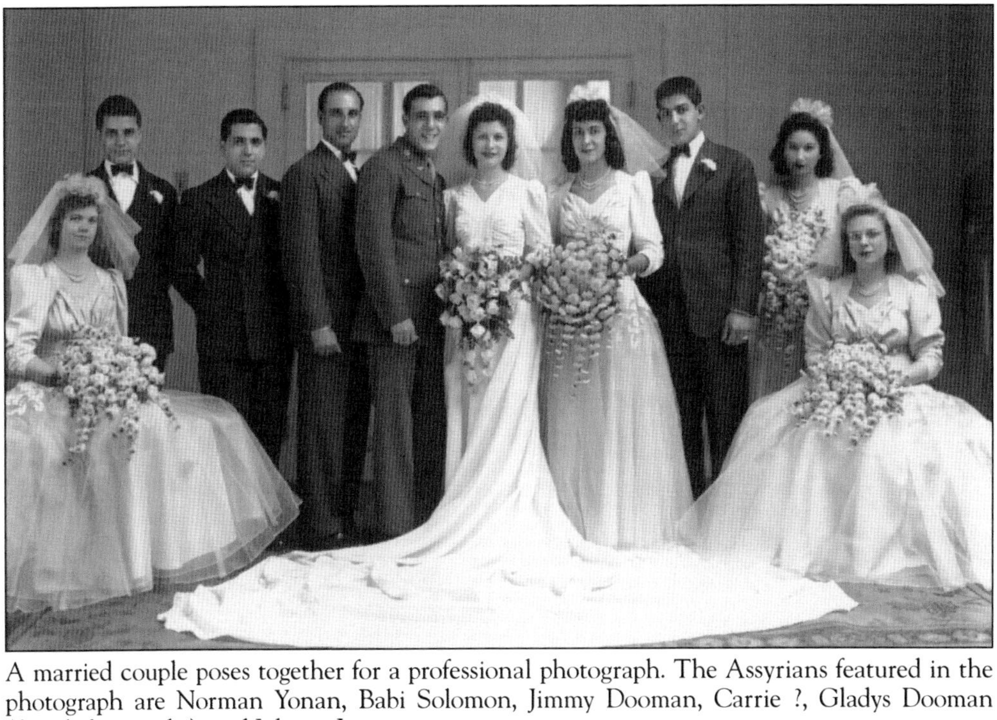

A married couple poses together for a professional photograph. The Assyrians featured in the photograph are Norman Yonan, Babi Solomon, Jimmy Dooman, Carrie ?, Gladys Dooman (fourth from right), and Johnny Jones.

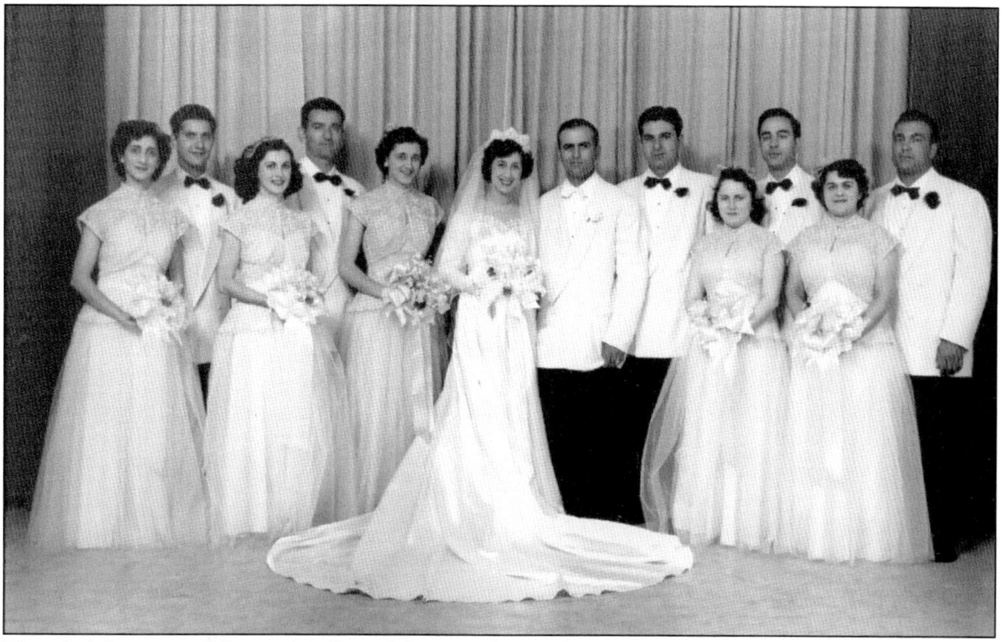

The California wedding of Lillian Ishoo is shown here. In attendance is the bride's sister, Connecticut resident Lucy Abraham (fifth from left) and another sister of the bride Mary Nimrod (left).

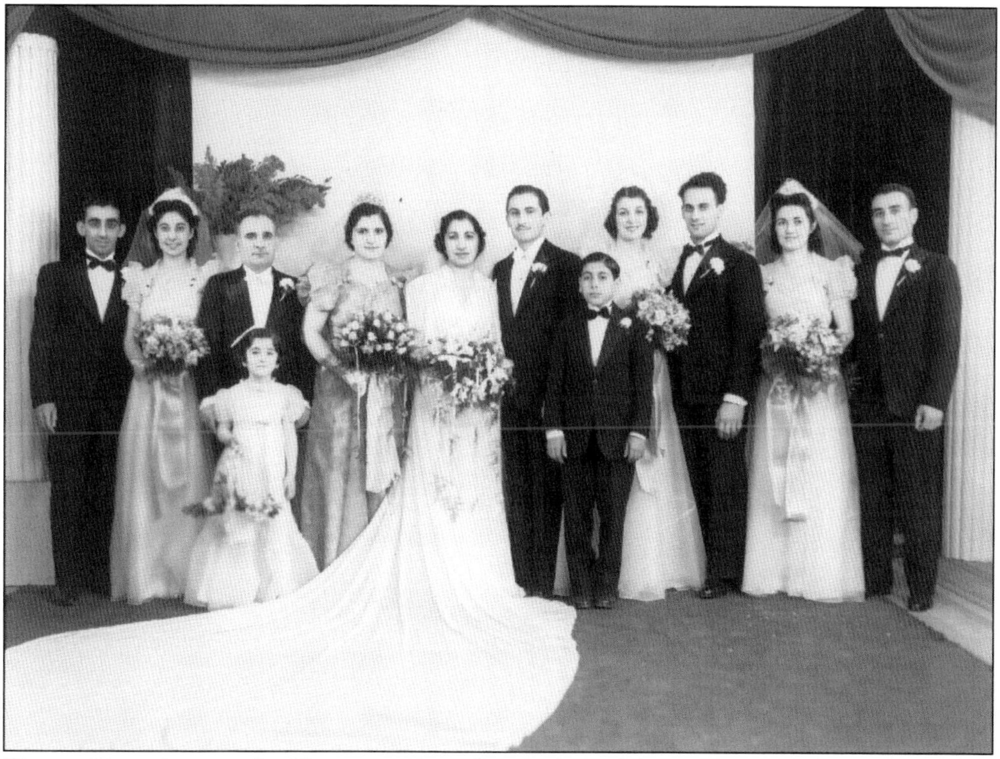

This wedding photograph of Jennie and Mooshie "Jack" Badal was taken on May 29, 1940. It was taken at Collomb Studio in New Britain.

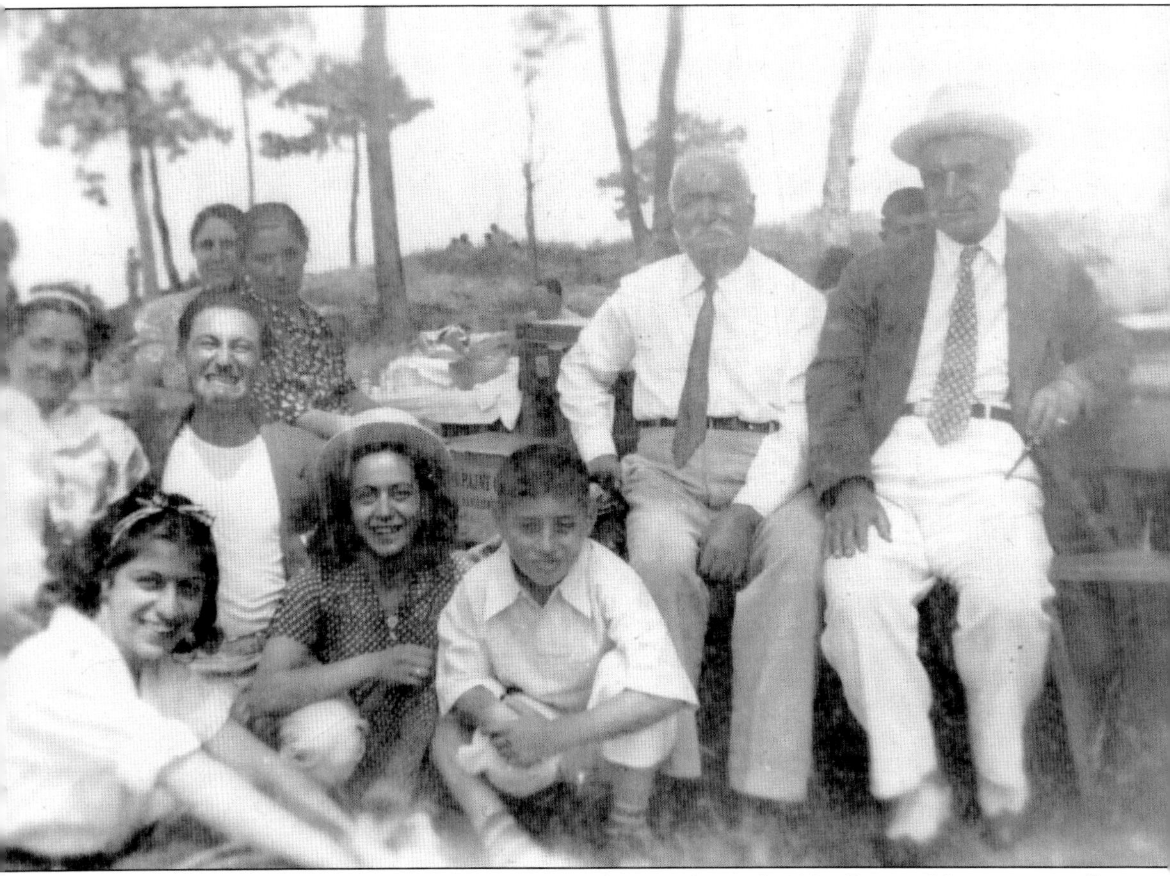

This is a photograph of an Assyrian picnic, taken in the mid-1920s. Featured here is a small group of adults in Batterson Park in New Britain.

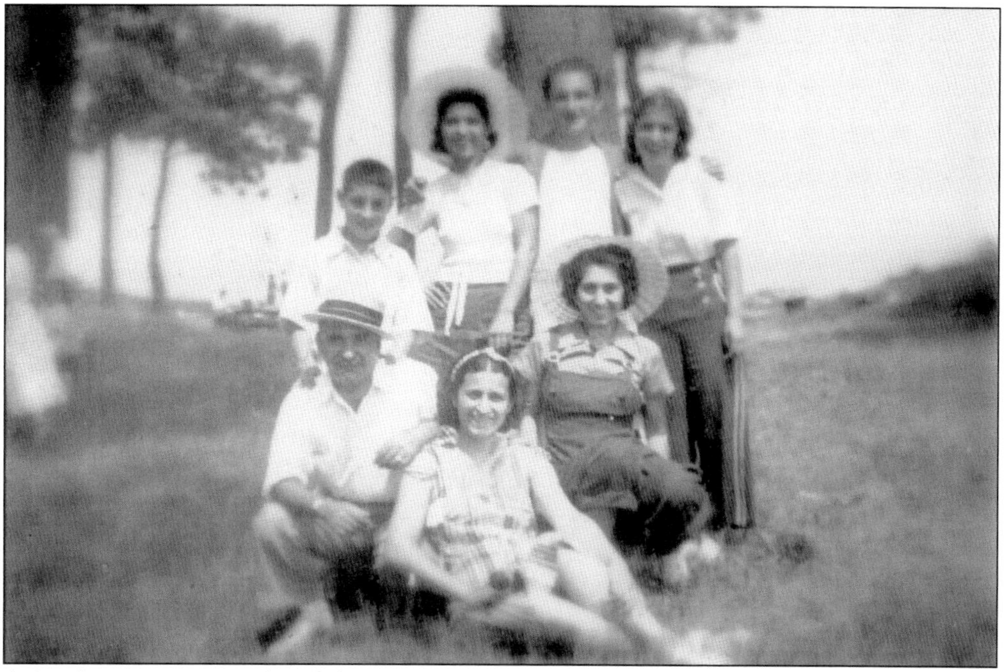

A family group poses in front of a tree at an Assyrian picnic in Batterson Park in New Britain. The photograph was taken in the mid-1920s.

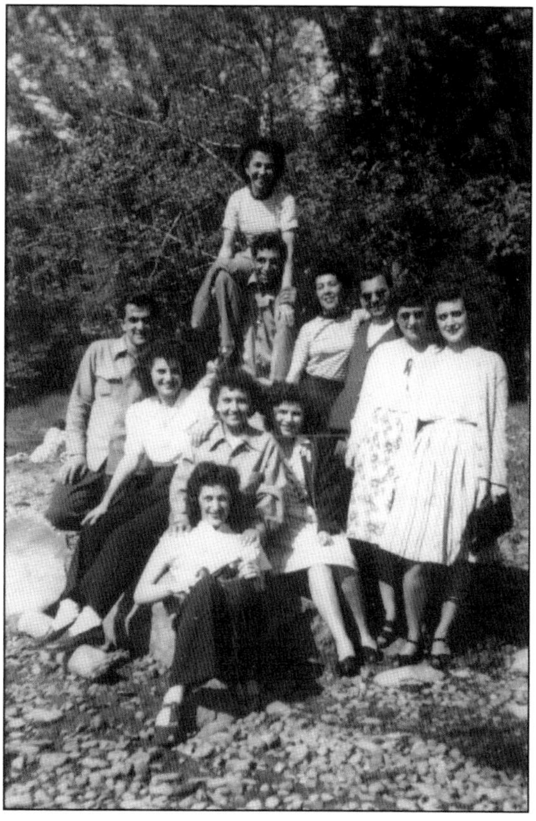

Assyrian young adults have taken a day trip to a lake in this photograph. They are shown here during a lunch break.

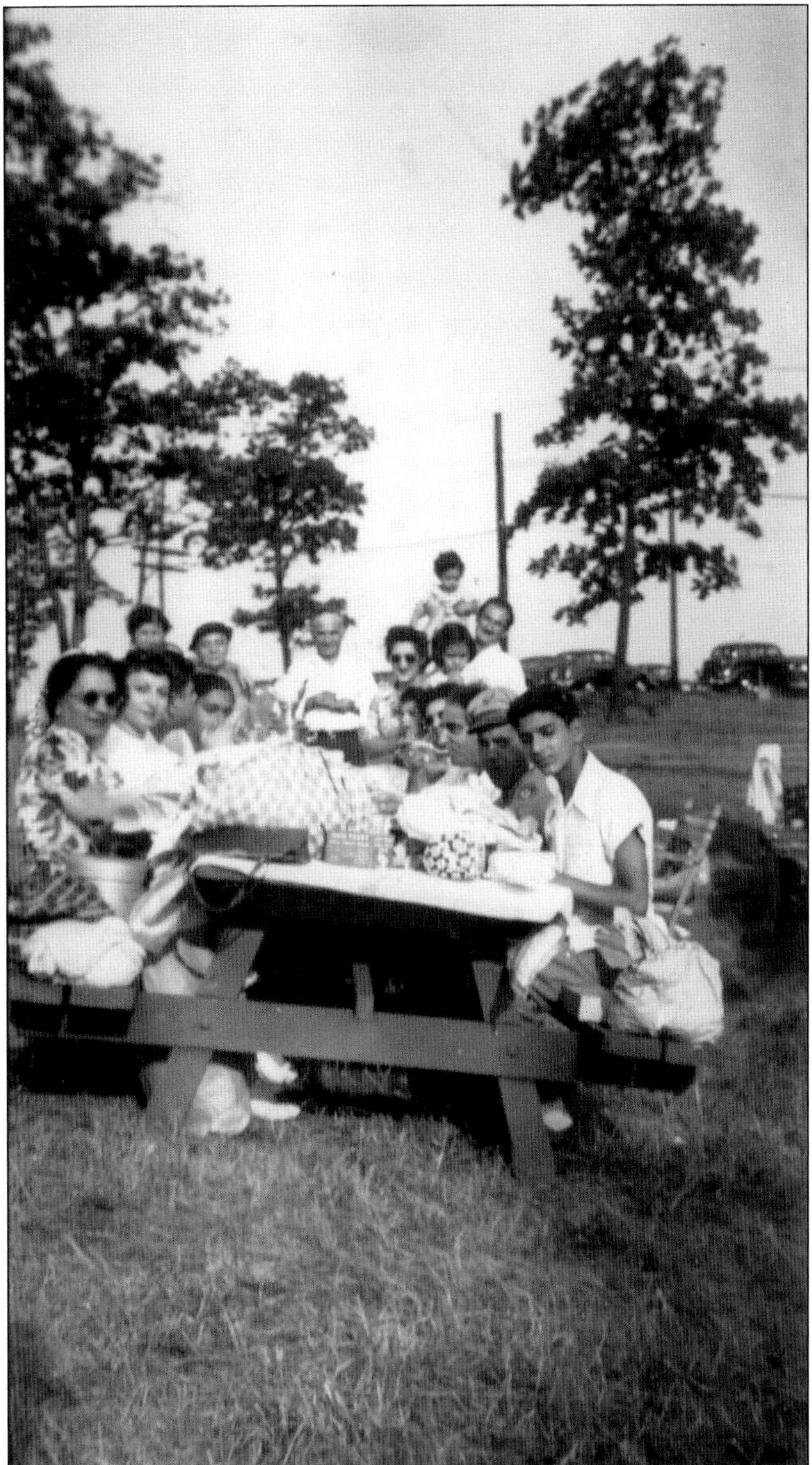

This is a photograph of an Assyrian picnic at Batterson Park in New Britain, taken upon the return of the veteran who is shown second on the right side.

This photograph portrays Joel (left) and his brother John Khamis. This was taken prior to World War II, which is when Joel was killed while serving as a pilot. Assyrian citizens were increasingly active in American activities and duties, and not long after the war, an Assyrian-American veteran group was established.

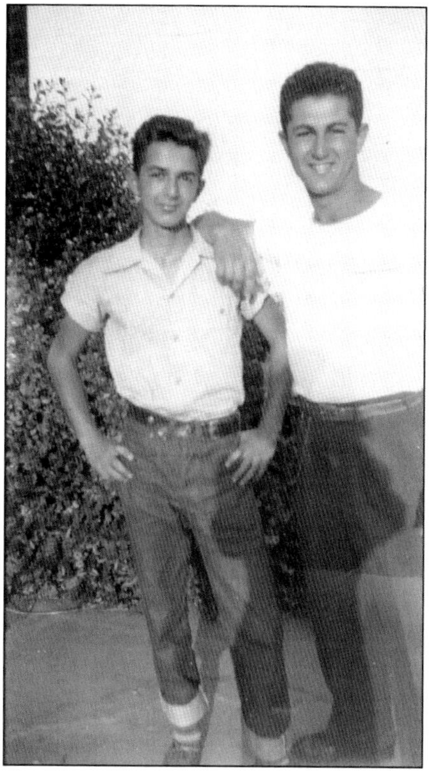

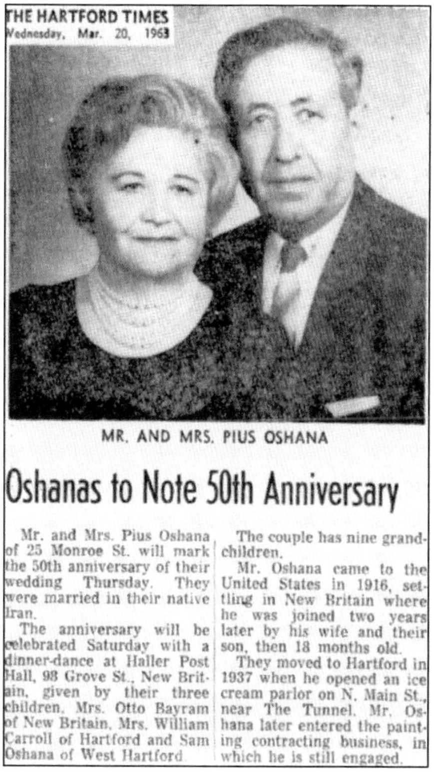

THE HARTFORD TIMES
Wednesday, Mar. 20, 1963

MR. AND MRS. PIUS OSHANA

Oshanas to Note 50th Anniversary

Mr. and Mrs. Pius Oshana of 25 Monroe St. will mark the 50th anniversary of their wedding Thursday. They were married in their native Iran.

The anniversary will be celebrated Saturday with a dinner-dance at Haller Post Hall, 98 Grove St., New Britain, given by their three children, Mrs. Otto Bayram of New Britain, Mrs. William Carroll of Hartford and Sam Oshana of West Hartford.

The couple has nine grandchildren.

Mr. Oshana came to the United States in 1916, settling in New Britain where he was joined two years later by his wife and their son, then 18 months old.

They moved to Hartford in 1937 when he opened an ice cream parlor on N. Main St., near The Tunnel. Mr. Oshana later entered the painting contracting business, in which he is still engaged.

The 50th anniversary announcement of Pius and Martha Oshana appeared in the *Hartford Times* newspaper in 1963. This gives a brief description of his journey to New Britain in 1916 and his wife and son's journey two years later.

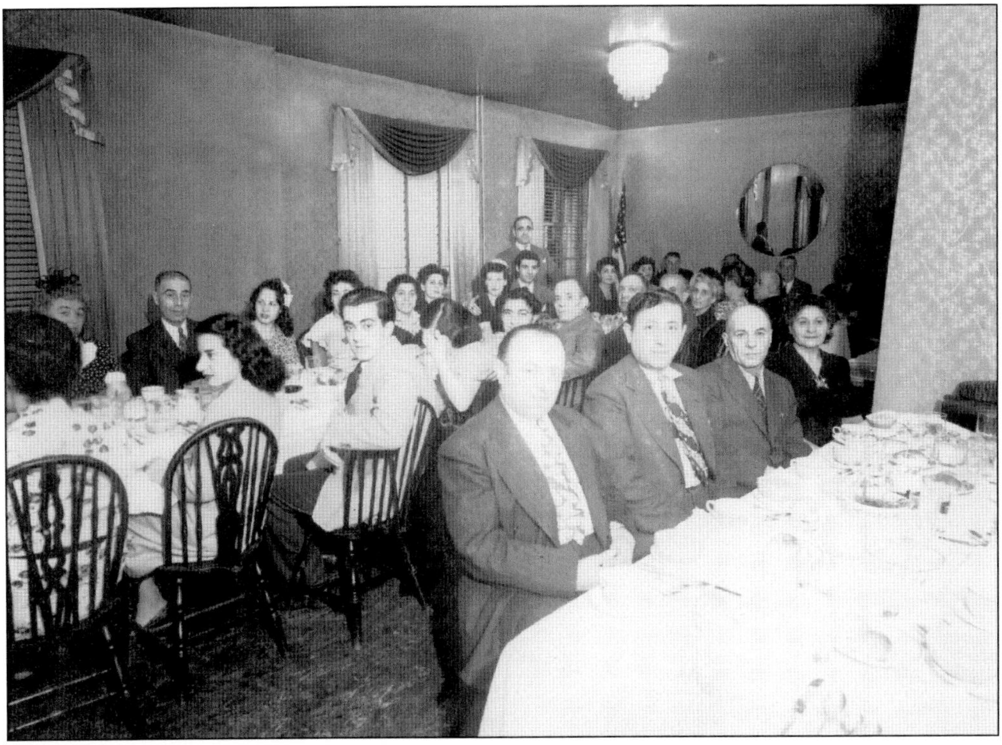

An Assyrian wedding event is shown in this photograph. Featured on the left are Pius Oshana and Joe Yonan, among others.

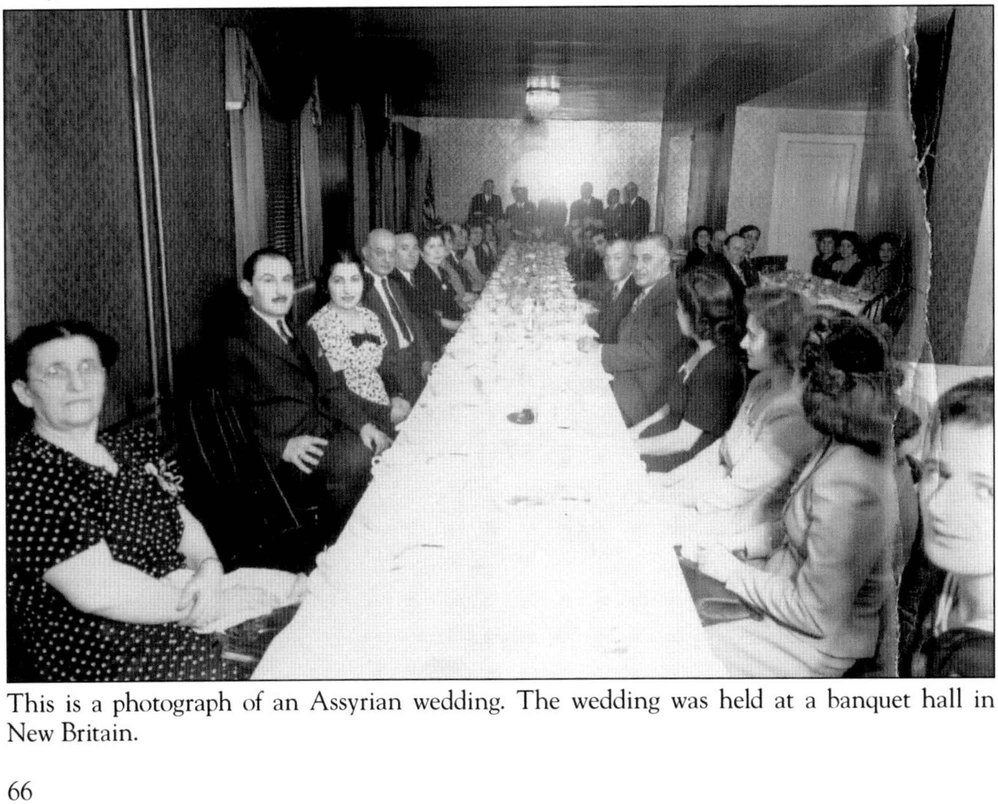

This is a photograph of an Assyrian wedding. The wedding was held at a banquet hall in New Britain.

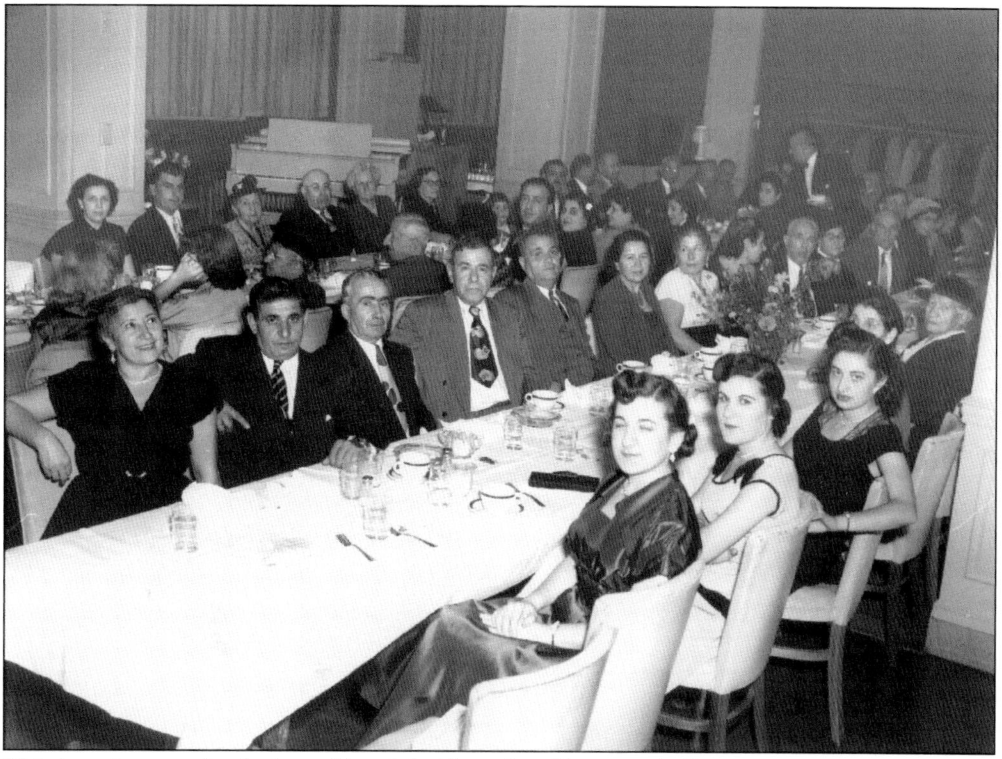

This is a photograph of a formal lunch held at a local banquet hall.

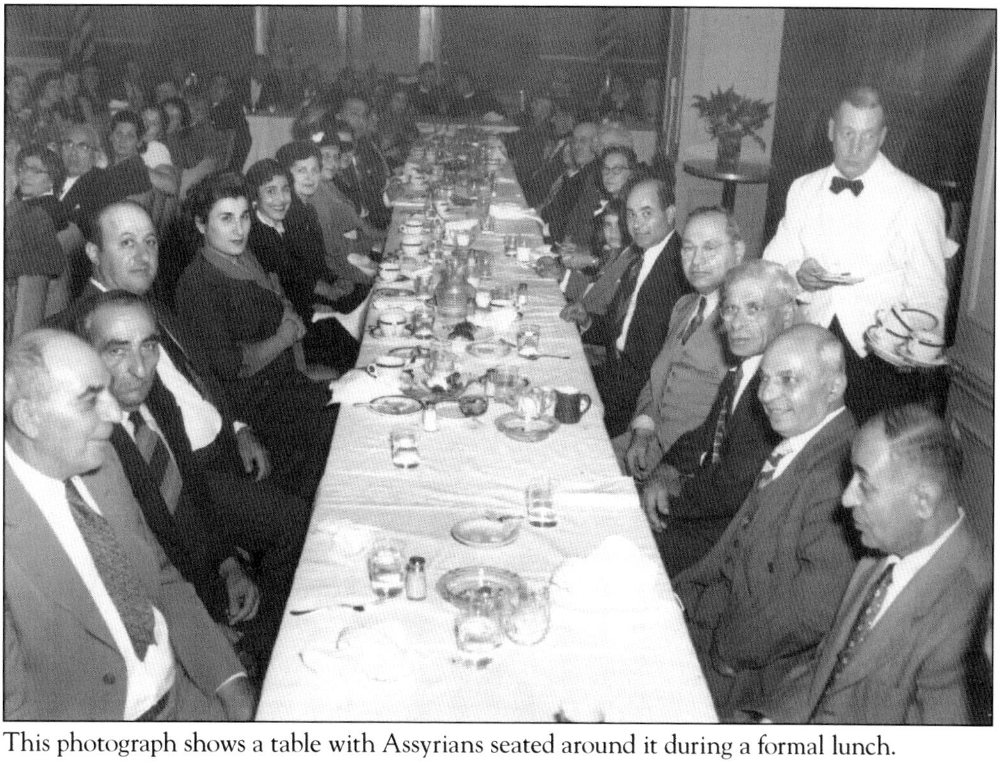

This photograph shows a table with Assyrians seated around it during a formal lunch.

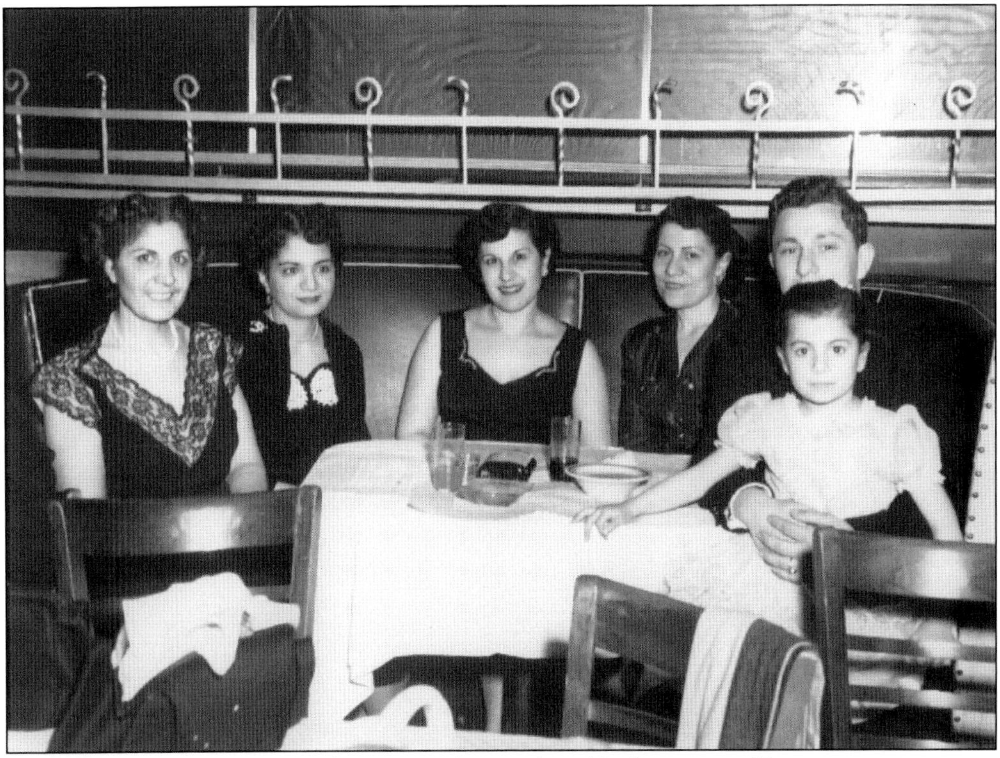

In this photograph, a family is shown seated around a table during a wedding.

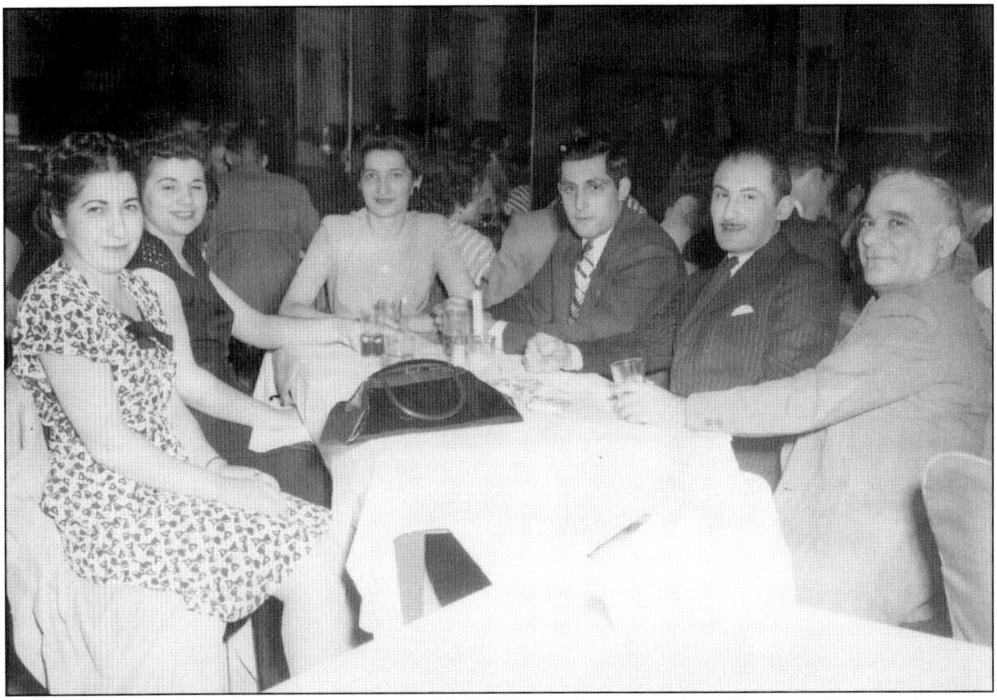

Jack (second from right) and Jennie Badal (left) are shown in this photograph seated with a group of friends at an Assyrian banquet event.

Three

CHURCH HAPPENINGS

The first Assyrian to preach at the South Church of New Britain, Elisha E. Adams, began his service upon Baba Jones's efforts to secure the services of an Assyrian minister in 1911. Adams was brought to New Britain from Yonkers, New York, and continued preaching until 1936.

The second Assyrian minister, Richard G. Pera, of the University of Chicago, served from 1937 until 1947. It is written in South Church of New Britain documents that he served the needs of both older and younger generations of Assyrians very well.

The final Assyrian minister at the South Church of New Britain, Stephen O. Khoobyar, served from 1948 to 1956. Reverend Khoobyar, in 1956, gave a speech on the history of the Assyrian mission within the South Church of New Britain.

Portraits of the Assyrian pastors, along with one of Ozora S. Davis, now hang in the Assyrian parlor of the South Church of New Britain, a room that was dedicated in 1981. The room continues to host many gatherings within the church, both Assyrian events and those of South Congregational Church's business.

The parish of St. Thomas Church of the East was established in New Britain in 1919, though church services for the St. Thomas Church of the East were held at St. Mark's Episcopal Church. The church was placed at the disposal of the Assyrians of the St. Thomas Church of the East for their services and events. Within some years, the parish purchased a home on South High Street, with the intent of building a church on the land. Rev. Saul K. Neesan and his family took up residence there, and for a time Assyrian school and bible studies were taught there.

St. Thomas Church of the East has welcomed and seen off seven Assyrian priests. The first was Rev. Shimun Yonan, who served from 1919 until 1923, and the most recent of which has been in service since 2000.

Prior to 1995, the Church of the East and Catholicism were considered separate practicing branches of Christianity, but in a meeting between Pope John Paul II and the Assyrian patriarch Mar Dinkha, the Pope declared that both religions were the same. The first Catholic priest to preach in a Church of the East was Ghasha Benny Yadegar, at St. Thomas Church of the East in New Britain.

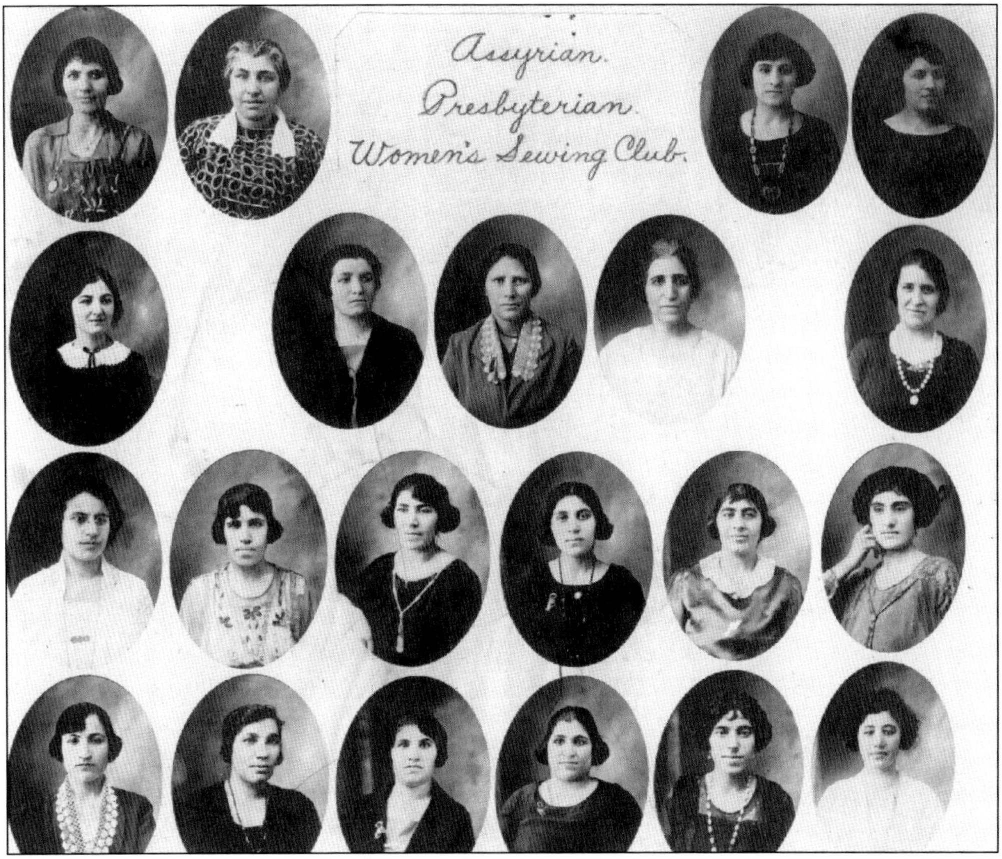

This group of Assyrians attended St. Mark's Episcopal Church in downtown New Britain. They created the Assyrian Presbyterian sewing group. While it was, overall, a group created for Assyrian-American women to socialize and create things, there was a small number of American women who were a part of the group as well.

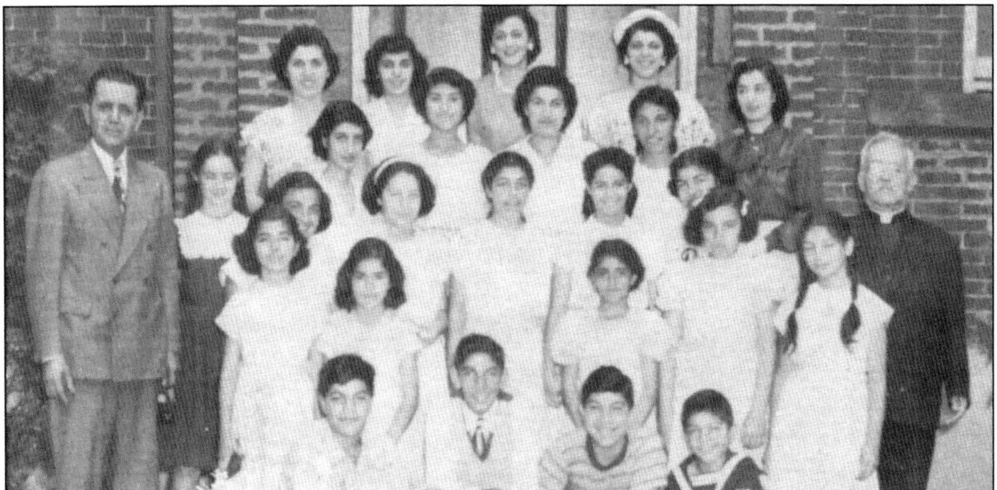

Shown in this photograph is the New Britain Assyrian Choir Group. The minister also stands in the photograph.

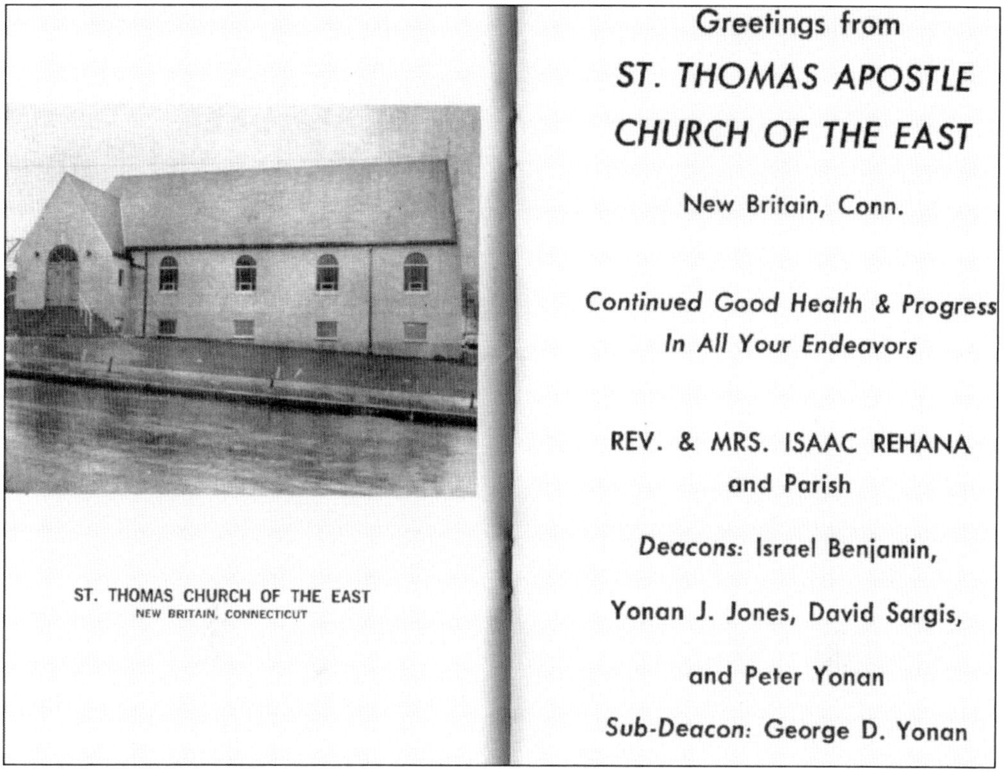

Each year, an Assyrian convention is held in a different large city in the United States. This photograph of St. Thomas Church of the East was put in the advertisement book of the 1957 convention to announce the establishment of a new church.

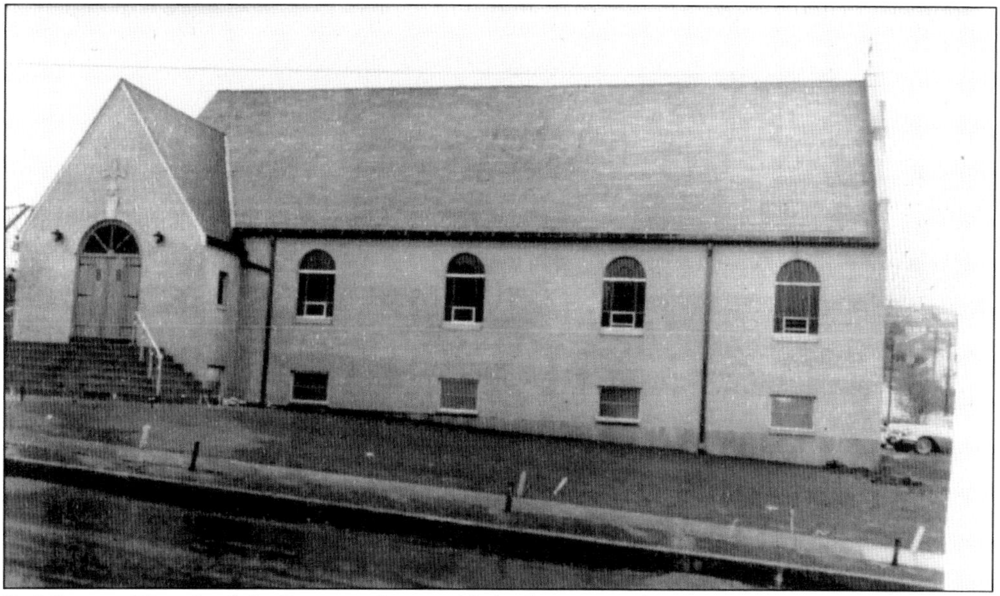

St. Thomas Church of the East was first established in November 1957. Prior to the construction of this church, Assyrians had attended various churches in New Britain, mainly South Church of New Britain and St. Mark's Episcopal Church.

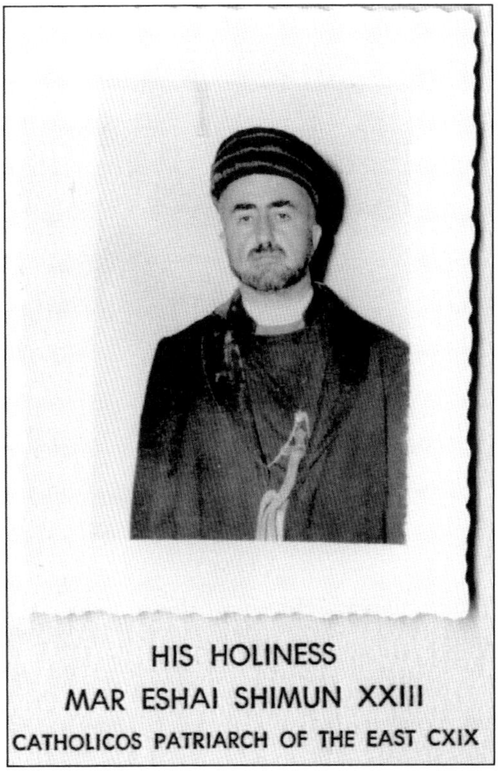

This is a photograph of Mar Eshai Shimun XXIII, the patriarch of the Assyrian Church of the East. He attended the unveiling and participated in blessing St. Thomas Church of the East in November 1957. He was very active in church related Assyrian affairs in New Britain.

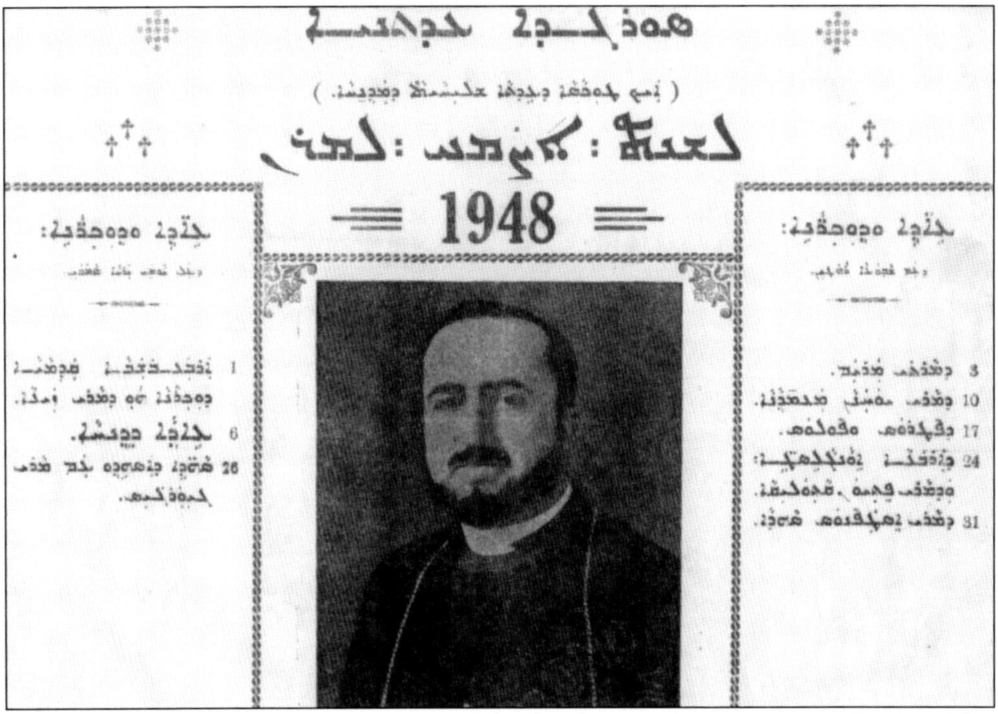

This copy of the first page from a 1948 calendar features Assyrian patriarch Mar Eshia Shimun XXIII.

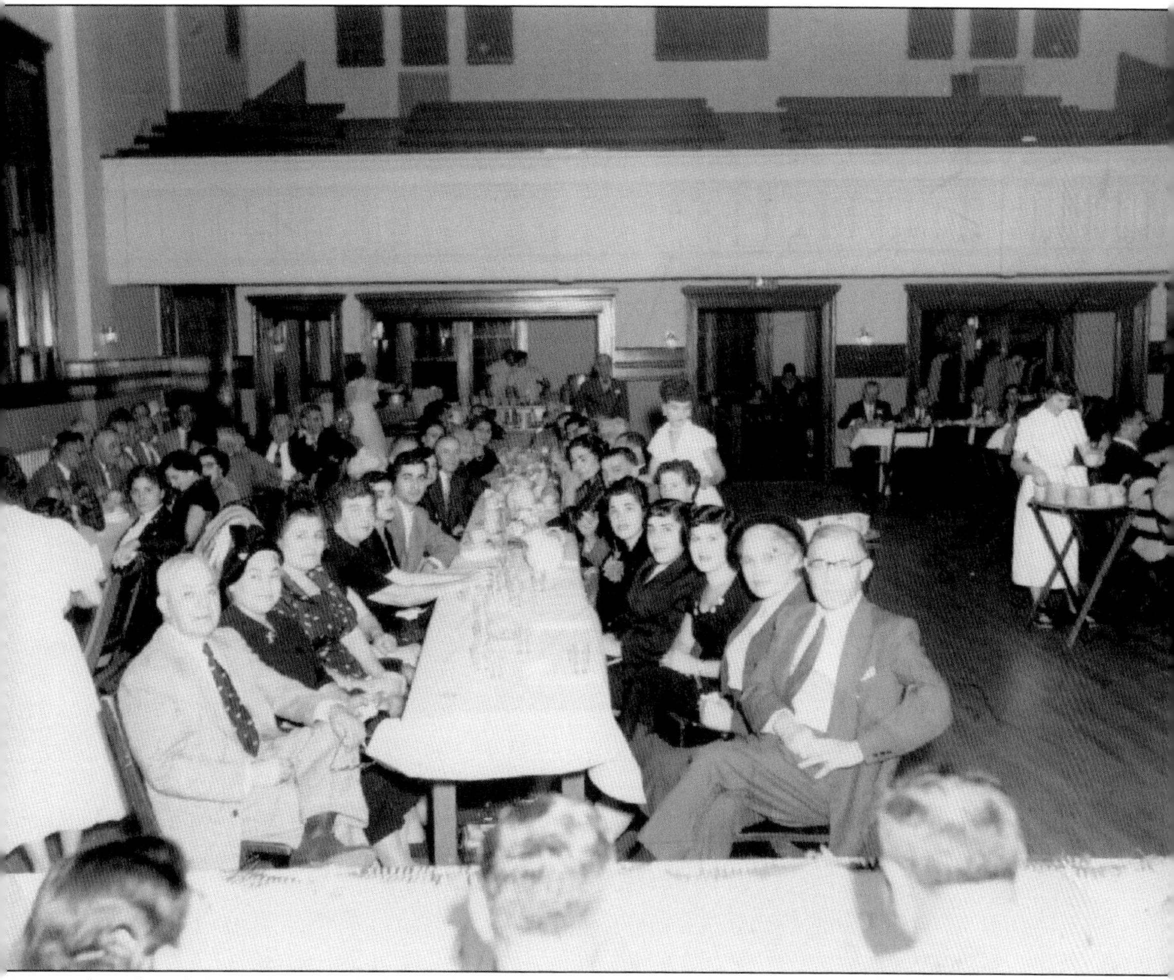

This church banquet included a large group of Assyrians from a number of different churches. (Courtesy of the Eshia family collection.)

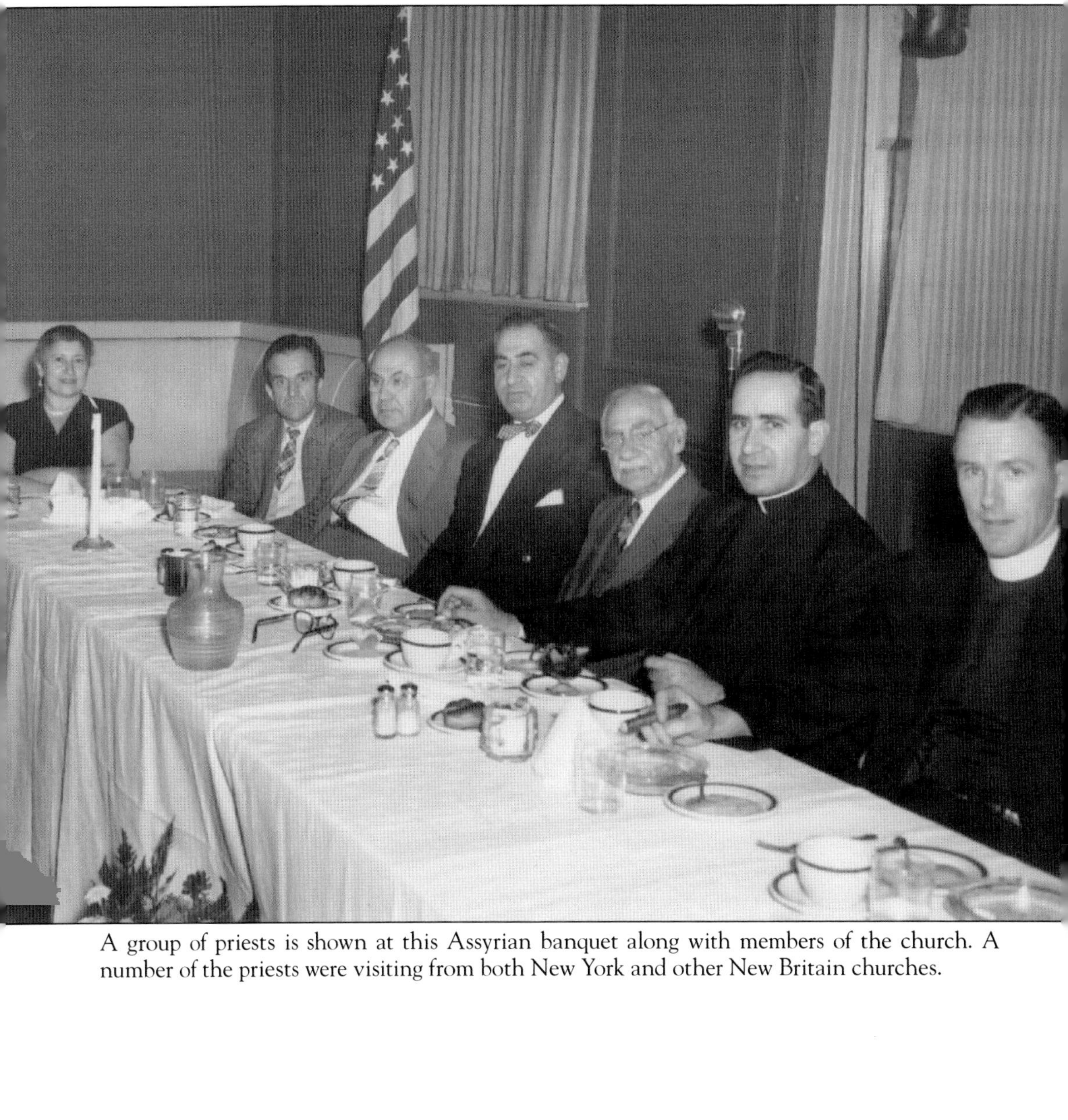

A group of priests is shown at this Assyrian banquet along with members of the church. A number of the priests were visiting from both New York and other New Britain churches.

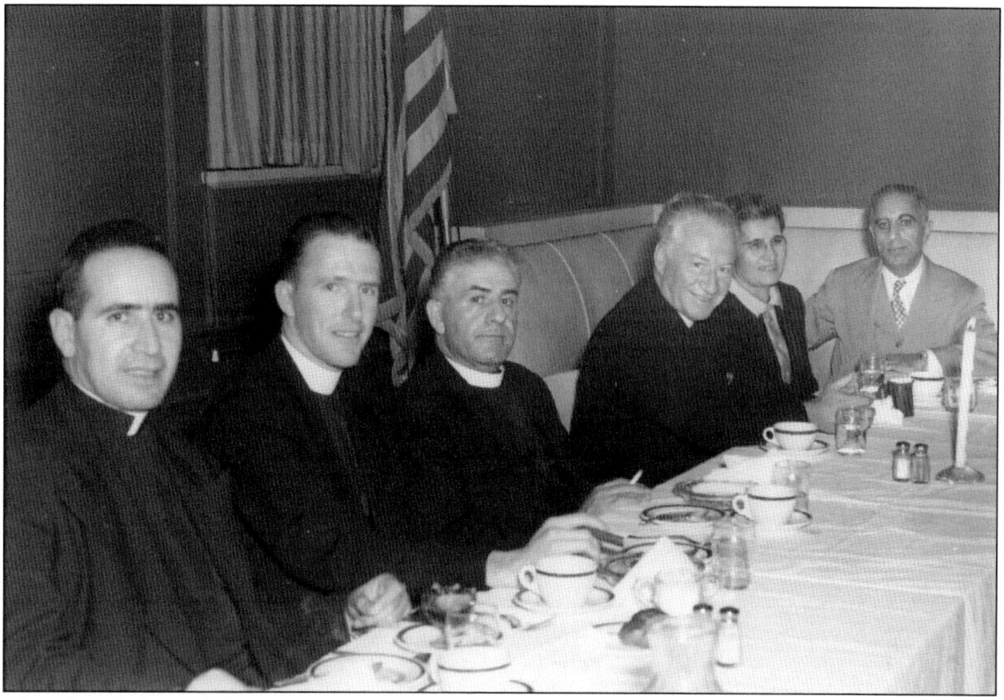

This church-hosted dinner included visiting Assyrian priests and notable guests from around the United States. The event took place four years prior to the establishment of St. Thomas Assyrian Church in 1953.

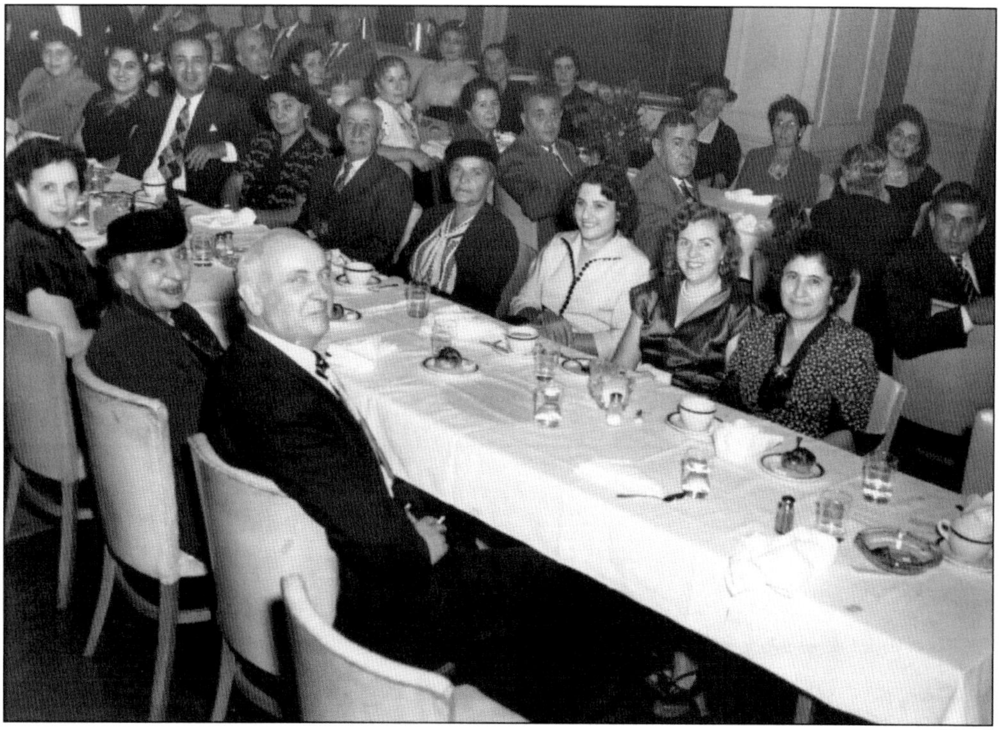

Guests are shown at one of the tables at a church banquet.

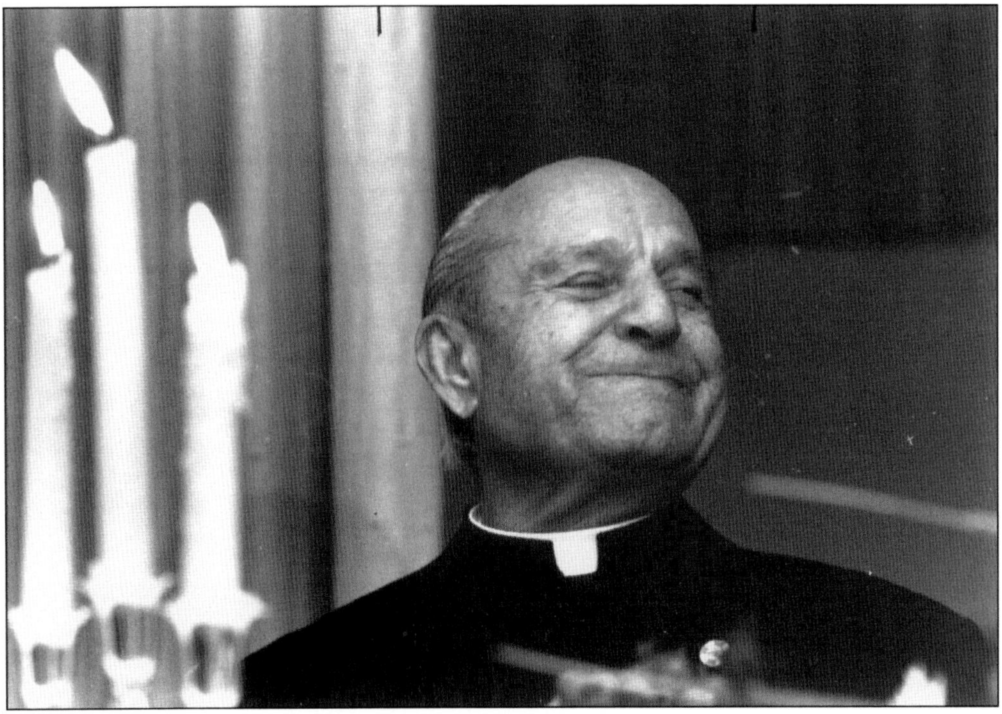

Rev. Isaac Rehana is shown here during a dinner held to honor his services to the Assyrian church.

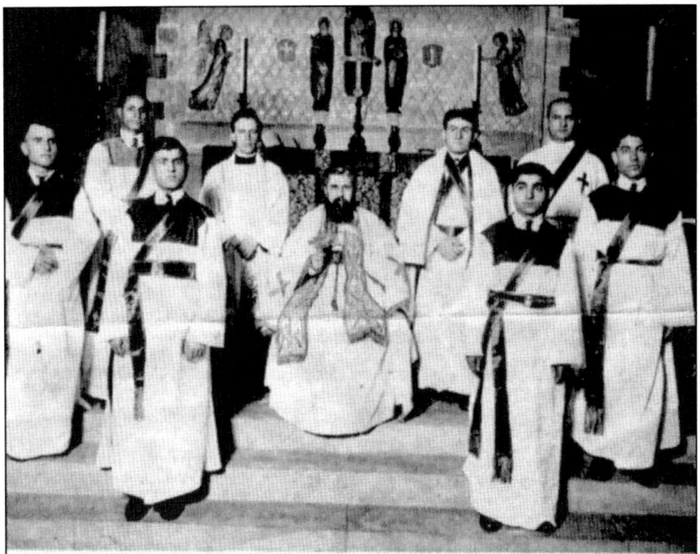

Ordination rites half-century ago

Participants in ordination ceremonies of St. Thomas Church of the East (Assyrian) at St. Mark's Episcopal Church, 147 W. Main St., 50 years ago were: the late Mar Timotheos, metropolitan of India, seated, who ordained the deacons and a priest while visiting the parish; bottom row, Deacon David Sargis, left, Deacon Israel Benjamin, right; second row, the late Deacon David Yonan, Deacon Ephraim Shuman of Yonkers, N.Y.; third row, Deacon Putrus Yacob, India, who assisted with the ordination, and the late Rev. Samuel Sutliffe of St. Mark's, the late Rev. Saul Neesan and Deacon Peter Yonan, who also assisted with the ordination. The late Father Neesan became the parish priest here upon his ordination in 1924, serving 20 years. He died in 1958.

Shown here is an ordination ceremony that occurred in the early half of the 20th century.

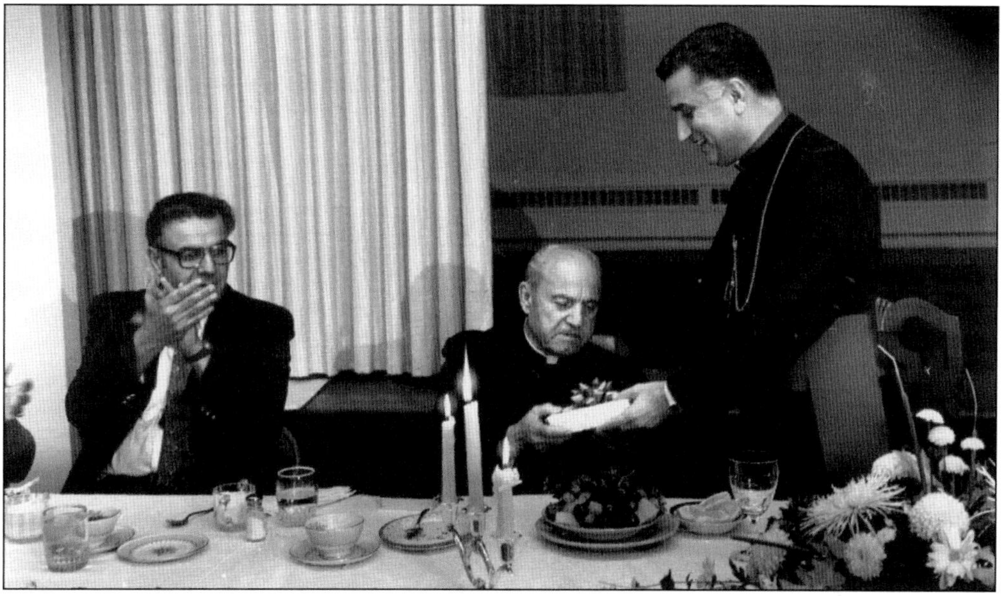

Reverend Rehana (center) is being honored by visiting Assyrian patriarch Mar Aprim Khamas (right) at a dinner held in his honor.On the left is George Lounadam.

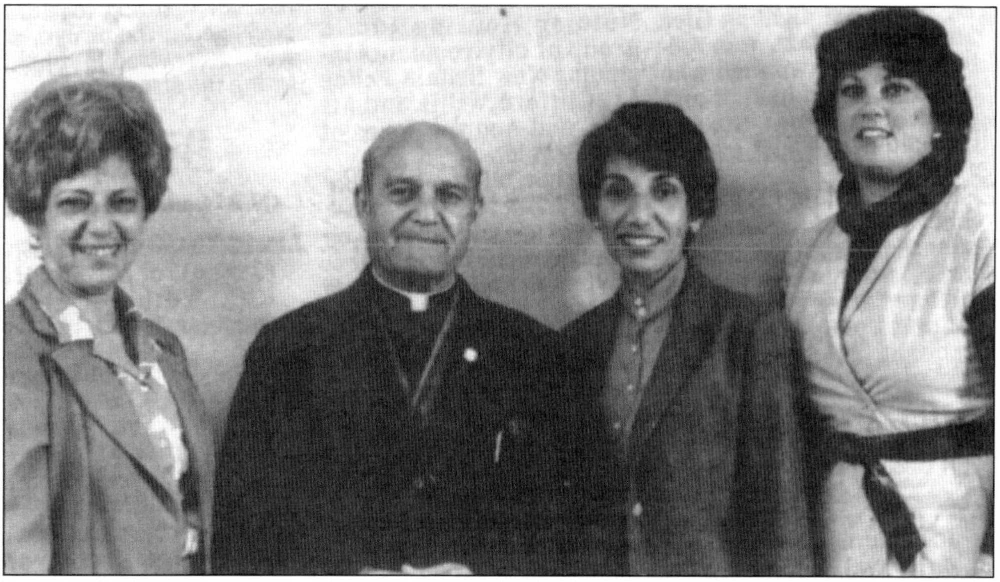

Reverend Rehana is shown with Agnes Sargis (left), Shamie Thomas (second from right), and Marsha Gallo (right), all members of St. Thomas Church of the East.

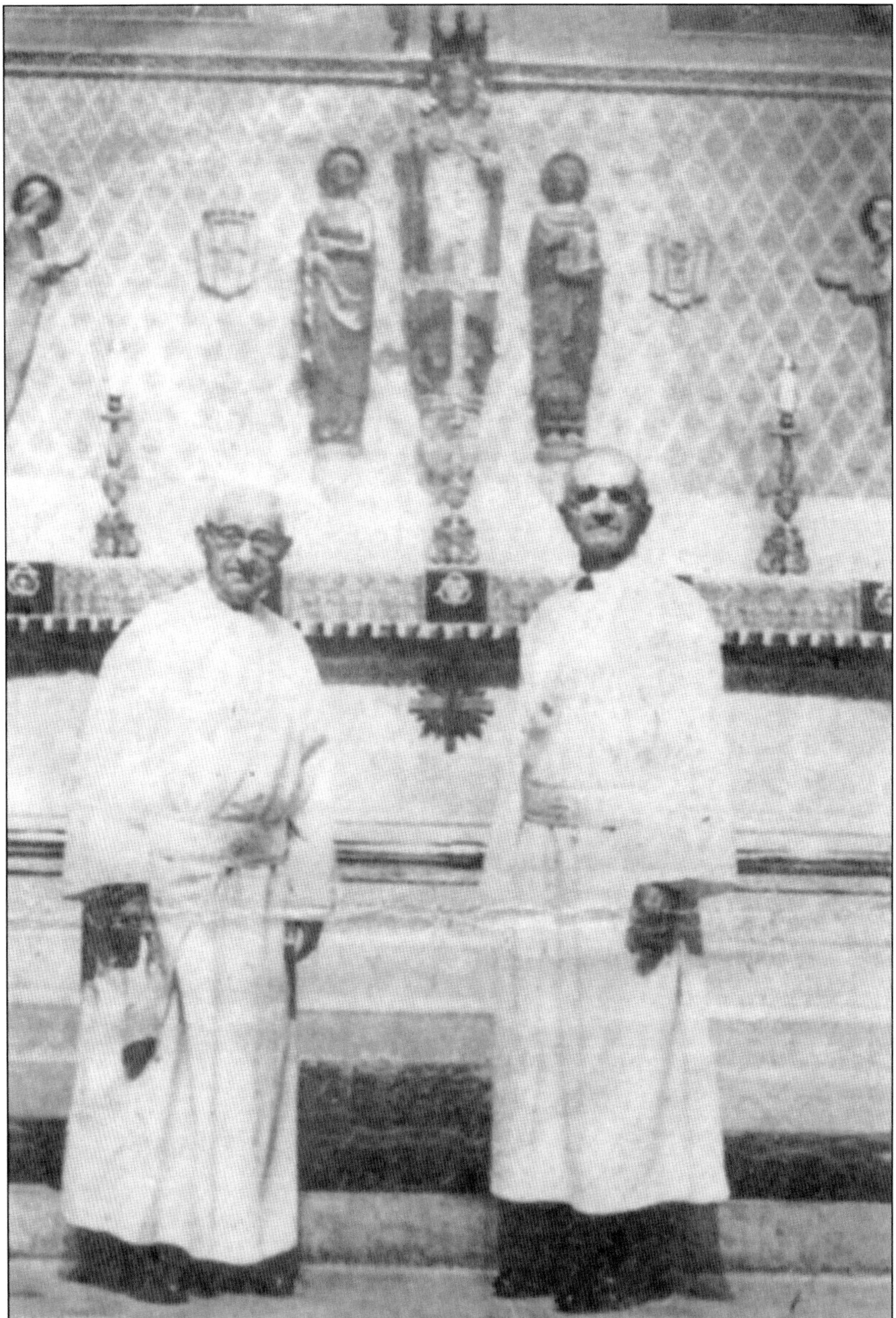

Deacons Israel Benjamin and David Sargis of St. Thomas Church of the East are shown here in St. Mark's Episcopal Church, where they were ordained in 1924.

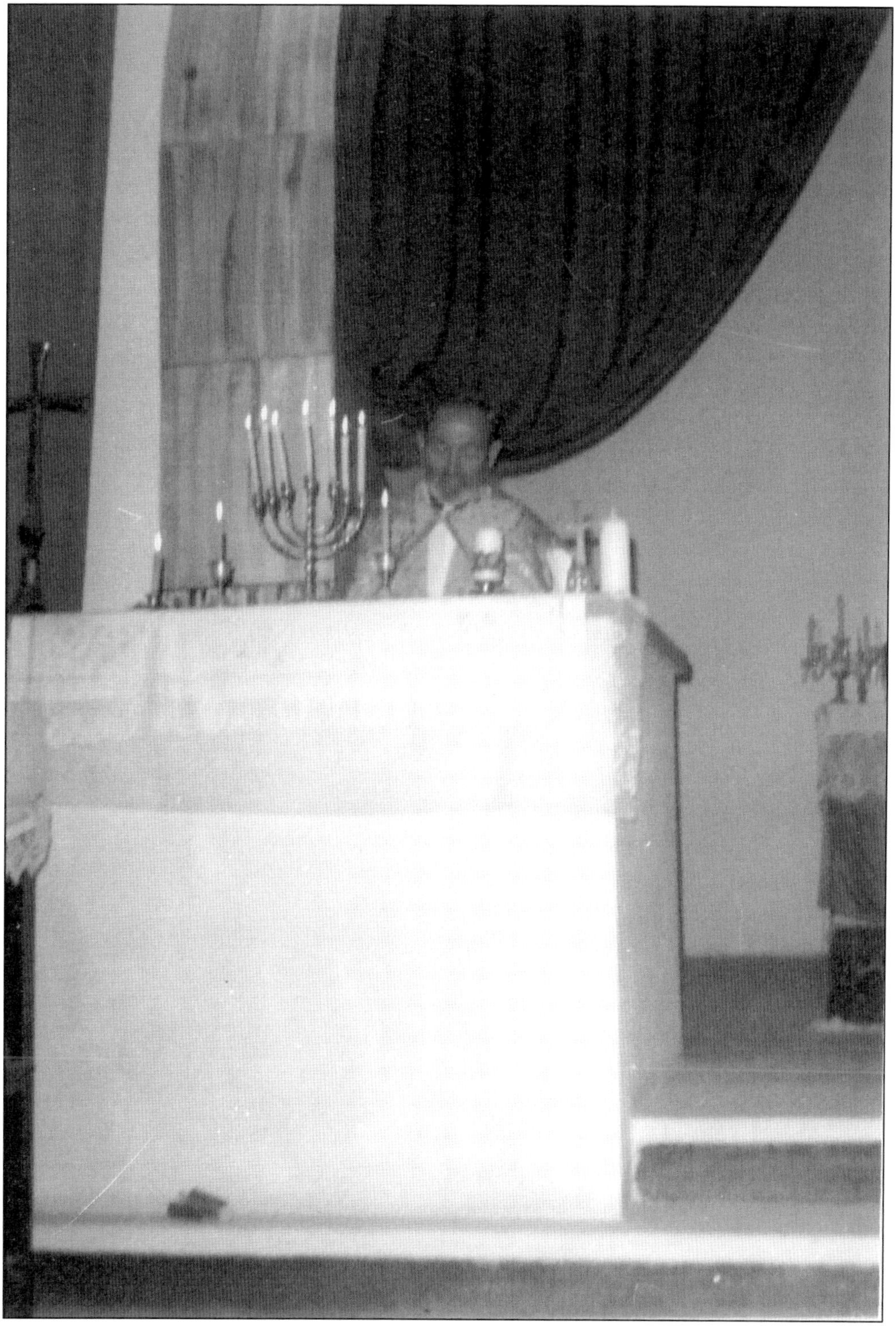

This Sunday morning service was led by Rev. Isaac Rehana. This photograph was taken at St. Thomas Church of the East.

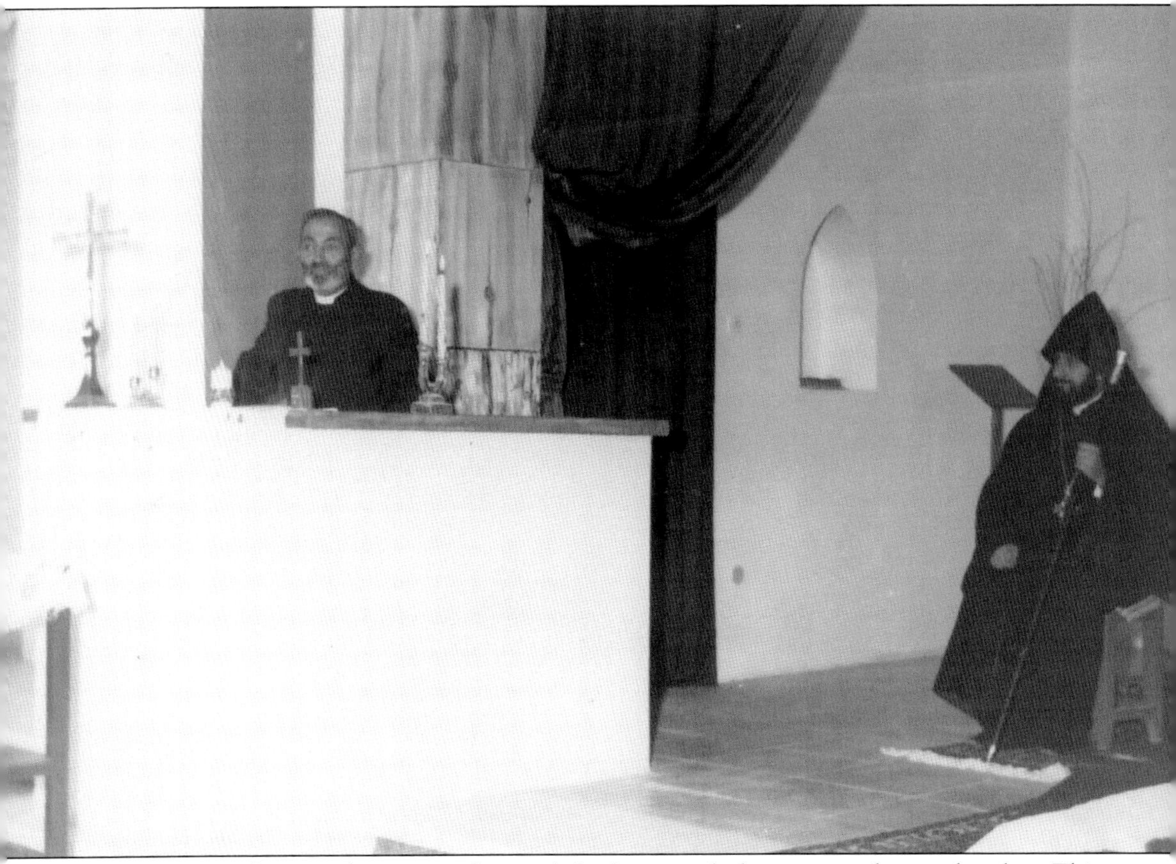

Rev. Isaac Rehana is shown preaching, while the guest bishop is seated near the alter. This photograph was taken at St. Thomas Church of the East.

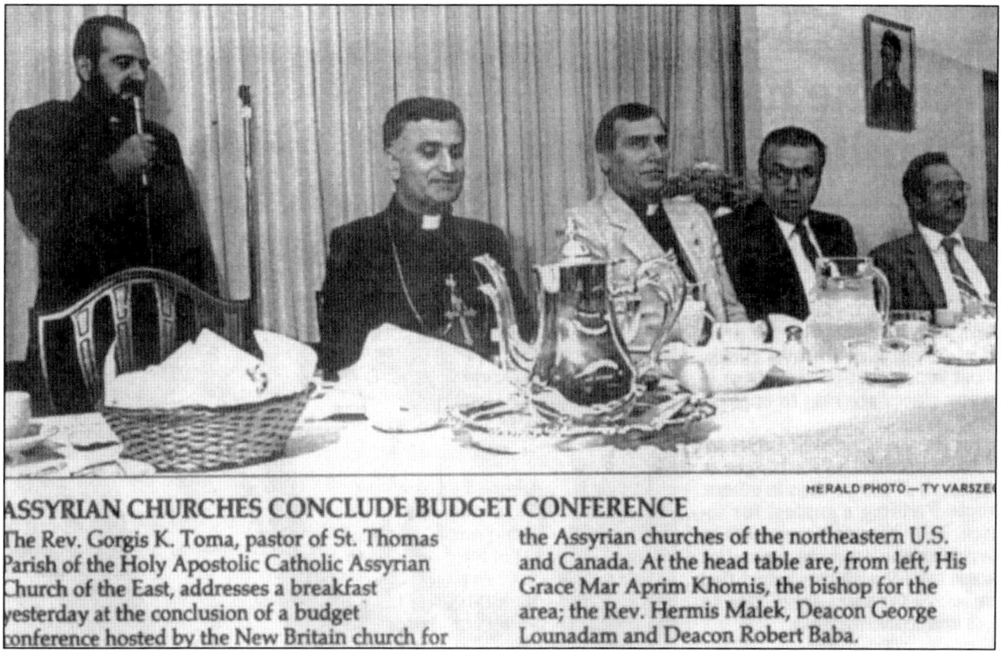
HERALD PHOTO—TY VARSZE

ASSYRIAN CHURCHES CONCLUDE BUDGET CONFERENCE

The Rev. Gorgis K. Toma, pastor of St. Thomas Parish of the Holy Apostolic Catholic Assyrian Church of the East, addresses a breakfast yesterday at the conclusion of a budget conference hosted by the New Britain church for the Assyrian churches of the northeastern U.S. and Canada. At the head table are, from left, His Grace Mar Aprim Khomis, the bishop for the area; the Rev. Hermis Malek, Deacon George Lounadam and Deacon Robert Baba.

This photograph, taken in the 1980s, shows the pastor of St. Thomas Church of the East speaking at a conference of northeastern United States Assyrian churches. (Courtesy of the Solieman family collection.)

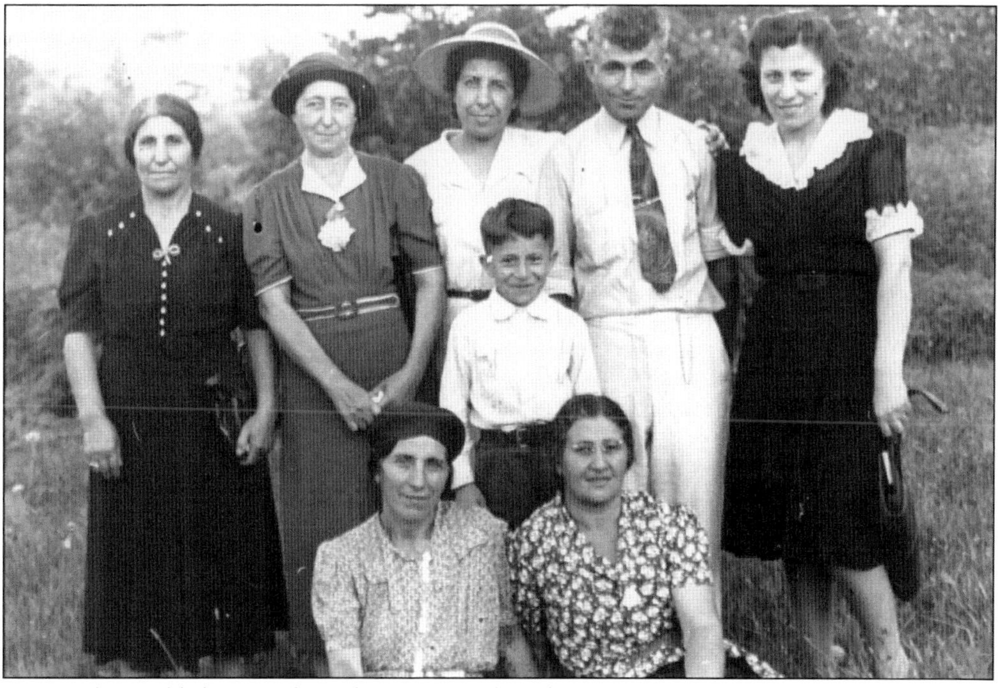

Prior to the establishment of St. Thomas Church of the East, Assyrians held their church picnics at different park locations in New Britain. Pictured from left to right are the following: (first row) Mayo Badel, Michael Yonan, and Esiat Sargis; (second row) Esther Benjamin, Rebecca Alkhas, Yonatan Benjamin, and Shamiran Yonan.

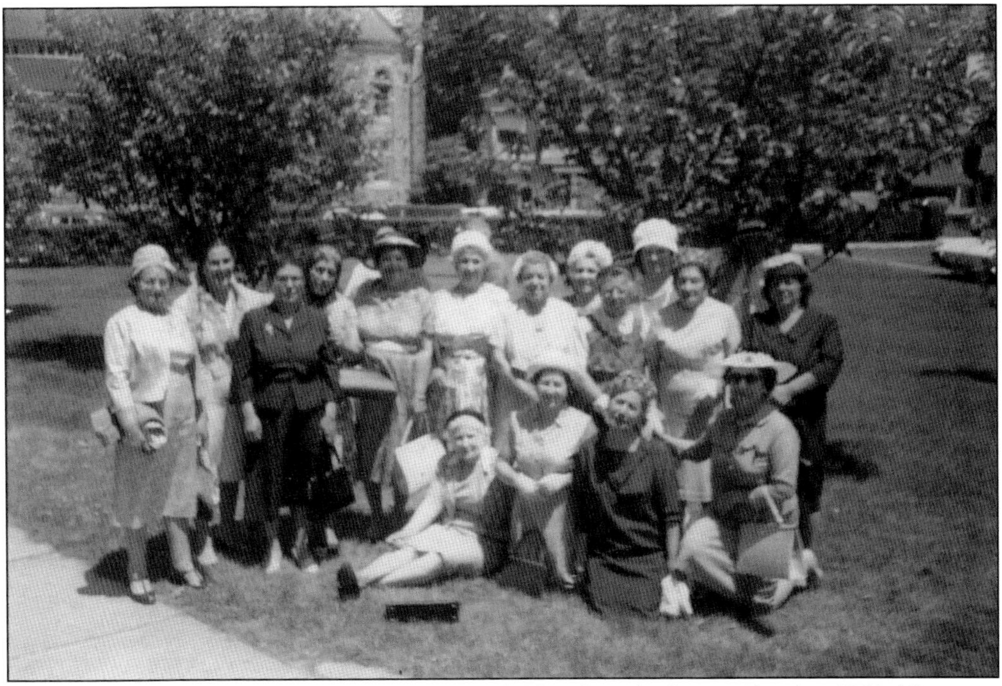

This Assyrian picnic nearby St. Mark's Episcopal Church took place in October 1965. (Courtesy of the Dooman Family collection.)

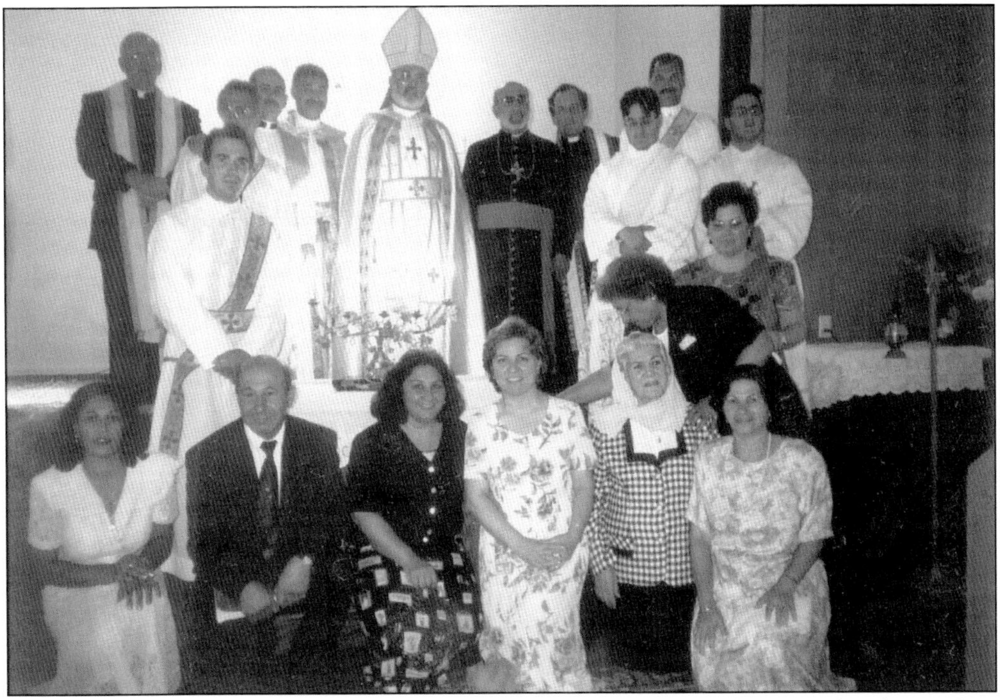

The deacons and priest of St. Thomas Church of the East are pictured among church members following a service honoring the visit of Assyrian patriarch Mar Dinkha.

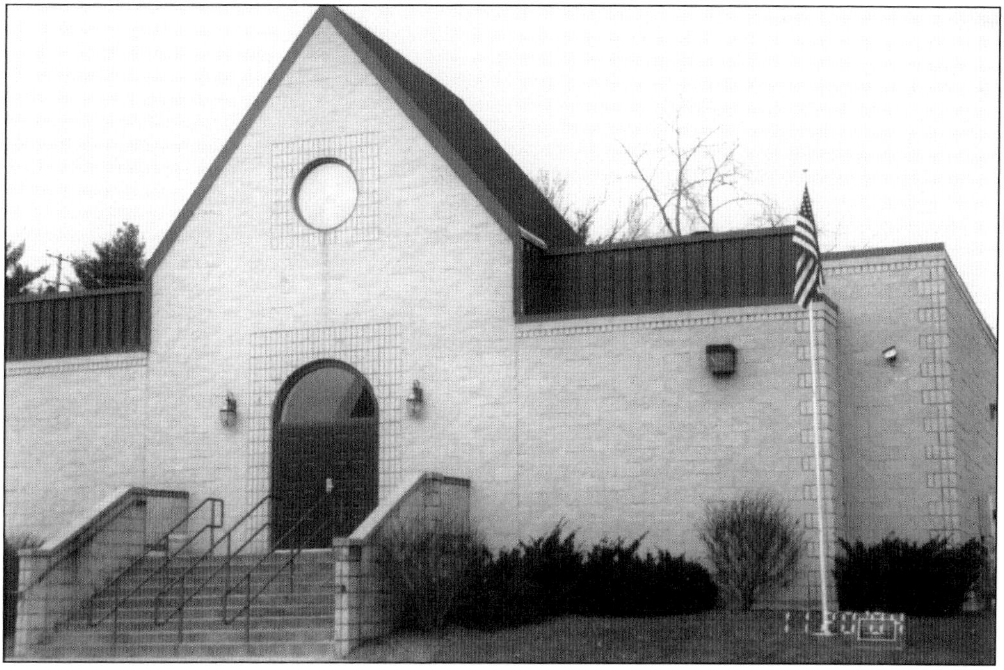

In April 1995, an Assyrian cultural center and ballroom was built and dedicated on the last four acres of St. Thomas Church of the East property. The hall is regularly rented out for both Assyrian and non-Assyrian events.

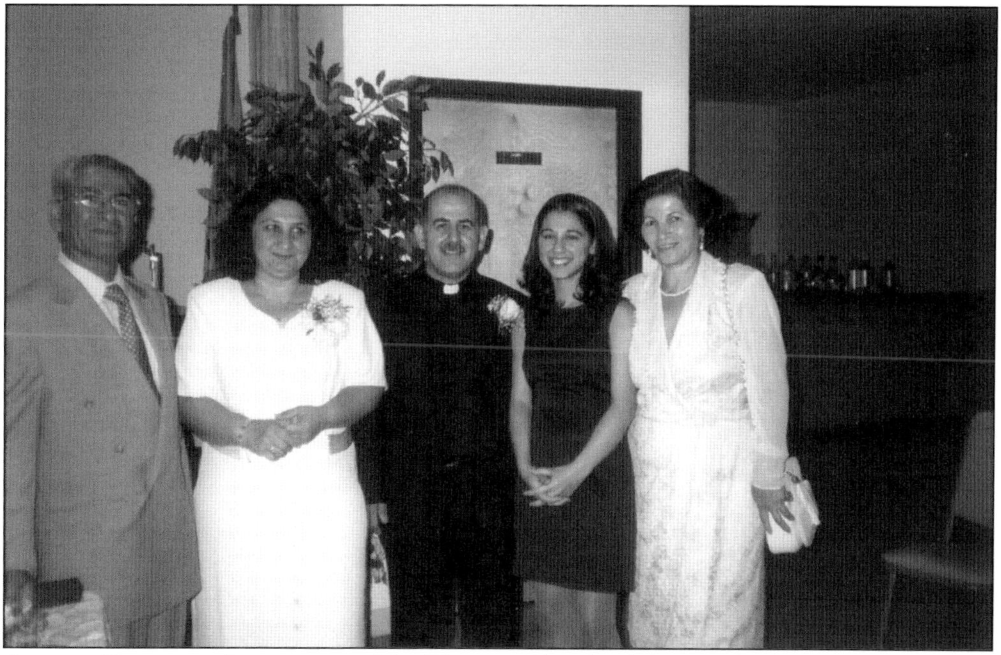

Gevargis Toma was the minister of St. Thomas Church of the East between the early 1980s and mid-1990s. In the photograph, from left to right, are George BetGeorge, Hilda Toma, Rev. Gevargis Toma, Nseebin Toma, and Florence BetIshoo.

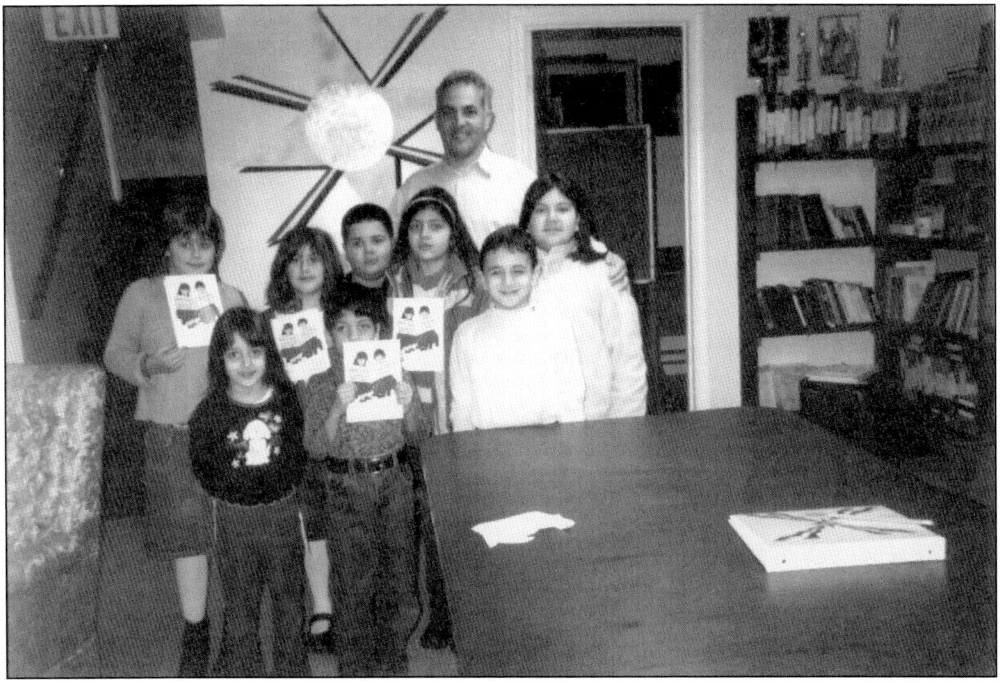

Sunday school students at St. Thomas Church of the East hold up their most recently learned Bible lessons. On display behind them is the Assyrian flag.

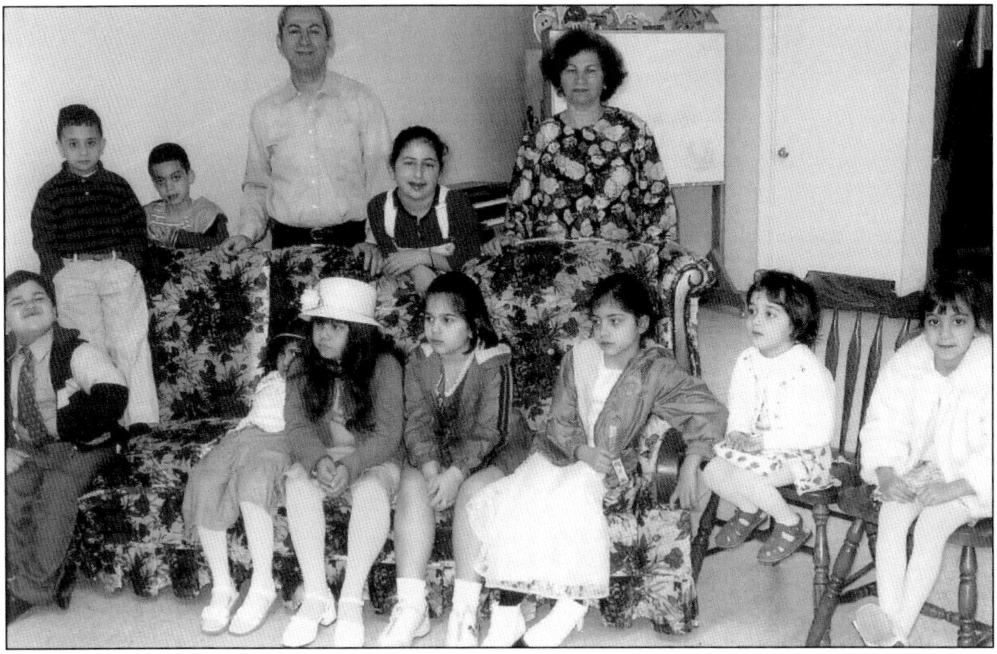

Students of the Sunday school at St. Thomas Church of the East are pictured with their teacher, Florence BetGeorge, standing on the right.

Four

SECULAR ORGANIZATIONS

Due to the rising amounts of Assyrians in New Britain, the Assyrian National Association (ANA) was formed in 1915. This organization originally began with the aims to assist Assyrians abroad as well as to provide recent Assyrian immigrants with shelter, jobs, and education for their children.

On October 1, 1933, the delegates and presidents of the ANA of Connecticut, the ANA of Yonkers, and the ANA of America of Newark gathered in Newark to discuss the recent Assyrian genocide that had occurred in Simele. They also worked together to write a common set of bylaws. Their next meeting location was Yonkers, where they continued to meet and discuss these two aspects. The final location of the meeting was New Britain, where they chose the first president of the Assyrian National Federation (ANF), Alex Ameer. New Britain is also the site in which they held fund-raisers and gathered a significant amount of money to send to the Assyrians of the Simele massacre in Simele, Iraq. The final event to take place at the end of this month-and-a-half-long string of meetings was the first annual ANF convention, which took place in New Britain on November 19, 1933.

The ANA of New Britain has always had a place of residence. When they were first established, they purchased a three-story house and conducted their business there until they purchased the Assyrian Club in 1977. This building is still used for their business and various Assyrian and non-Assyrian events.

During the mid- to late 1920s, an Assyrian theatre group called the Assyrian American Citizen's Club was established. They put on many plays of both Assyrian and American origin.

A women's club, known as the Ladies Association, was based in the Assyrian Club of New Britain. In various files at the club, are several full accounts of their minutes, correspondence, and budget with a full list of their members between the years 1948 and 1956. But the main organization based in the Assyrian Club was the ANA.

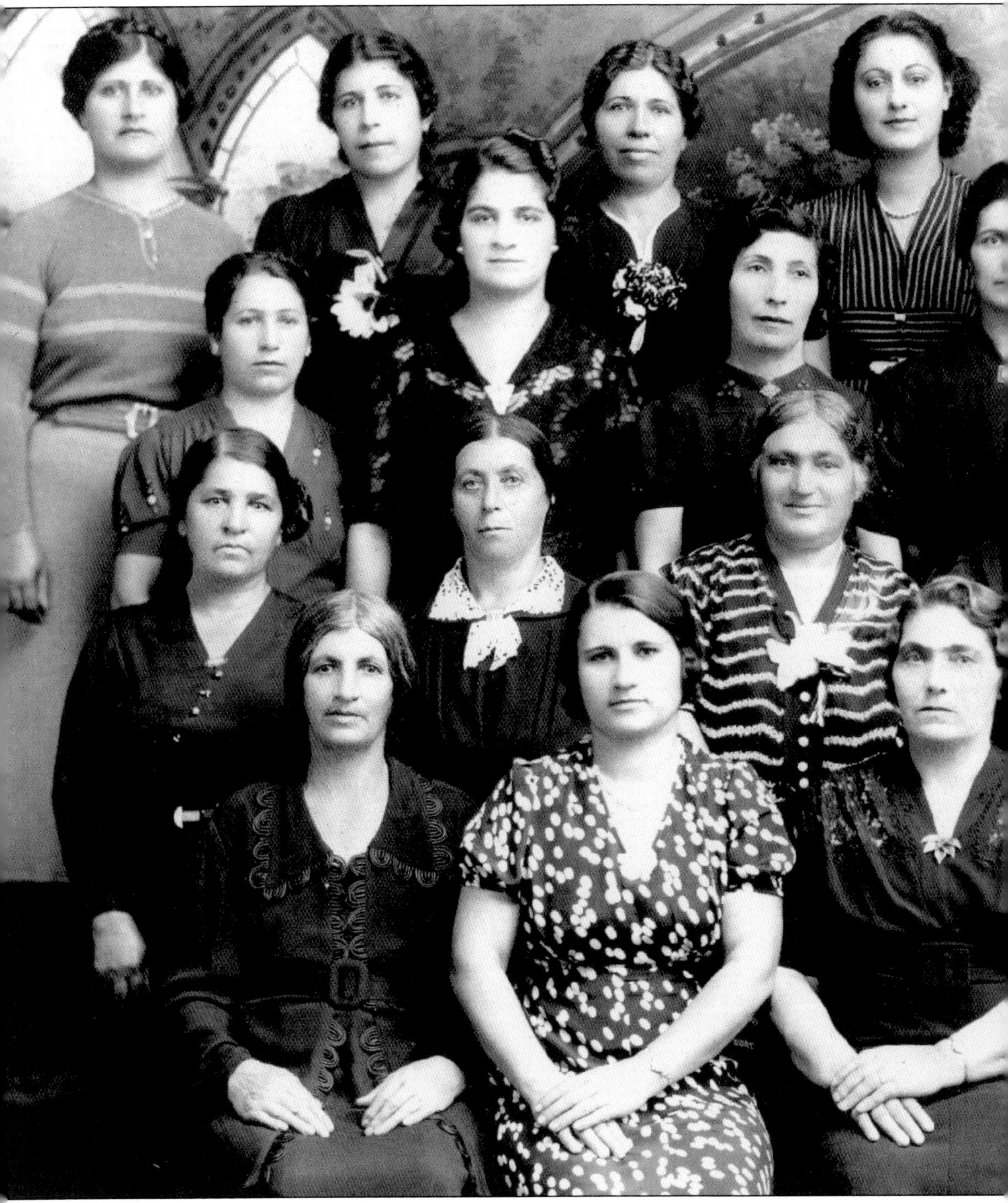

The Tek Ardishai Women's Society was created during World War II by a group of women who were all from the Iranian village Ardishai. At this time, most Assyrian organizations in New Britain were organized based on the village that the members had migrated from. The society was created in order to send aid to Assyrians in the Middle East during the war. This photograph was taken in 1945 and shows the following individuals: Ester Sayadof, Rose Benjamin,

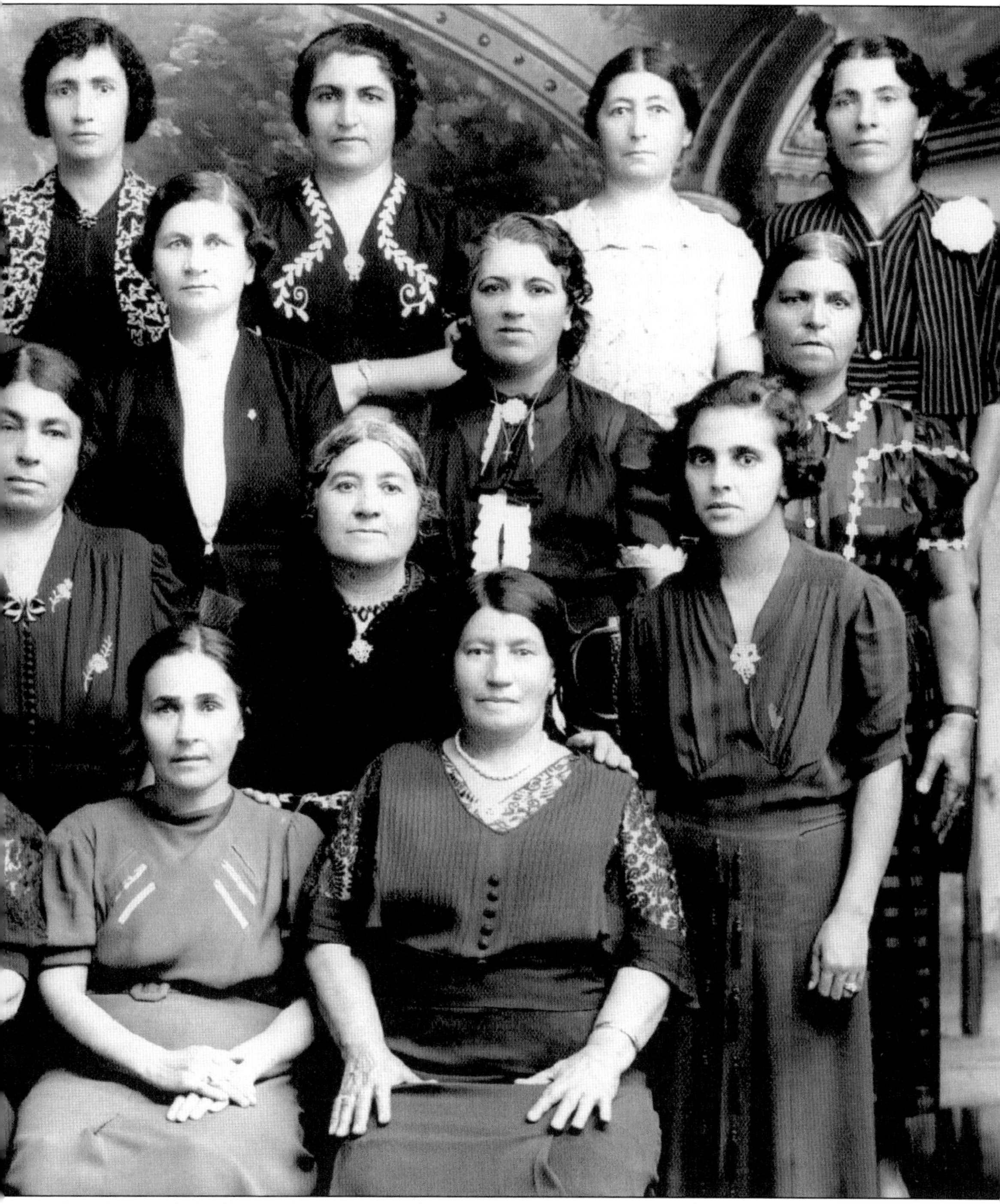

Eslie Yonan, Esho Yonan, Marta Eshoo, Eslie Benjamin, Mayo Sargis, Ana Elia, Marta George, Khena George, Eslie Baba, Jeanette Sayadoff, Ana Lazar, Botishva Azizian, Esiet Eshoo, Mary David, Esho Havel, Rachel "Nano" Abraham, Alice Benjamin, Marganita Ives, Ana Isaac, Milenia Aziz, Nabat Benjamin, Rebkah Ishoo, and Mayo BetGichoo.

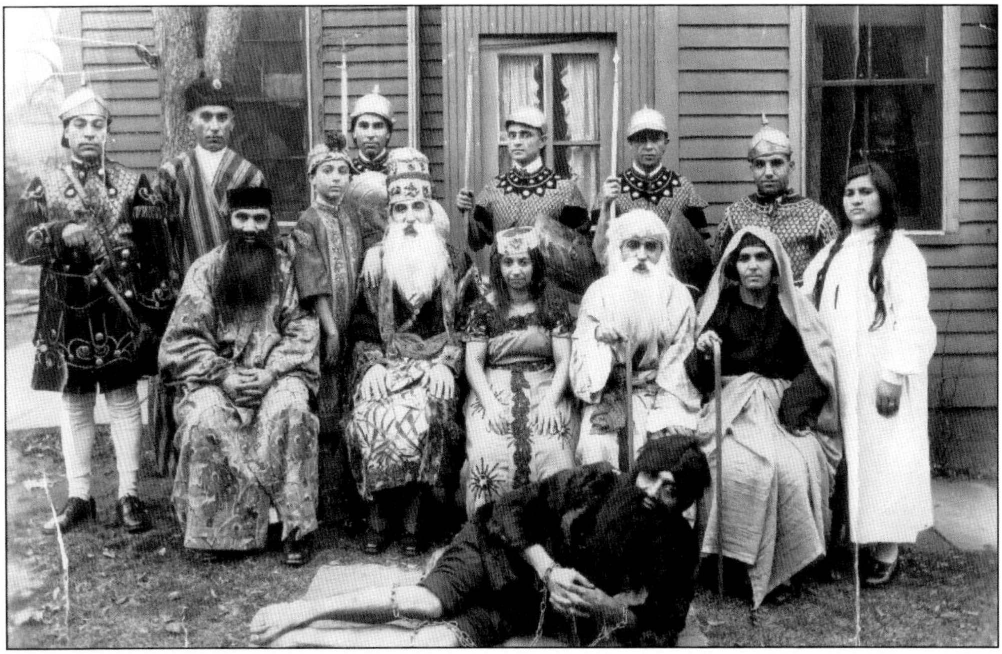

This is a portrayal of the story of Samson and Delilah, which in this instance was directed by the Rev. Saul K. Neesan. Shamasha Yonan Jones is Samson in chains, Susamber Yohannan is Delilah, Anna A. Solomon is Samson's Mother, and Rose Benjamin is shown in white. The remaining people shown here are Peter Baba, Sargis George, Joel Joseph, John Akasie, Israel Benjamin, and Ricky Benjamin.

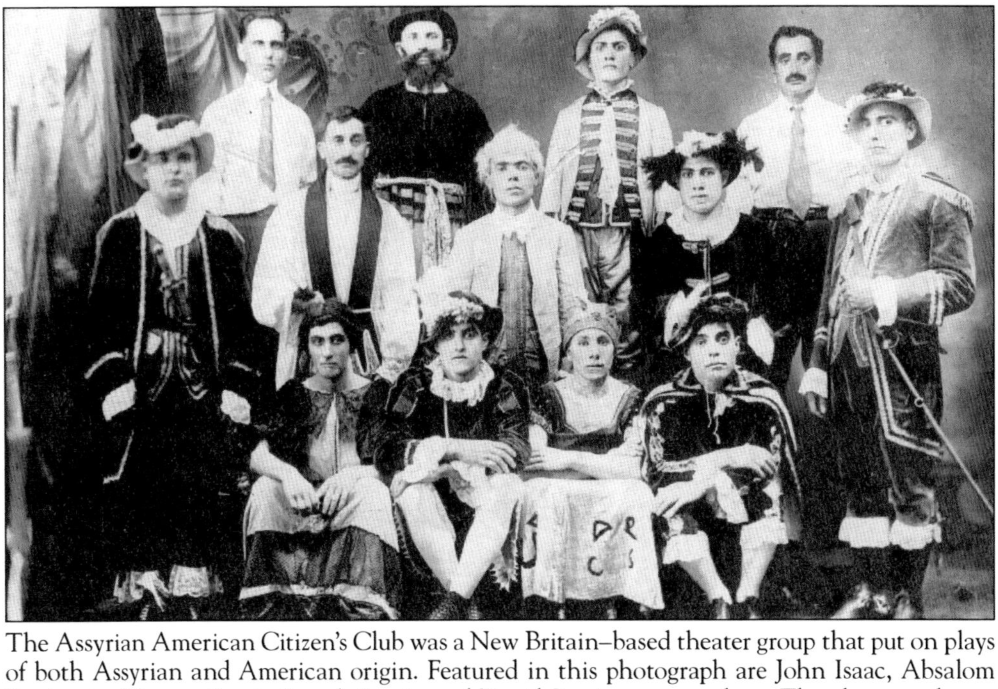

The Assyrian American Citizen's Club was a New Britain–based theater group that put on plays of both Assyrian and American origin. Featured in this photograph are John Isaac, Absalom Benjamin, Khoona Sargis, Joseph Sargis, and David Sargis, among others. The photograph was taken at Benjamin Brothers Studio on Main Street in New Britain.

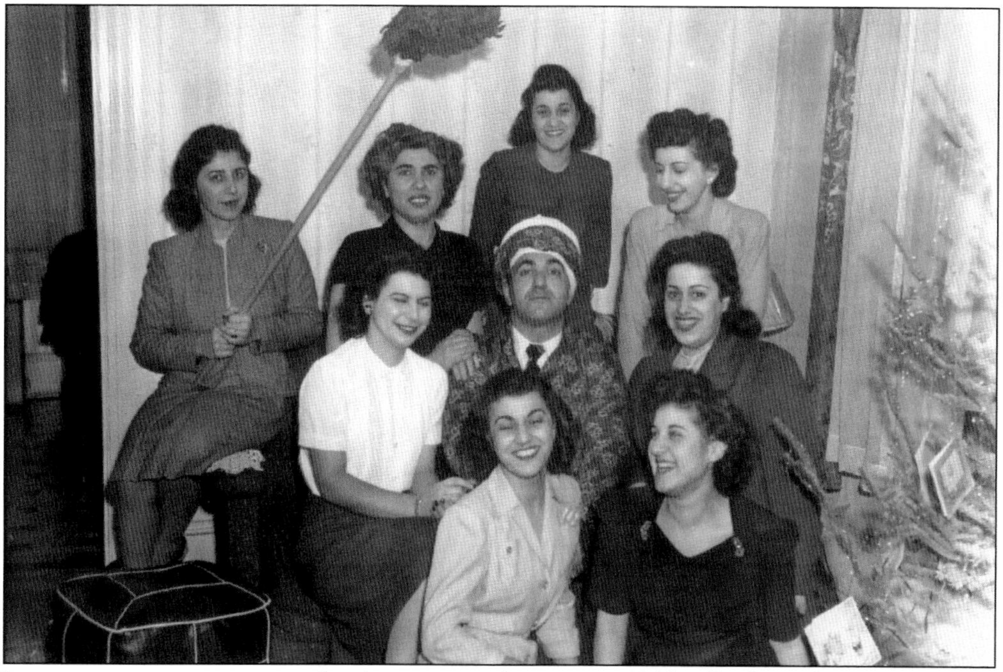

It was a common occurrence for Assyrian youth to put on Biblically themed plays during the Christmas season. Here a group is shown posing beside a Christmas tree dressed for their play.

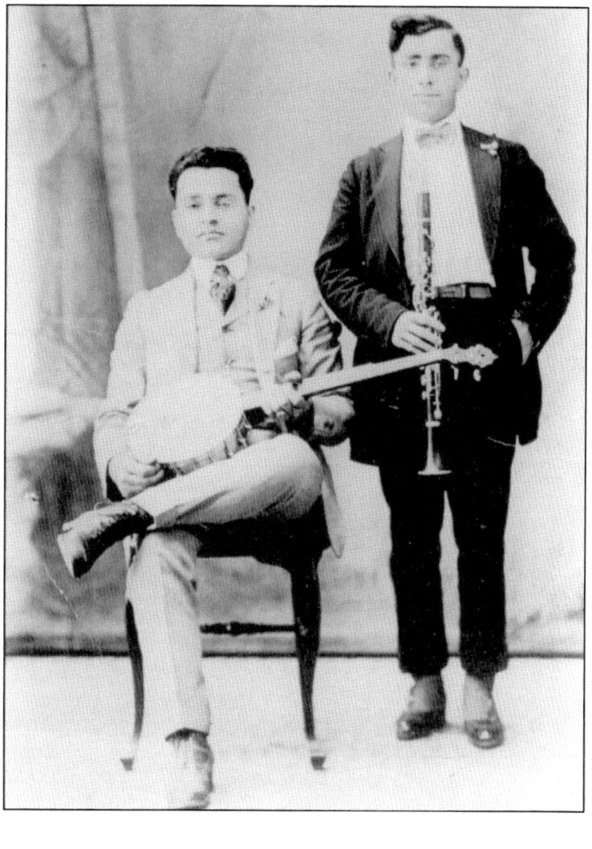

Yosep Niyas was a talented Assyrian musician in New Britain. Here he is shown with an Assyrian-Armenian man with whom he regularly played.

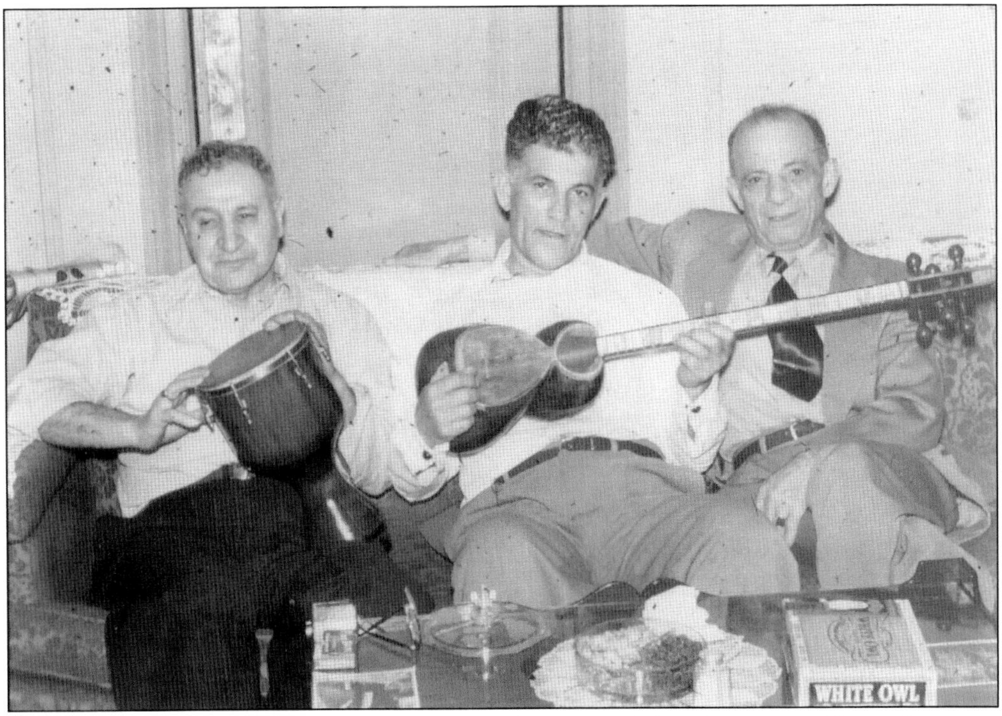

Seated here is a group of Assyrian musicians by the names of David, Jerry, and Sam. They were all local to New Britain and played often during the mid-20th century.

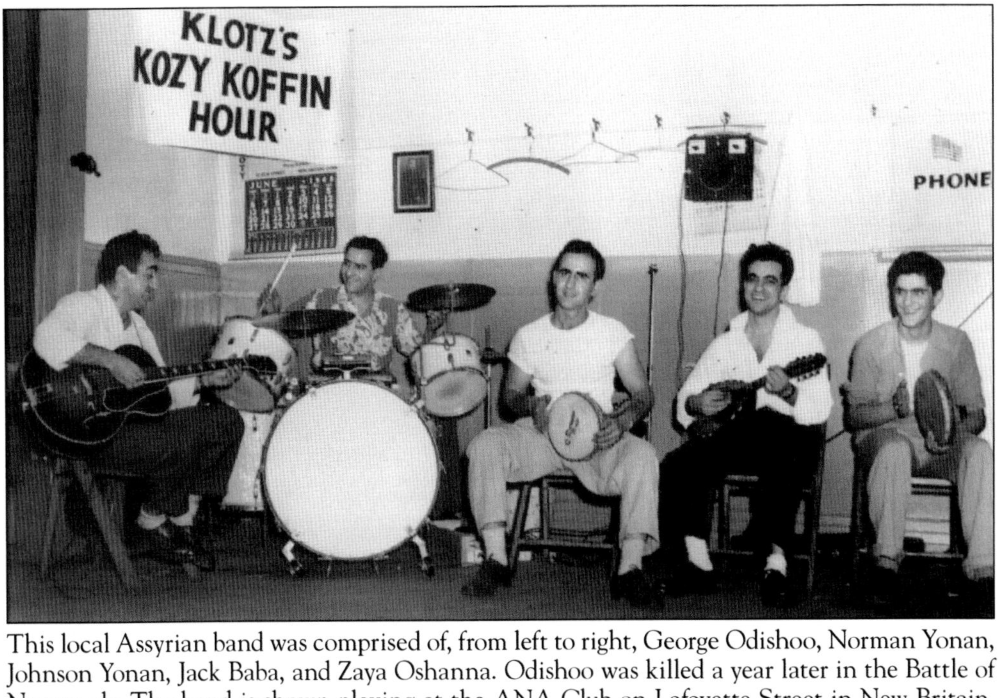

This local Assyrian band was comprised of, from left to right, George Odishoo, Norman Yonan, Johnson Yonan, Jack Baba, and Zaya Oshanna. Odishoo was killed a year later in the Battle of Normandy. The band is shown playing at the ANA Club on Lafayette Street in New Britain. The ANA Club was located there until its new location was purchased in the 1970s. The new location is still used today.

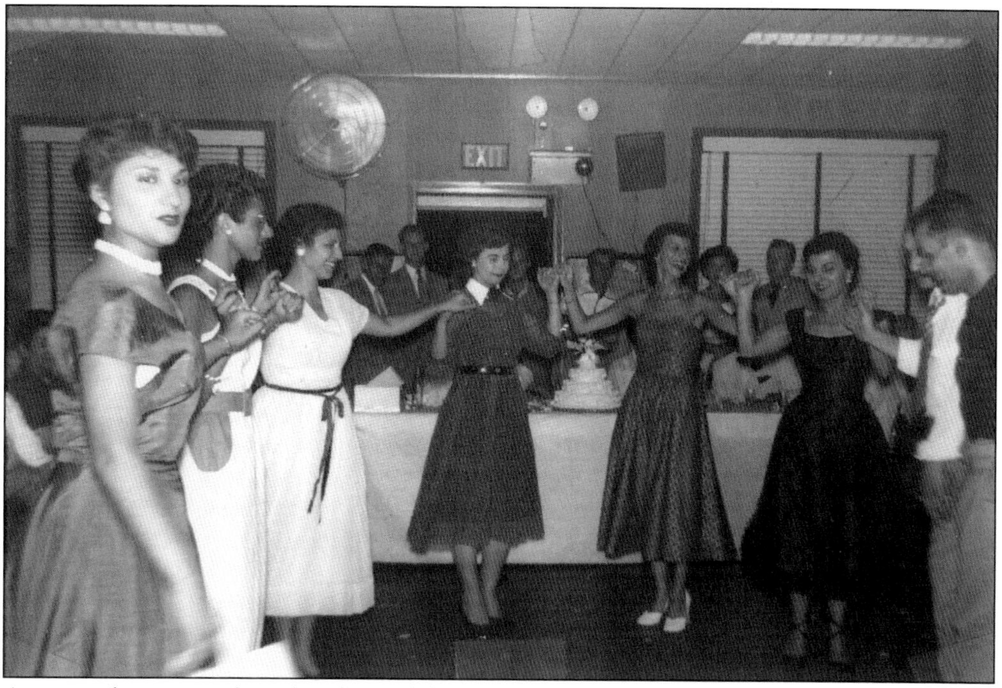

Assyrians have a number of traditional dances that involve clasped hands and quick and agile steps. Here a group of individuals is shown doing one of these traditional Assyrian dances at the ANA Club during a party.

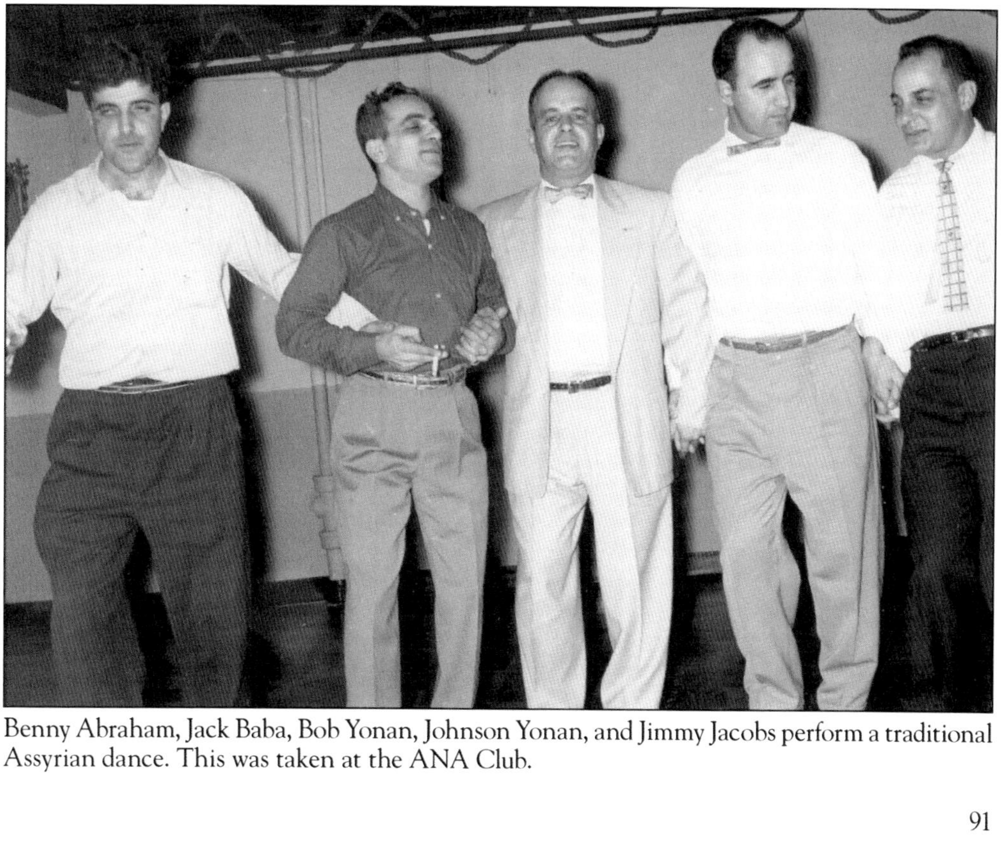

Benny Abraham, Jack Baba, Bob Yonan, Johnson Yonan, and Jimmy Jacobs perform a traditional Assyrian dance. This was taken at the ANA Club.

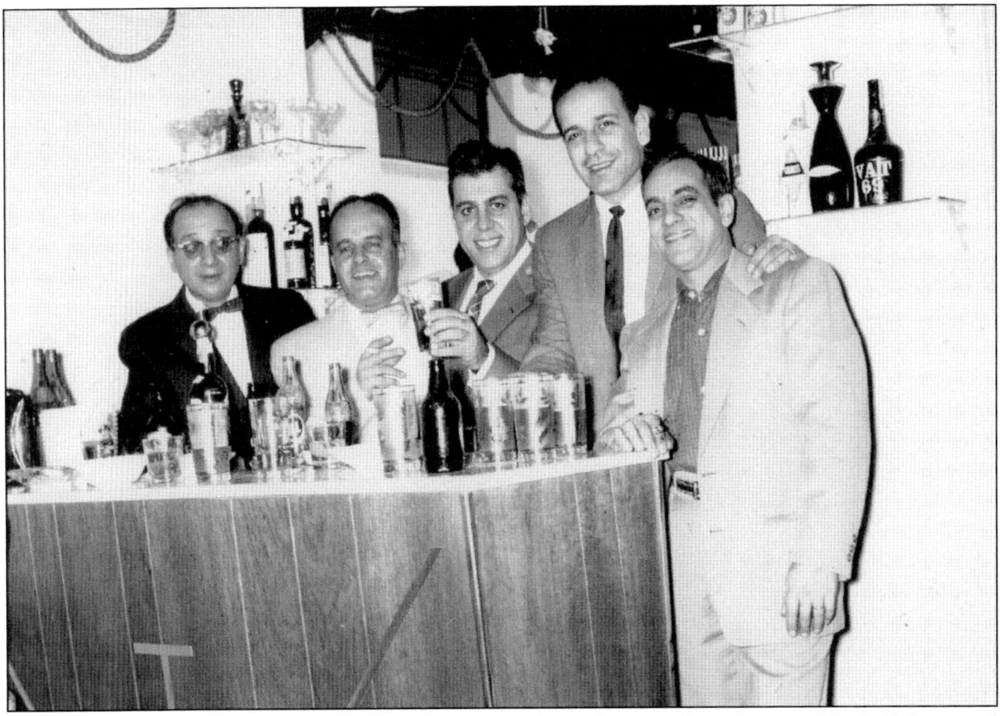

From left to right, Warren Bayram, Bob Yonan, John Eshia, unidentified, and Jack Baba stand around the bar at the ANA Club.

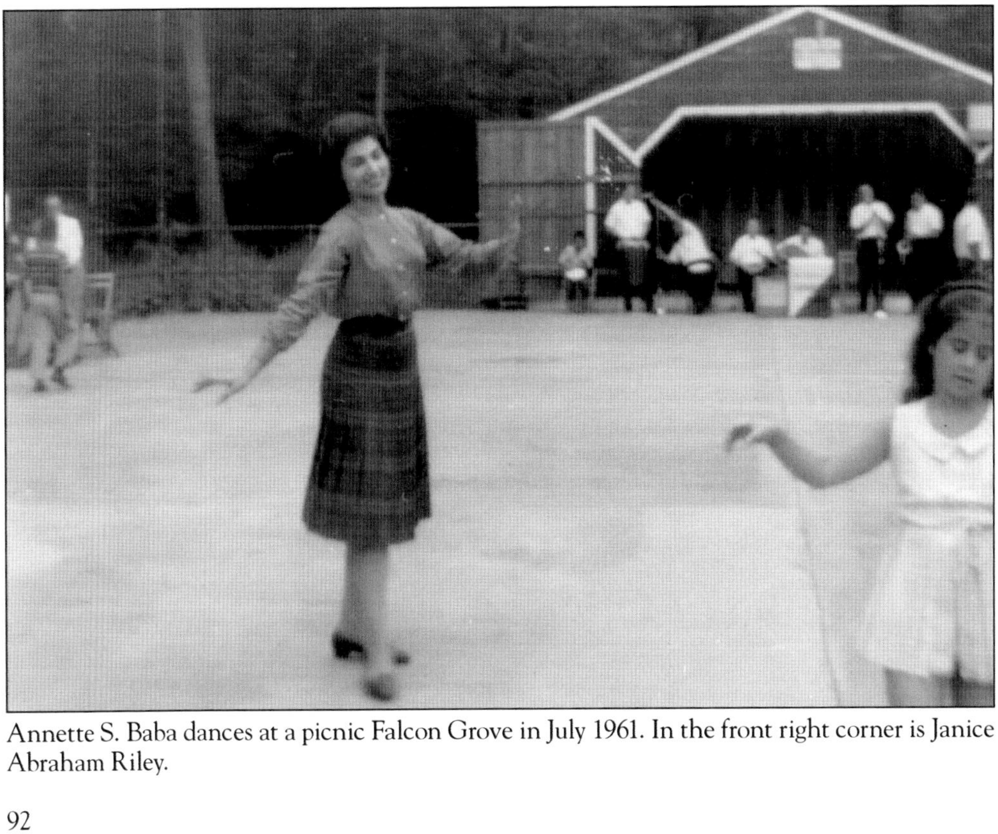

Annette S. Baba dances at a picnic Falcon Grove in July 1961. In the front right corner is Janice Abraham Riley.

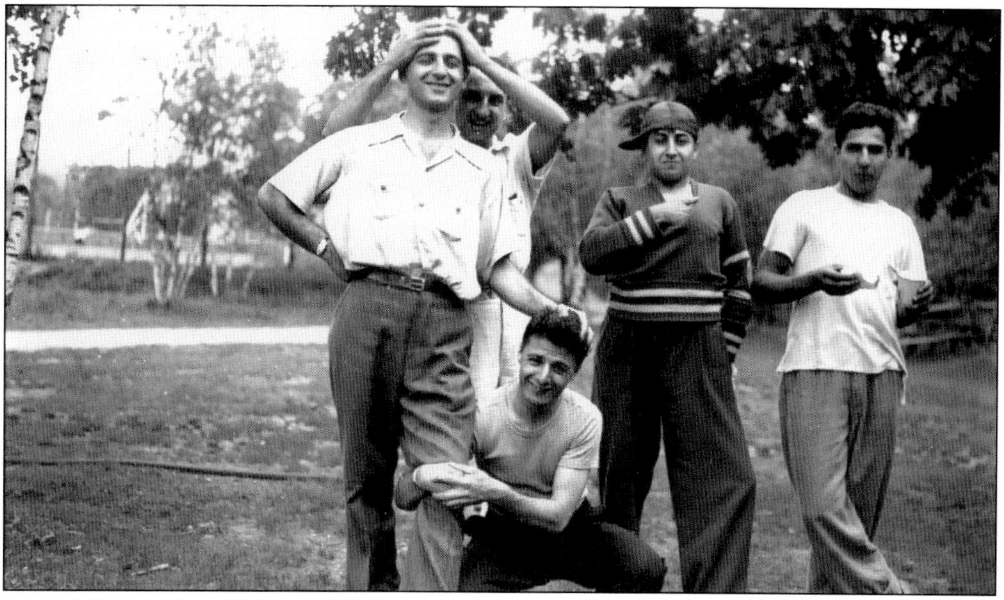

From left to right, Howie Odishoo, Bob Solomon, Sam Oshanna, Otto Bayram, and an unidentified young man are shown at Assyrian picnic grounds in New Britain. This photograph was taken during the early 1930s.

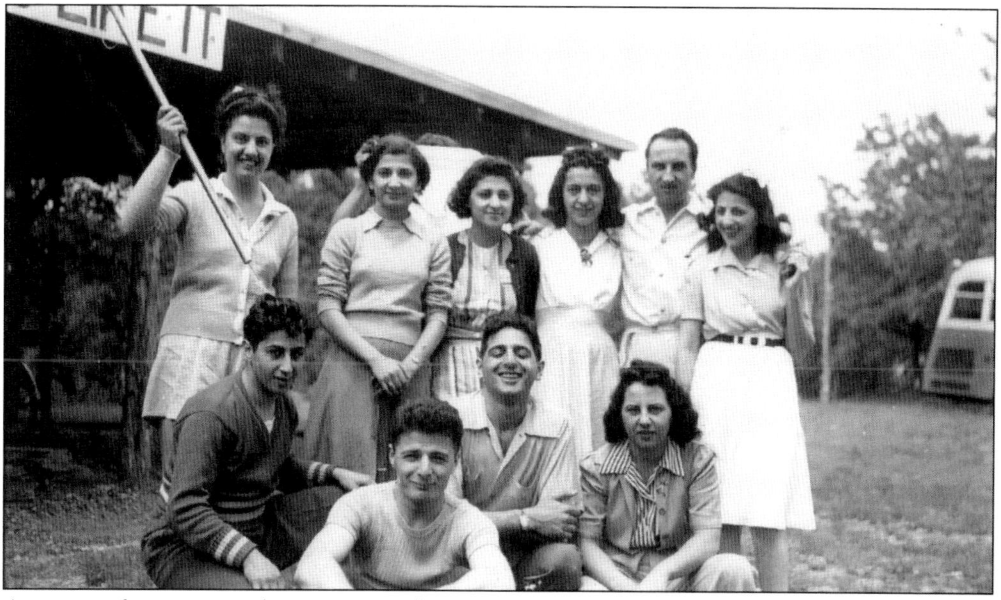

A group of young people are pictured at an Assyrian picnic grounds that was located on Farmington Avenue in New Britain. The photograph was taken in the early 1930s and features the following people from left to right: (first row) Sam Oshanna, Howie Odishoo, Otto Bayram, and Millie Solomon; (second row) Elaine Solomon, Margaret Jones, Mary Bayram, Gladys Dooman, Bob Solomon, and Helen Isaac. (Courtesy of Doris Jones.)

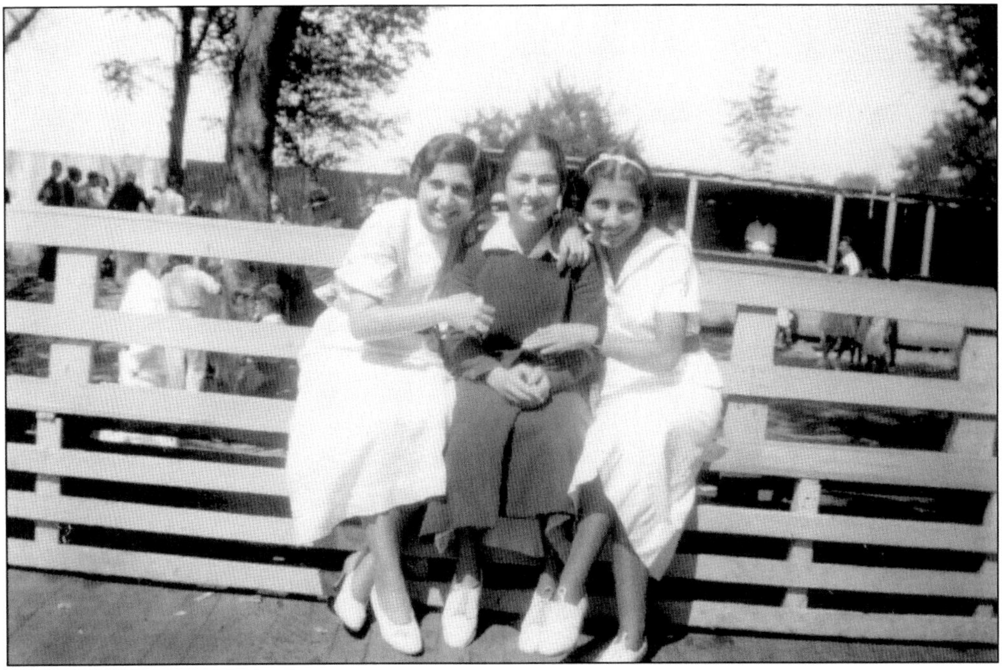

This family snapshot was taken at a picnic at the Assyrian picnic grounds on Farmington Avenue. The picnic grounds were Assyrian-owned until the establishment of Pulaski Middle School, which now occupies this location.

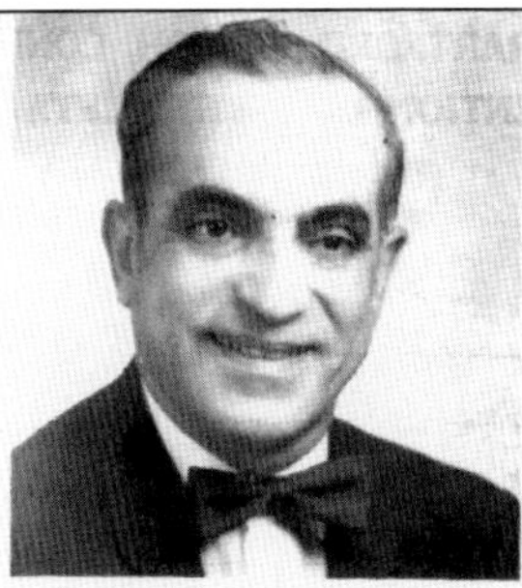

DEAR FRIENDS:

On behalf of the Assyrian National Association and its Ladies Auxiliary of New Britain, Connecticut, may we extend to you the Officers and Delegates of the Assyrian American Federation a most cordial welcome to the Nutmeg State and the 37th. annual Convention, which is being held in the Capitol city of Hartford, Connecticut.

To those who will be busy in the business meetings of this convention we wish you success in your endeavours and help the Federation to achieve its goals, only you can do this, and it must be done like Brothers and Sisters.

As President of this Affiliate, Iwish to thank very much the Members and Ladies who have worked many months in the preparations needed in planning this Convention, and making it most successful one, again thank you all very much.

Jack P. Baba, *President*
Assyrian National Association
New Britain, Connecticut.

Here is a welcoming statement written by Jack Baba, a Connecticut resident who was president of the New Britain–based Assyrian National Association at the time of this annual convention.

ASSYRIAN AMERICAN FEDERATION
37 ANNUAL CONVENTION
HARTFORD, HILTON, CONN.
CONVENTION BANQUET SEPT. 6, 1970

PROGRAM

Welcome .... William G. Yonan, *General Chairman*

Presentation of Colors .... Joe Eshoo, Post No. 1.

Pledge of Allegiance .... Assemblage

God Bless America by .... Mrs. Gloria Tuttle

Invocation by .... Rev. Youel Solomon

Introduction of Master of Ceremonies .... William G. Yonan

DINNER

Introductions .... Joseph David, *Master of Ceremonies*

Jack P. Baba .... Co-Chairman, *Convention*
President, Local Affiliate

Honorable, Paul Manafort, Mayor of New Britain, Connecticut - Atty. Gen., Robert K. Killian, for Governor Dempsey - Alexander P. Evans, President, Assyrian American Federation

Song by .... Edward Baba, Yonkers, N.Y.

Honorable Thomas A. Meskill, Congressman - Honorable Ann Ucello, Mayor of Hartford, Connecticut - Honorable Ella Grasso, Sec. of State, Connecticut - His Excellency, Talib El-Shibb, Permanent Mission of Iraq to the U. N. - The Honorable Abdul Hameed Al-Gree, Acting Consul General - The Honorable Mohammed Hassan El-Zayyat, United Arab Republic, U. N. - The Honorable Khabil Haddad, Consulate General of Lebanon - The Honorable Dr. Mehdi Vakil, Permanent Mission of Iran to the U.N. - The Honorable George J. Tomeh Permanent Mission of the Syrian Arabb Republic, U.N

ASSYRIAN AMERICAN FEDERATION
37 ANNUAL CONVENTION
HARTFORD, HILTON, CONN.

PROGRAM

REGISTRATION:- Mezzanine Thur. Sept 3, 1:00 p.m. to 6:00 p.m. and Friday all day. Vicky Badal, *Chairman.*

OPEN HOUSE Thur. Sept. 3. John Badal, *Chairman*, 8:00 p.m. until Knights of Columbus Hall, East Street New Britain, Connecticut.

Free admission to all, Buffet Dinner. Music by: The Assyrian Knights Band

FRIDAY NIGHT DANCE MAIN BALLROOM Julie Yonan, *Chairman* 9.00 p.m. until. — Music by: The New England Ararat Band American and Oriental Music.

BACKGAMMON & PING PONG Golfers may play at Goodwin Park, or attend the G.H.O at the Wethersfield Country Club.
Bus Tour Hi-Lites of Hartford - Leaves Hotel at 1:00 p.m. returns 5:00 p.m.
See the Elizabeth Park Garden, famous for its Roses through-out the United States, and many other Historical Sites.

SATURDAY - PRESIDENTIAL BALL. MAIN BALLROOM Geo. Isaac, *Chairman*, 9:00 P.M. until. Music by the New England Ararat Band, American and Oriental music.

LADIES LUNCHEON: 11.30 a.m. Champagne Brunch will be served Cities Room & Fashion Show. Lucy Abraham, *Chairman.*

DELEGATES LUNCHEON: Presentation of awards. Jack P. Baba, *Chairman.*

BACKGAMMON AND PING PONG

SUNDAY DINNER & DANCE Sept. 6, MAIN BALLROOM, 4:00P.M. until Music by the Vanites Band, American and Oriental Music. - Johnson Yonan, *Chm.*

MONDAY Sept. 7, ALL DAY PICNIC Wilson S. Baba, *Chm.*
Falcon Picnic Grounds, Farmington Ave. New Britain, Conn. — Transportation for Hotel Guests will be available. Music by the Vanites Band.

The 37th annual Assyrian American Federation convention was held in Hartford in 1970, as illustrated by the program.

ASSYRIANS

BY JACK BADAL
Secretary of the State's Ethnic Advisory Council

A close look at the personal stories of Assyrian immigrants who came to the United States in the early 20th century shows that their reasons for immigration were similar to those of other ethnic groups, chiefly to escape religious persecution.

The majority of Assyrians came to this country after World War I when the need for labor in the United States was so marked.

In Connecticut, the majority of this group settled in Hartford County. Because most were denied formal education in the countries of their origin, they joined the pool of unskilled laborers who accepted the hardest and lowest paying jobs. Many lived in the urban areas of the state but there were some who became successful farmers.

As with many immigrant groups, the original Assyrians who came here were impoverished and uneducated. Those who have arrived in the last decade are both more affluent and educated.

Religion

The Christian religion is the dominant theme of the Assyrian culture. Together with other groups which practice orthodox rituals, the Assyrians use the Julian calendar. However, recognizing the need to assimilate to a degree with that of the majority of Connecticut, the Assyrians have adjusted their calendar and generally observe holidays at the same time as others in the state.

Assyrians maintain their ties with the old world by teaching their children their ancient language which is Aramaic or the more common dialects in Assyrian. Members of the group subscribe to newspapers and other periodicals which have been written and published by their own Connecticut residents.

The religious makeup of the Assyrian community includes orthodox, Protestant and Catholic. Their church is Holy Apostolic Church of the East in New Britain. The American Assyrian National Association is also located in New Britain.

Assyrian youths have become professionals — lawyers, doctors and teachers who have struggled for respect and prosperity.

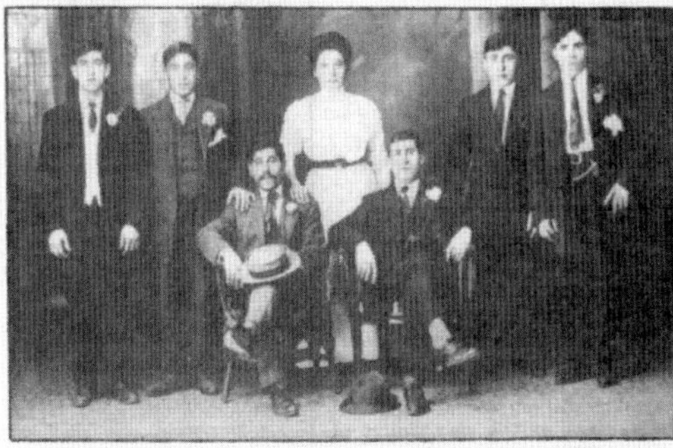

This photograph of an Assyrian family was taken in 1909 in New Britain. The author's father, Abraham Badal, is seated at right.

Jack Badal came to the United States towards the early 20th century. He wrote this article, featured in the *Hartford Current*, about the history and immigration process of Assyrians.

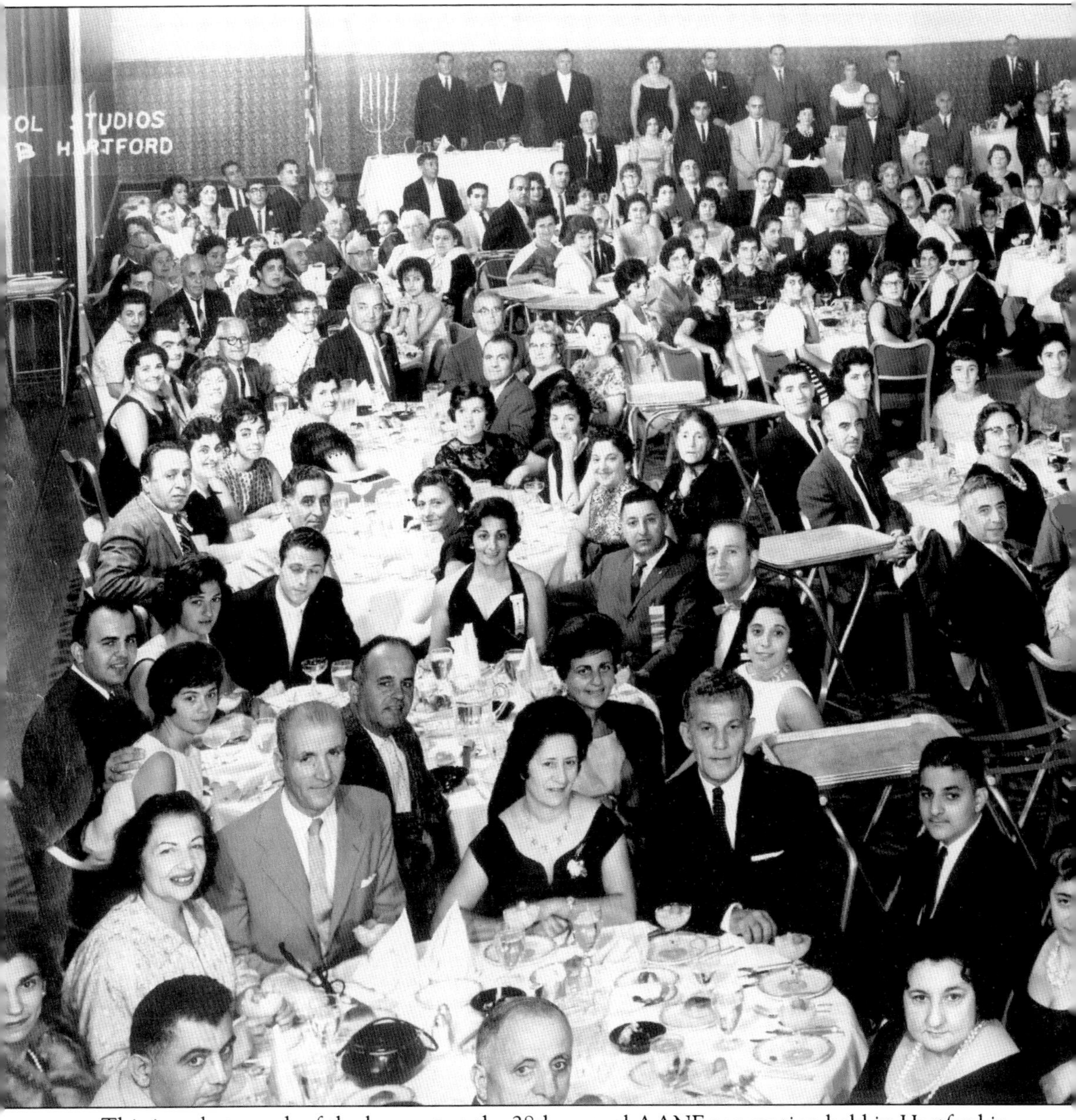

This is a photograph of the banquet at the 28th annual AANF convention held in Hartford in

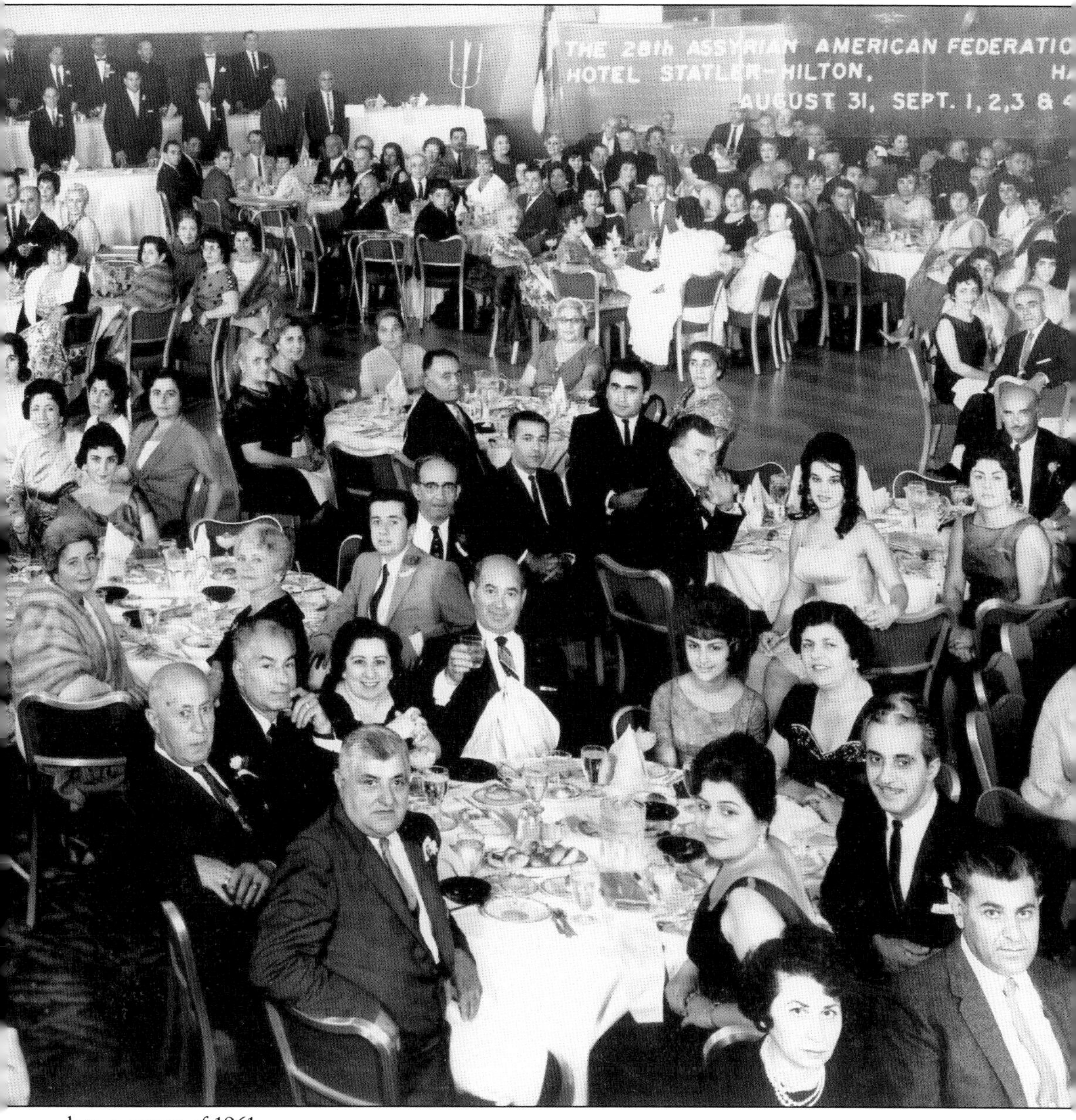

late summer of 1961.

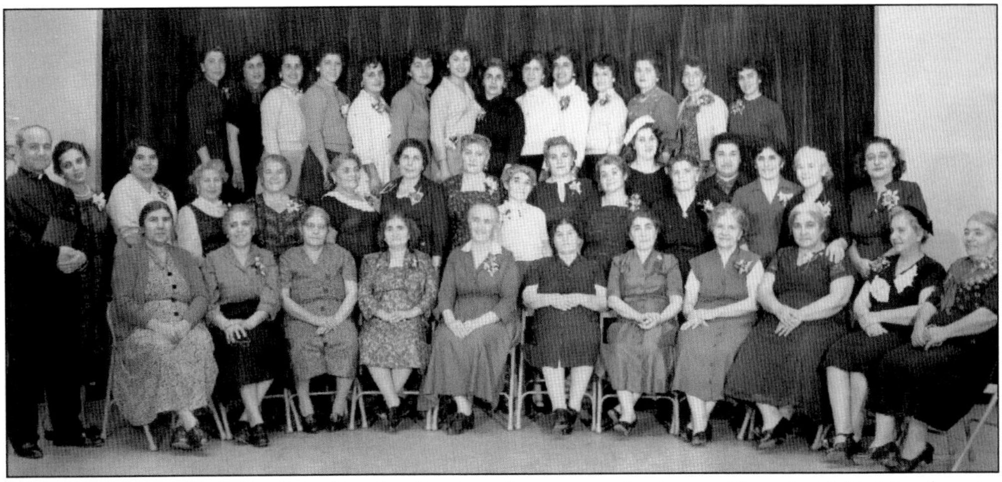

The St. Thomas Church of the East Ladies Auxiliary group is pictured here in 1955. Members in the photograph include Shamie George, Annie Yonan, Mrs. Israel Borasha, Mary Nimrod, Gizbaz Baba, Shushan ?, Anna Benjamin, Marganita ?, Shaleem Jones, Gulnar ?, Rev. Isaac Rehana, Anna George, Nellie Benjamin, Eslie Baba, Mrs. Avraham, Elsie Yonan, Alice Benjamin, Aveegil Givargis, Mauro, Mrs. Totol, Esther, Julie Yonan, Anna BetSolieman, Kathrin Joseph, Sheerin Solieman, Nina, Anna Iskhagh, Mrs. Nimrod, Agnes Yonan, Lily Sargis, Agnes Sargis, Jonie Jones, Annette Baba, Mrs. Yonan, Norma Yonadan, Margaret Capsalaros, Lillian Baba, Mary Hurmuz, and Betty Oshana.

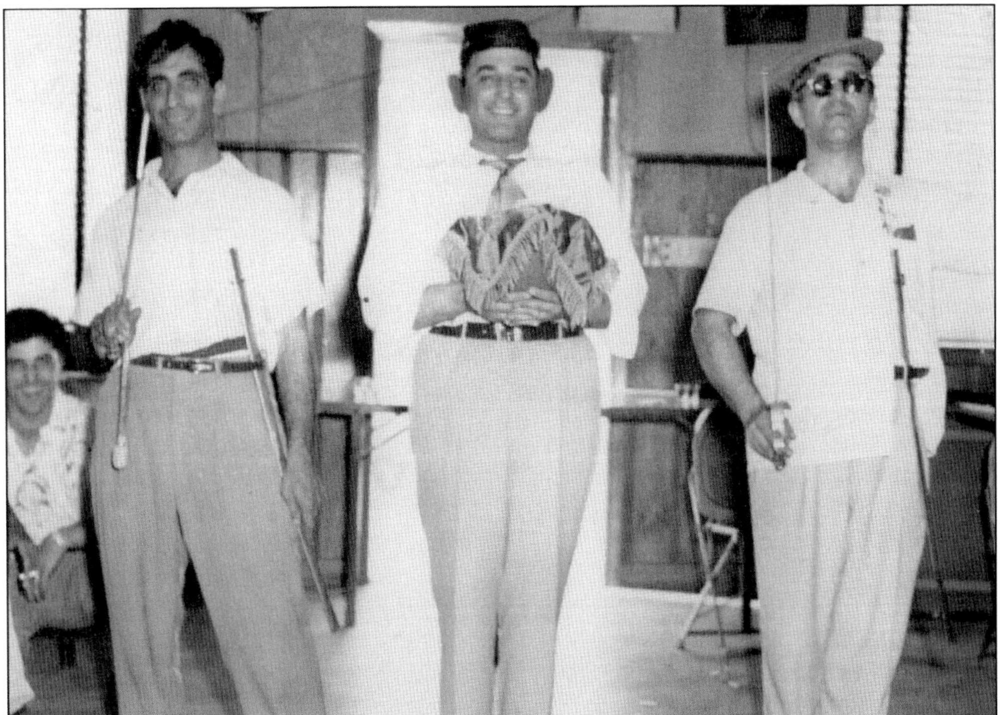

The Assyrian American Joel Eshoo Veteran's Post was established in 1946 and continued to hold meetings and host events until the mid-1970s. This photograph was taken during the 1960s and features, from left to right, Benny Abraham, Johhny Yonan, Karam Jacobs, and William Merza.

This awards ceremony was held by the Assyrian American Joel Eshoo Veteran's Post at the ANA Club in the 1960s. Here Karam Jacobs (left)congratulates Jimmy Dooman.

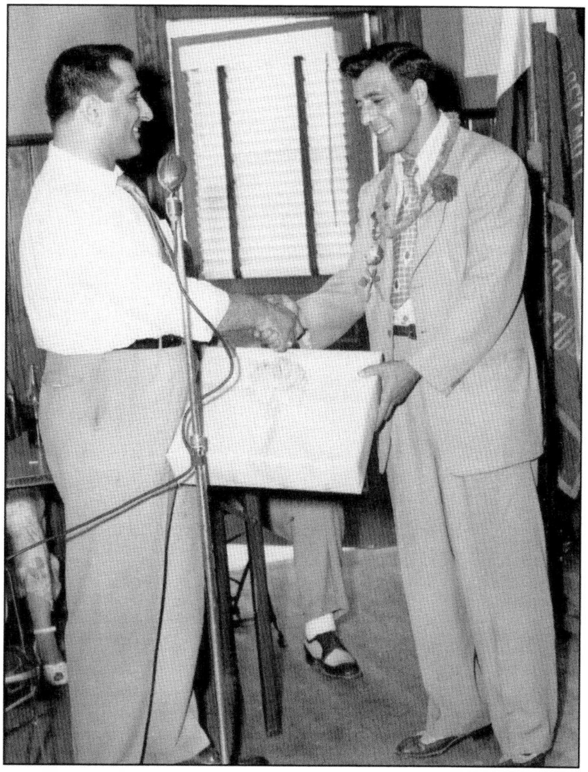

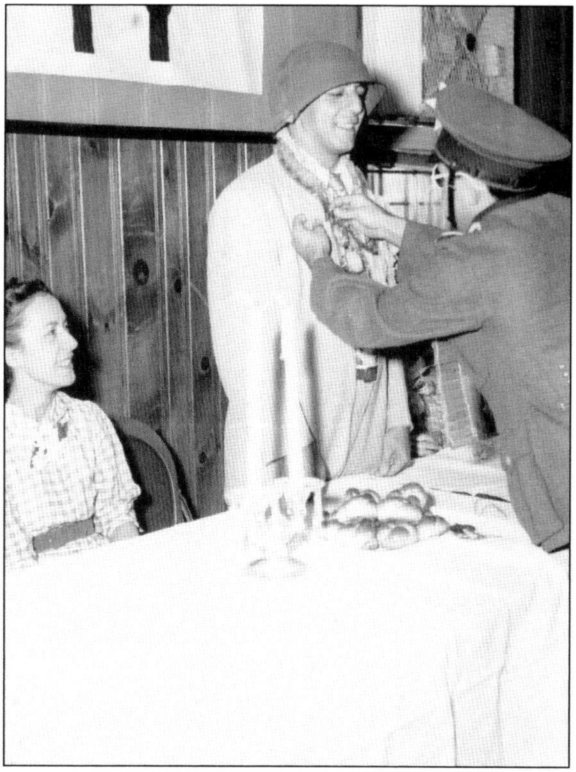

From left to right, Gladys Dooman, Jimmy Dooman, and Norman Vardanian are pictured at the Assyrian American Joel Eshoo Veteran's Post.

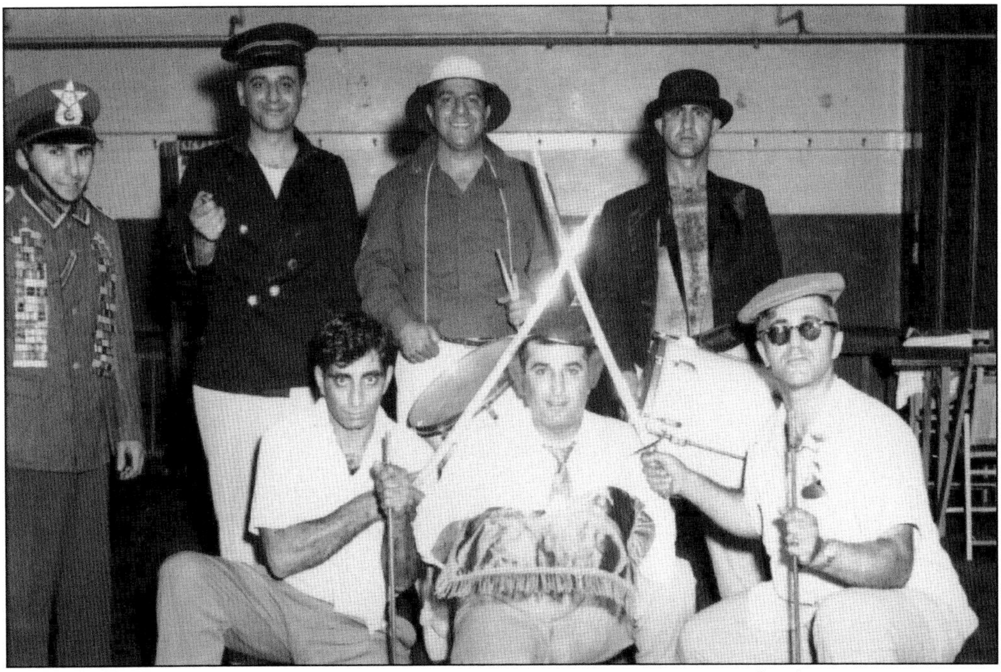

Pictured in the 1960s from left to right, at the Assyrian American Joel Eshoo Veteran's Post, are the following: (first row) Johnny Yonan, Karaim Jacobs, and Johnson Yonan; (second row) Norman Vardanian, Otto Bayram, Norman Yonan, and Johnson ?.

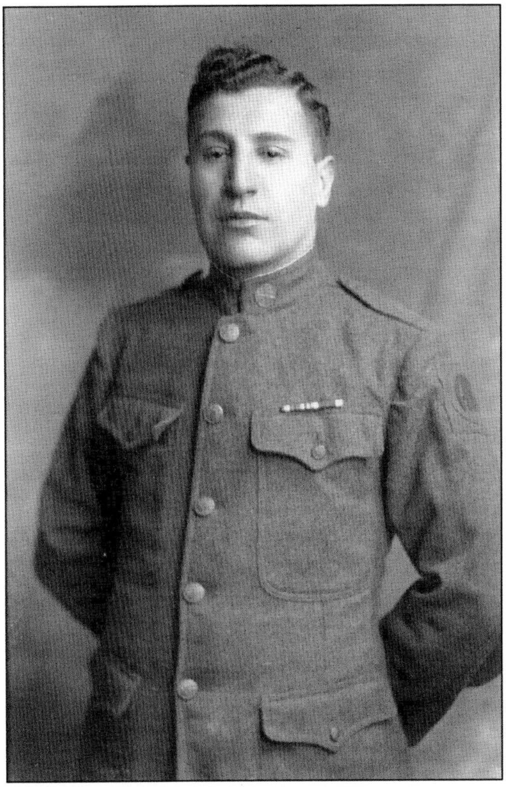

This is a photograph of veteran David Sargis in his World War I uniform. He married Julia Dooman of New Britain in Yonkers. Sargis worked as a police officer with the New York City Police Department, and he worked as a cabinet maker.

Lt. Norman Yonan was raised in New Britain and served with the United States during World War II. This photograph was taken in 1941.

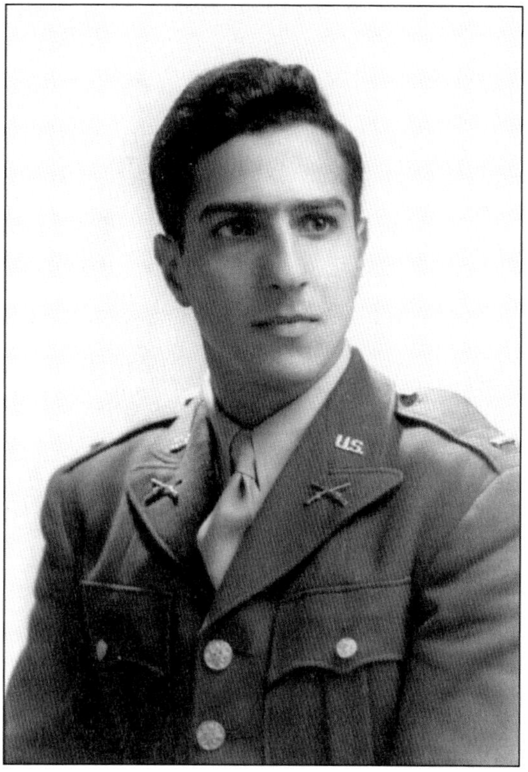

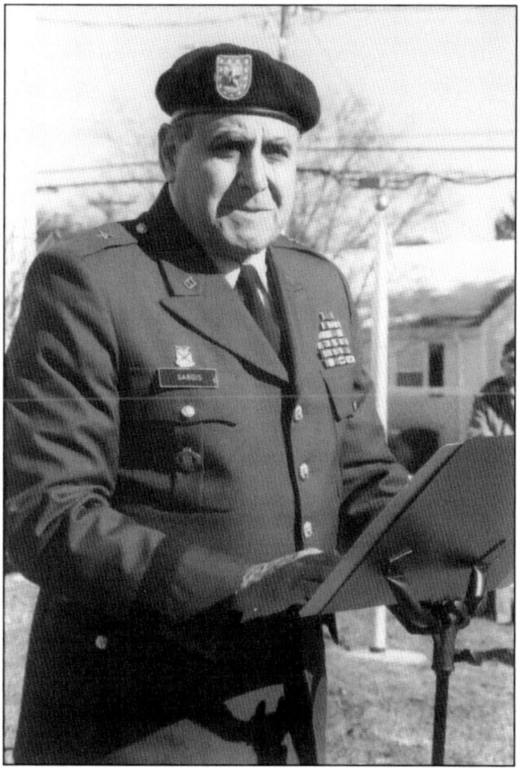

In 2004, St. Thomas Church of the East held a dedication ceremony for Assyrian veterans. Shown here is a veteran giving a speech directly outside of the church. The monument was dedicated in a ceremony on November 14, 2004.

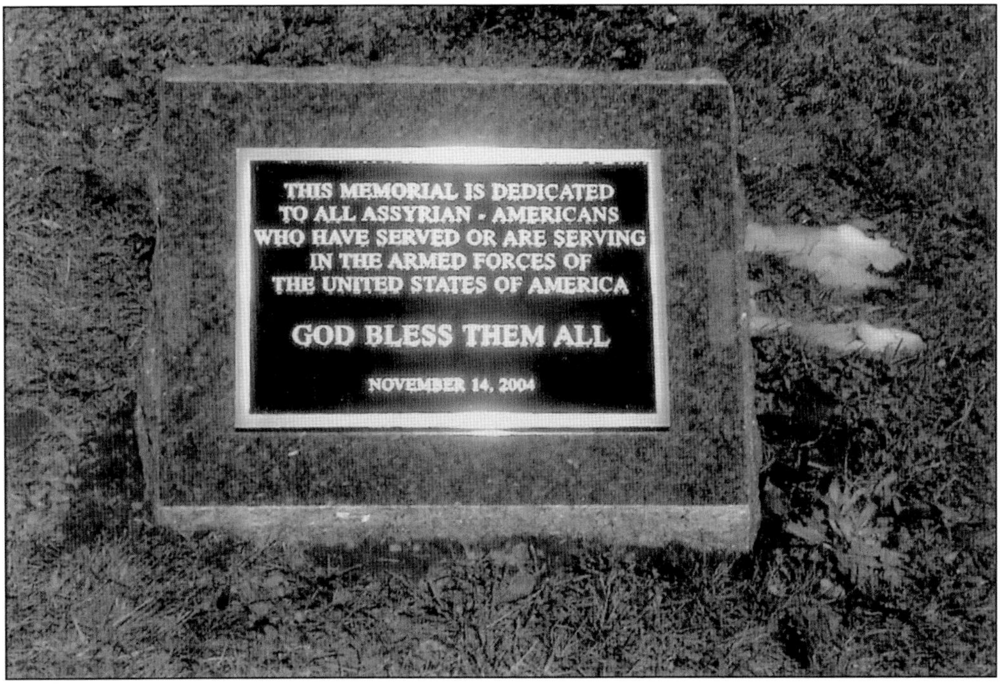

A large part of the veteran dedication ceremony was the establishment of a monument at St. Thomas Church of the East that displays the words, "This memorial is dedicated to all Assyrian-Americans who have served or are serving in the Armed Forces of the United States of America. God Bless Them All."

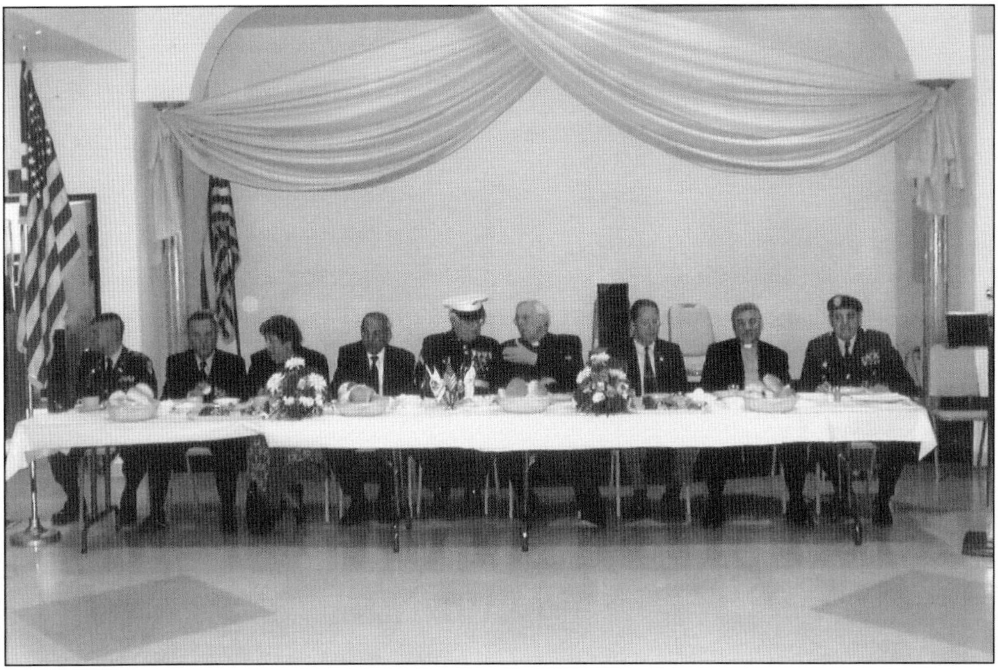

After the ceremony, a banquet was held inside of the church ballroom, which was open to all of the veterans, their families, and others who had attended the previous ceremony.

Five

Influential Persons in the Assyrian Community

New Britain has seen a number of influential Assyrians who are currently known for their involvement in Assyrian issues, as well as a number of people that are now known for their involvement in things outside of the Assyrian community.

Yonatan Bet Solieman was born in Iran in 1893 and made the decision to come to America in 1907, at the age of 14. In 1914, he helped to begin a number of Assyrian organizations that worked towards gathering money for Assyrian immigrant students, families, and those in need of health care.

Concerned that Assyrians risked losing knowledge of their language and heritage due to their rate of assimilation, he began an organization called Shamraya Dava, the objective of which was to gather together the various Assyrian refugees and continue learning and developing their knowledge of the Assyrian language. With the help of his wife, daughters, and an Assyrian correspondent in France, he began printing the newspaper *Atour*. This paper was delivered to the households of many Assyrians within the United States, Iraq, and Iran.

Frances Eshoo Jacobs spent 18 years writing "Connecticut Chit-Chat" for the *Assyrian Star*, a bimonthly periodical. Her column was featured in the section of the magazine dedicated to updating Assyrians of the local happenings of various United States towns and cities. Jacobs wrote of weddings, graduations, and family visits both locally and abroad, along with the events of local Assyrian organizations such as the church, club, veterans post, and ladies auxiliary. Her final column, along with her farewell, appeared in the July–August 1970 issue of the *Assyrian Star*. The column lasted from 1954 until 1970.

Another well-achieved Connecticut Assyrian Citizen is Philip Tamraz, a businessman of 43 years. He immigrated to the United States from Iran at the age of 14 and worked in a New Britain Factory until World War I broke out; he served in the war and briefly. He entered business in New Britain, with the establishment of his first store in 1921. Soon afterwards, he purchased his second store. He continued owning this business until his retirement in 1964.

Anna Eshoo was born in Connecticut in December of 1942, and is an American citizen of Assyrian and Armenian heritage. She currently resides in Atherton, California, where she is a Democratic member of the House of Representatives of California's 14th district.

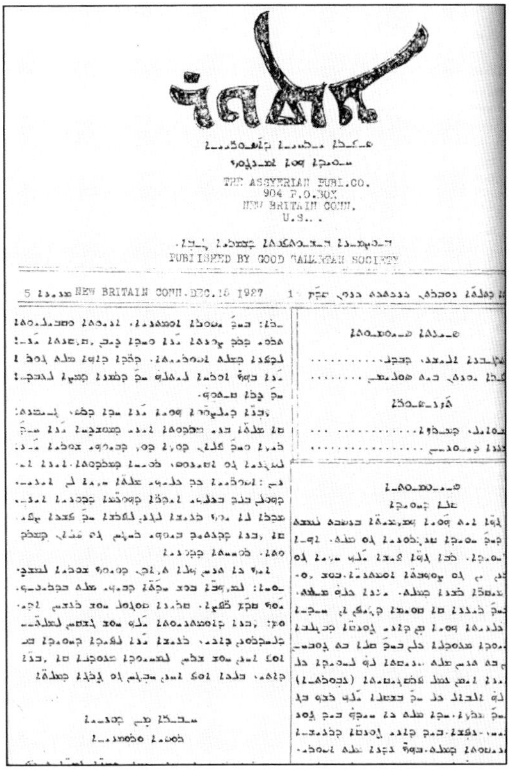

This is a sample of the newspaper *Atour* written by Yonatan BetSolieman, which was in circulation from 1925 until 1942. He also wrote a number of books, one of which was on the history of Assyrians in Christian times, which details the happenings of these people from the time of Christ onwards. Yonatan BetSolieman died in 1981, at the age of 88.

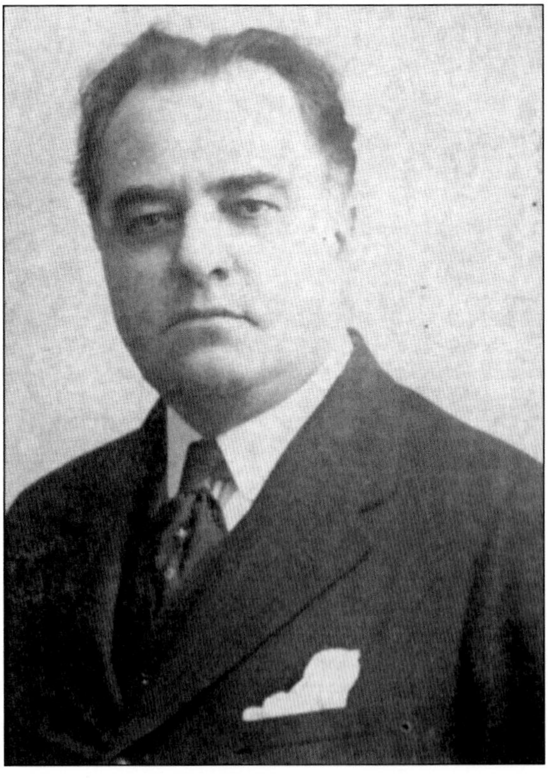

Joel E. Warda was the editor and publisher of the *Assyrian American Courier*, as well as the president of the ANA for a number of years. He is also known for having written a large number of books about the Assyrian people.

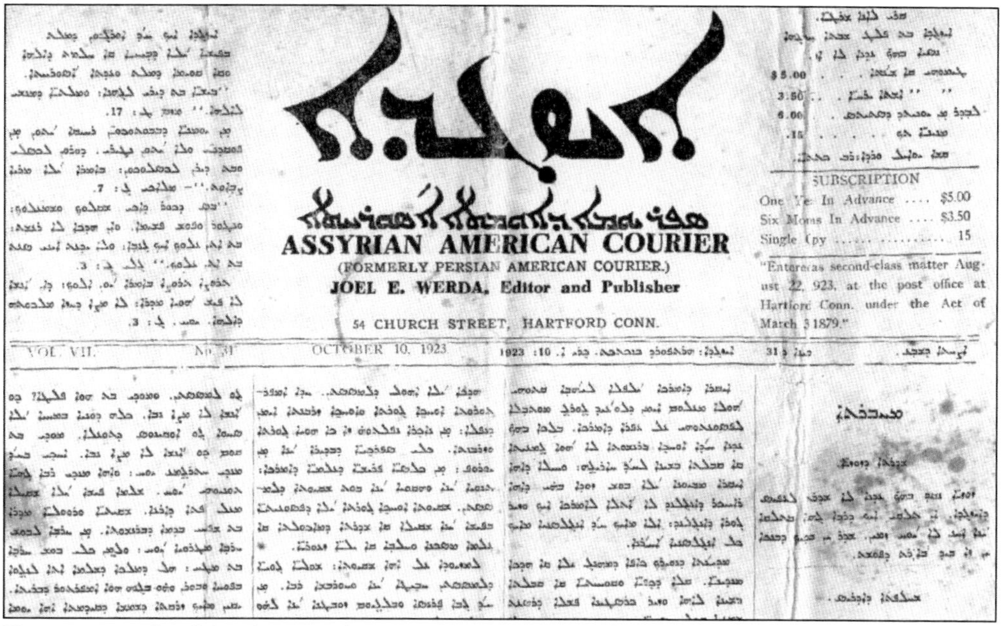

ASSYRIAN AMERICAN COURIER
(FORMERLY PERSIAN AMERICAN COURIER.)
JOEL E. WERDA, Editor and Publisher
54 CHURCH STREET, HARTFORD CONN.

SUBSCRIPTION
One Ye In Advance $5.00
Six Mons In Advance $3.50
Single Cpy 15

"Entere as second-class matter August 22, 923, at the post office at Hartford Conn. under the Act of March 3 1879."

VOL. VII. No. 31 OCTOBER 10, 1923

Here is a sample of the *Assyrian American Courier* written by Joel E. Warda. The newspaper was run out of Hartford during the early 20th century. As shown, it was written in Assyrian lettering and provided news on both Assyrian and American history, politics, and recent events. It was also used to advertise New Britain businesses. It held the title *Persian American Courier* until it was updated in the early 1920s.

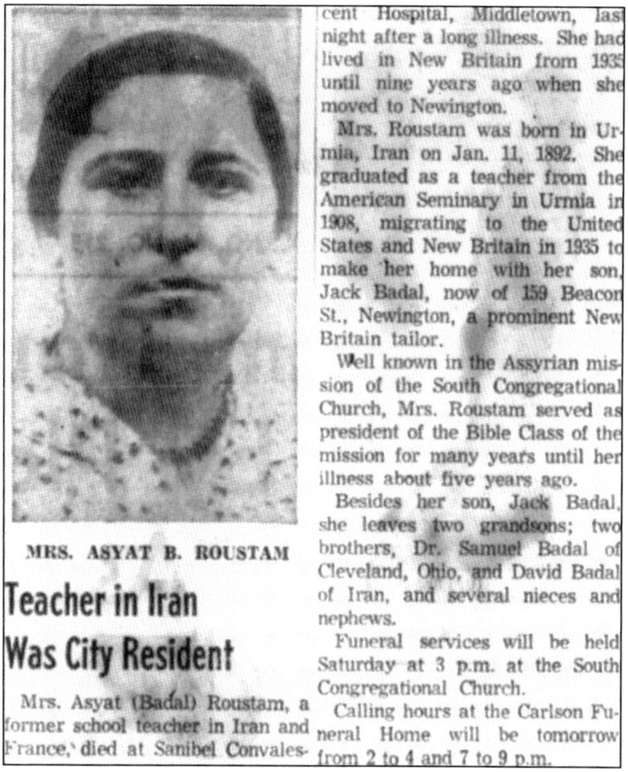

MRS. ASYAT B. ROUSTAM

Teacher in Iran Was City Resident

Mrs. Asyat (Badal) Roustam, a former school teacher in Iran and France, died at Sanibel Convalescent Hospital, Middletown, last night after a long illness. She had lived in New Britain from 1935 until nine years ago when she moved to Newington.

Mrs. Roustam was born in Urmia, Iran on Jan. 11, 1892. She graduated as a teacher from the American Seminary in Urmia in 1908, migrating to the United States and New Britain in 1935 to make her home with her son, Jack Badal, now of 159 Beacon St., Newington, a prominent New Britain tailor.

Well known in the Assyrian mission of the South Congregational Church, Mrs. Roustam served as president of the Bible Class of the mission for many years until her illness about five years ago.

Besides her son, Jack Badal, she leaves two grandsons; two brothers, Dr. Samuel Badal of Cleveland, Ohio, and David Badal of Iran, and several nieces and nephews.

Funeral services will be held Saturday at 3 p.m. at the South Congregational Church.

Calling hours at the Carlson Funeral Home will be tomorrow from 2 to 4 and 7 to 9 p.m.

Asyat Roustam received her high school degree at the American Presbyterian Seminary in Urmia, Iran, and moved on to become a teacher. She migrated to the United States and attended South Church of New Britain.

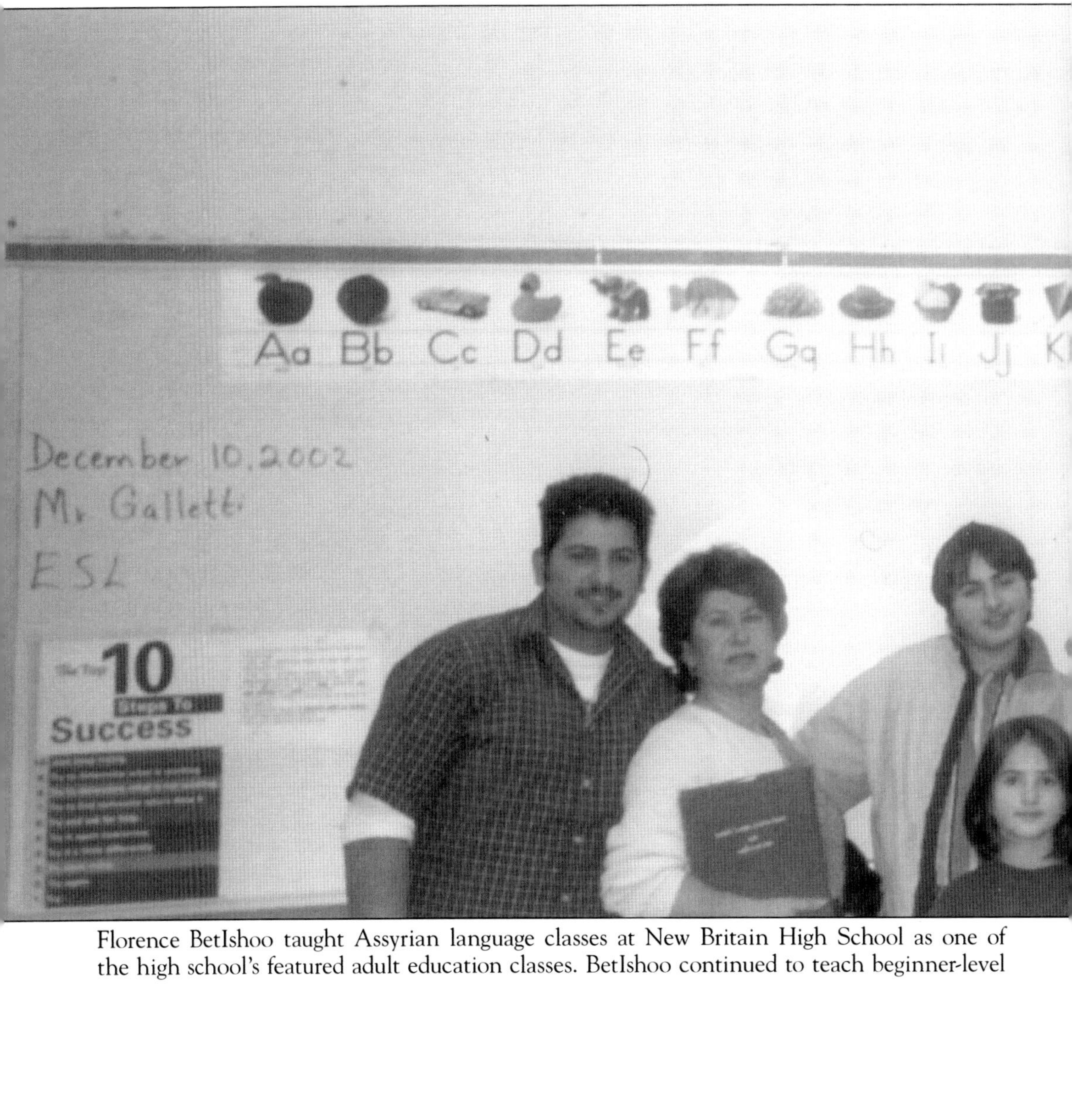

Florence BetIshoo taught Assyrian language classes at New Britain High School as one of the high school's featured adult education classes. BetIshoo continued to teach beginner-level

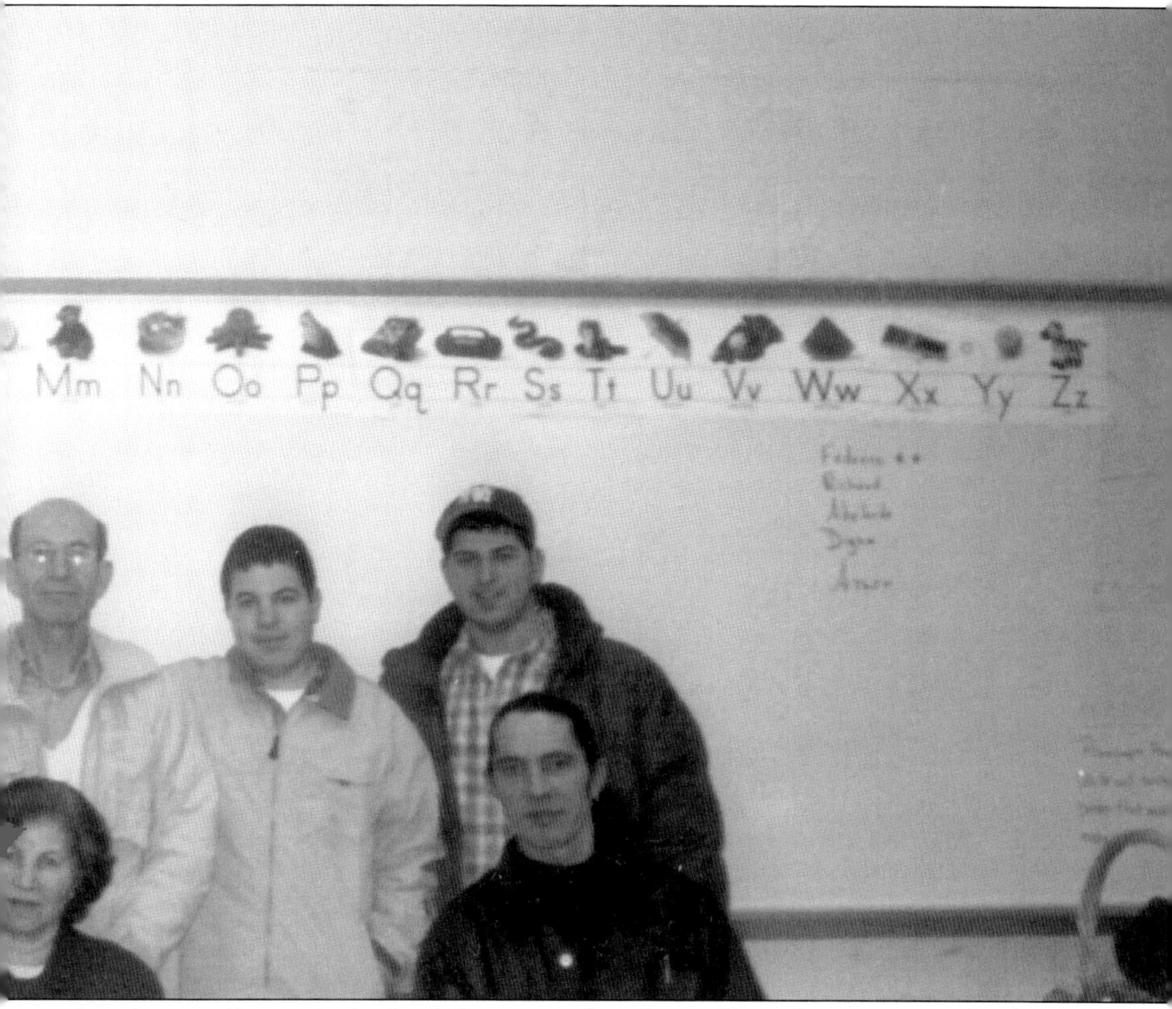

Assyrian as well as continuing-level classes a number of years. Shown here is a group of students with BetIshoo in the center of the first row.

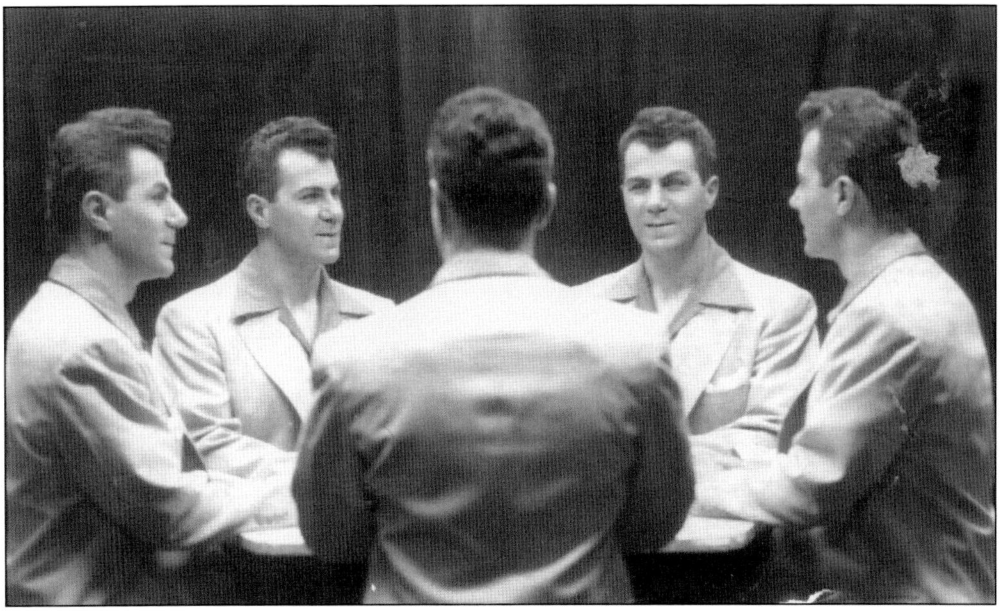

Charles W. Warda was an Assyrian citizen employed at Fafnir Bearing Company for 31 years. There he patented an invention for a ball-bearing locking device. He was a member of the Assyrian National Association of New Britain.

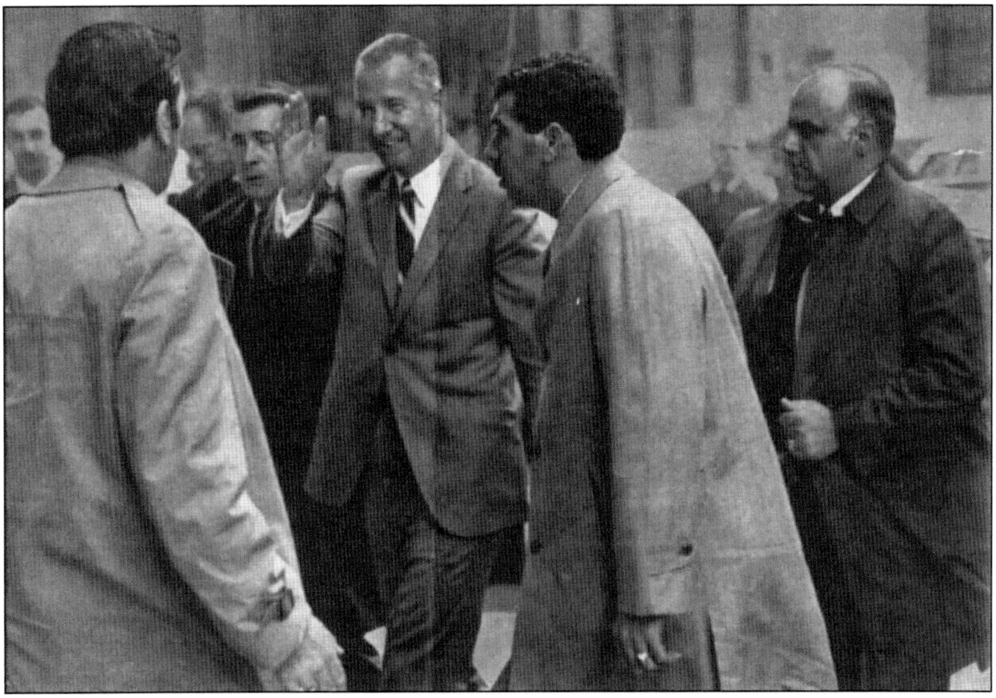

A headline in the *New Britain Herald* that stated "Spiro Agnew: Best Protected Vice President" was below this photograph. The vice president is shown flanked by a number of secret service men. On the far right is chief of detail, Assyrian-American Samuel Sulliman.

Six

The Community Now

Assyrians today use the Assyrian National Association club and the Assyrian church and its cultural center for their events and meetings. New Britain continues to have a vibrant Assyrian community that actively hold Assyrian celebrations as well as religious and secular events. Every year, on the first day of April, which happens to be the Assyrian New Year, an Assyrian flag is raised in the center of New Britain by the mayor in the Assyrian Flag Ceremony; Assyrians that wish to attend are welcome and many continue to do so. In January the Assyrian Club and St. Thomas Church of the East hold two separate New Year celebrations. Families from Connecticut as well as visitors from Massachusetts and other nearby states often attend this and many other New Britain–hosted Assyrian celebrations. Religious holidays are generally held at St. Thomas Church of the East, where there is often a special service and banquet to honor the occasion. Easter and Christmas are two holidays that are given most observance, and large groups of families and visitors are present for the service and the later festivities.

St. Thomas Church of the East currently owns a cemetery in New Britain that is maintained and open to those who wish to pay respect to family members and loved ones.

The groups that exist within New Britain are the Assyrian National Association, the Ashur Club, and the Ladies Association. They hold regular meetings and sponsor events.

Early in the 1990s there were four different Assyrian Television programs on the public access station in Connecticut. Church of the East was led by Rev. Gevargis Toma, who spoke about church news, Assyrian history, and gave bible lessons. Ishtar T.V. featured speakers, Agnes Pera, Abraham Zaya George, Remon George, and Elizabeth Yousefzada. The director of this program was Clyden Dooman.

Cynthia Besho was the speaker for Assyrian History and research; she would offer information to recent immigrants about gaining citizenship and learning United States History. Currently there is one program called Ashur TV which is put out by Ashur Association of New Britain. The director and editor for that is Wilson Baba.

Three recent AANF Eastern Regional Directors have been from the New Britain Area, Abraham Zaya George, Agnes Pera, and Zeena Tawfik-Yonkers, who served until 2006. As director, Tawfik-Yonkers put a lot of effort into educating people about the history of Assyrians and with involving young people of the Assyrian community.

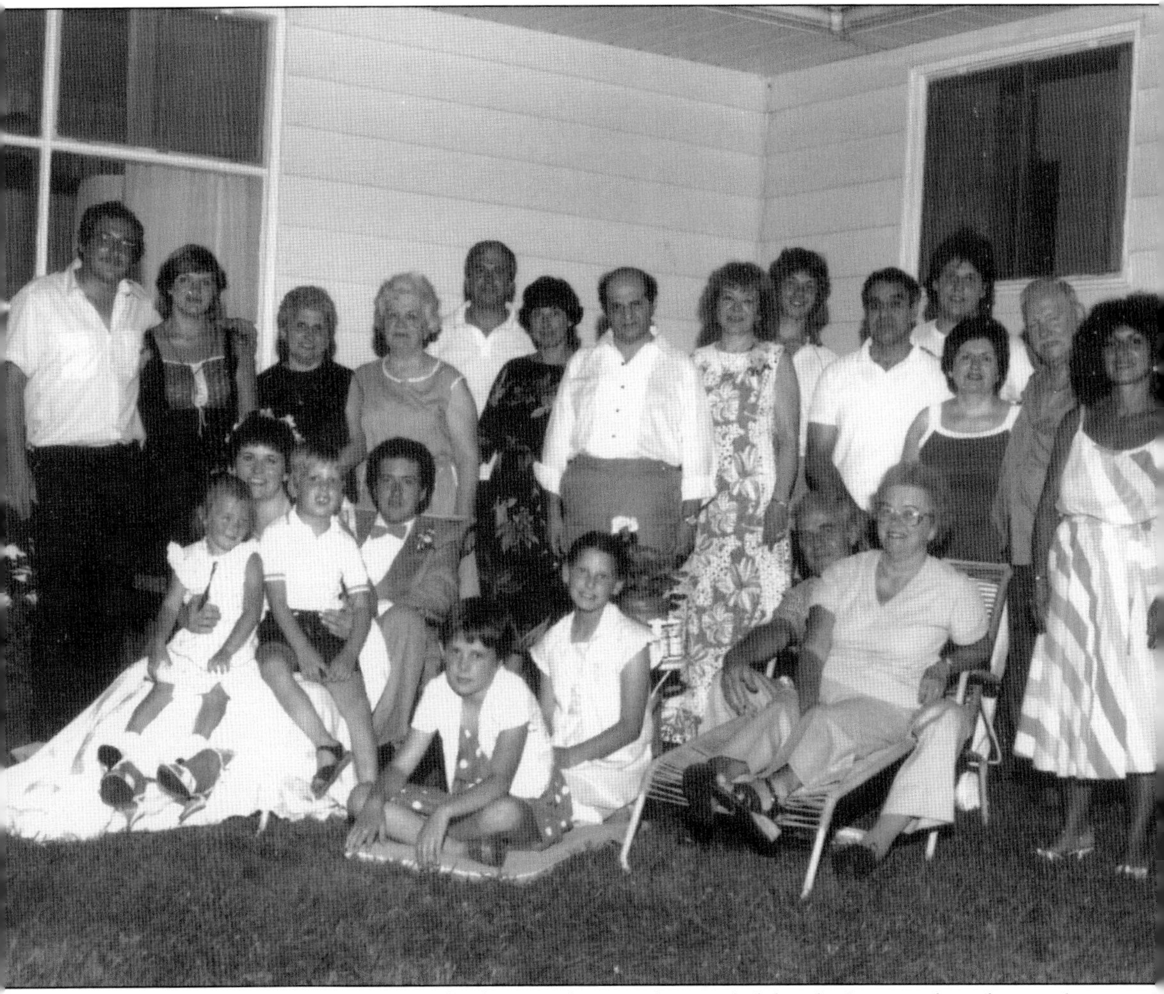

This family photograph features both immediate and extended family. It was taken during the 1980s after the wedding of the young couple in the front left. Also pictured are Shirly and William George, Mary and Bob George, and Seya George.

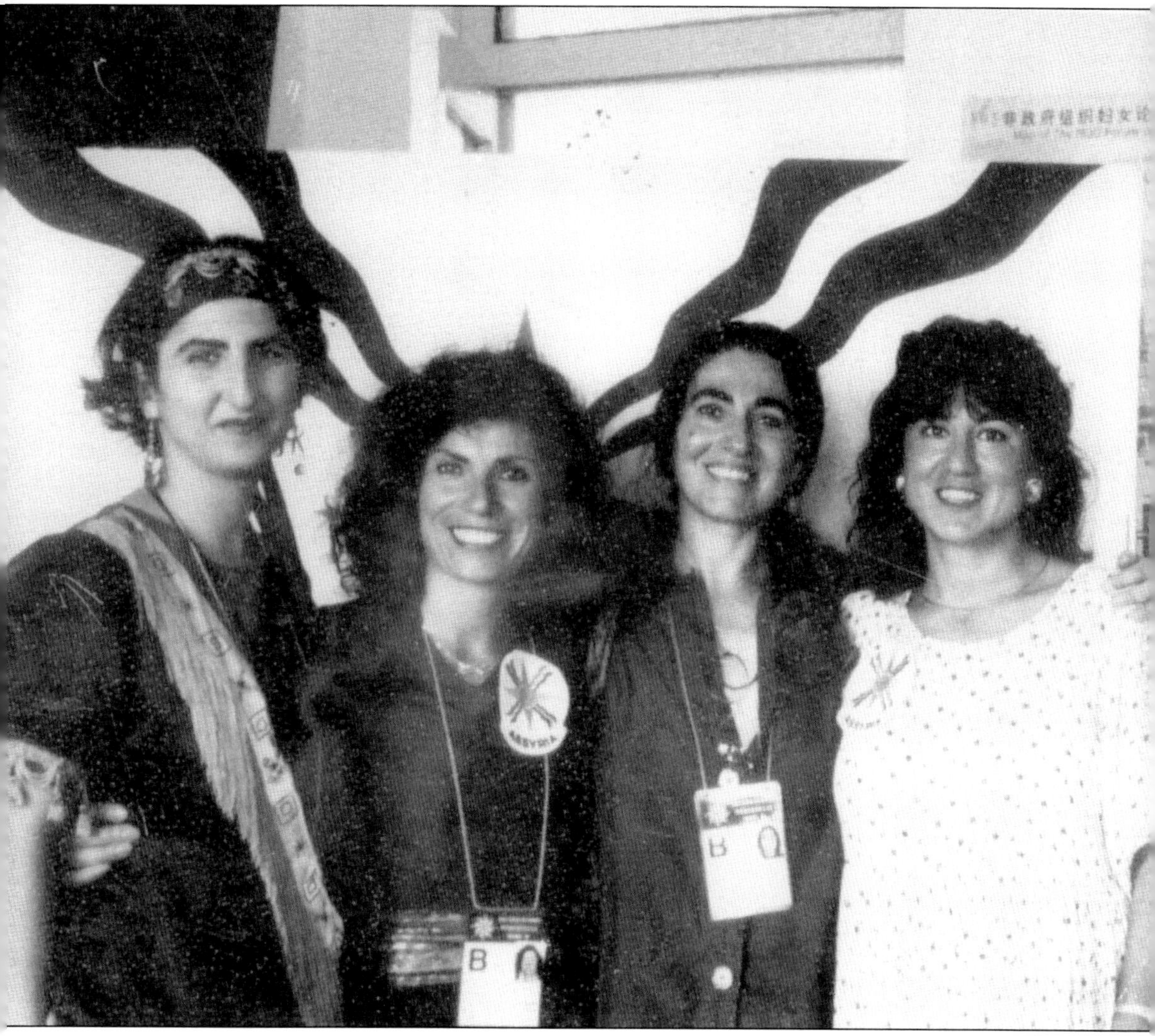

New Britain resident Sharokin Betgevargiz (left) attended the 1995 fourth World Conference on Women. She sat on a panel to discuss Assyrian women's issues. She is seen here with, from left to right, Edibe Yonan, Pamela Safir, and Sonia Aho.

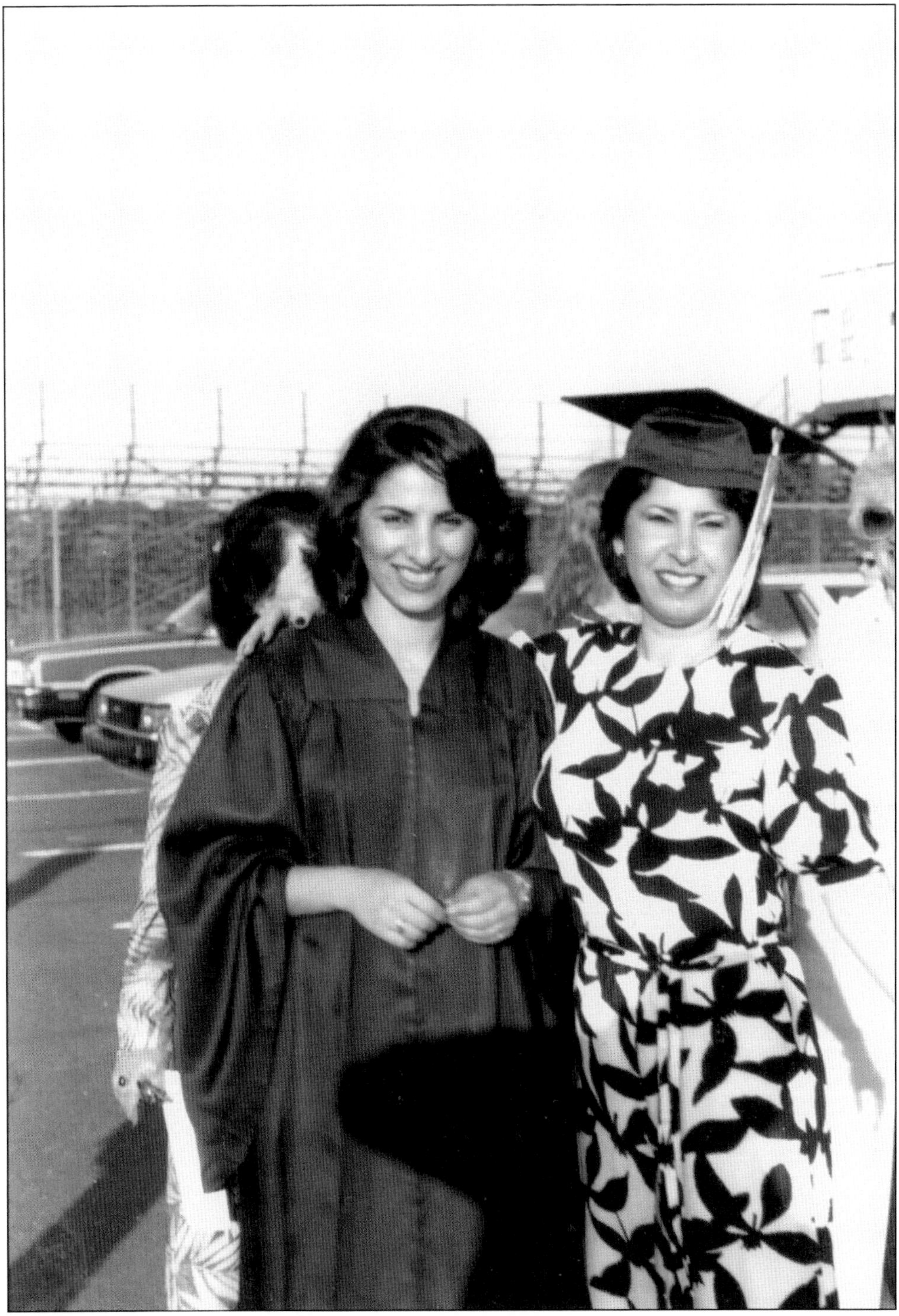

Helen BetGivargis (left) immigrated to the United States in the late 1970s. Her immediate family had not yet come to the states, so she stayed with extended family while attending Central Connecticut State University. Here she is shown on the day of her graduation while one of her cousins, Nahrin George, models her graduation cap.

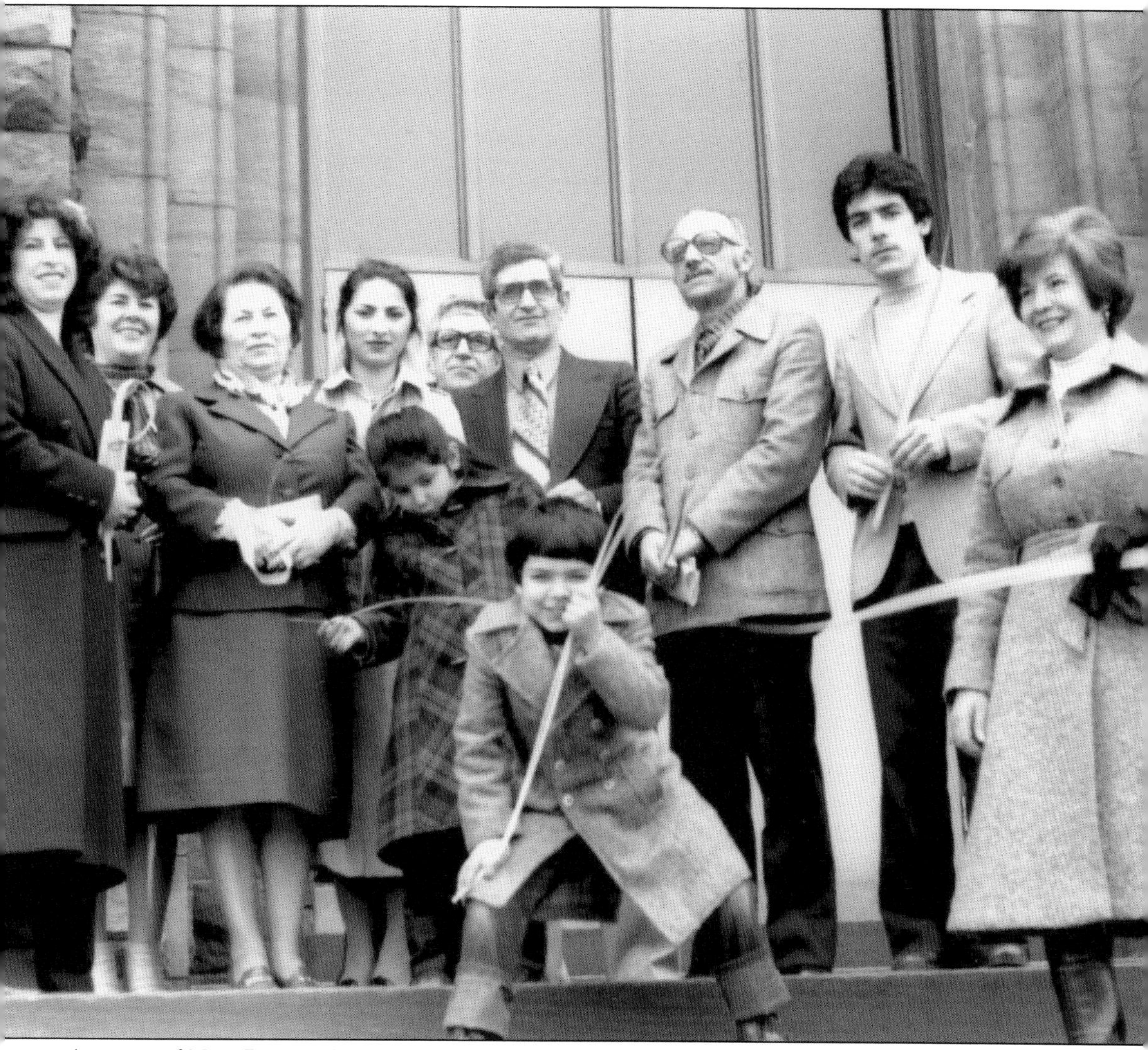

A group of New Britain Assyrians poses in front of St. Mary's church on Palm Sunday. From left to right are (first row) Helga and Henry Yosep; (second row) Nahrin George, Almas Toma, Nancy George, Helen BetGivargis, Yacob Toma, Albert George, Yosep Yosep, Daryush Alamsha, and Olga Yosep.

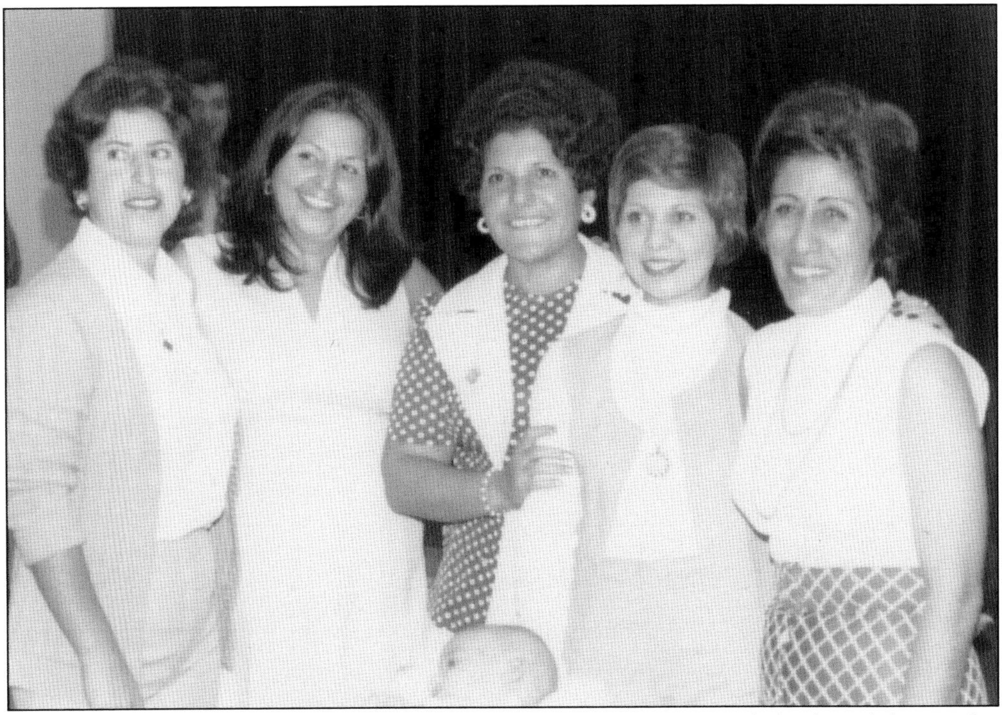

This group of Assyrian young women, all native to New Britain, include, from left to right, Nahrin George, Virginia Ebrahimi, Nagris ?, Shamiran Babazaya, and Elsie Donabed.

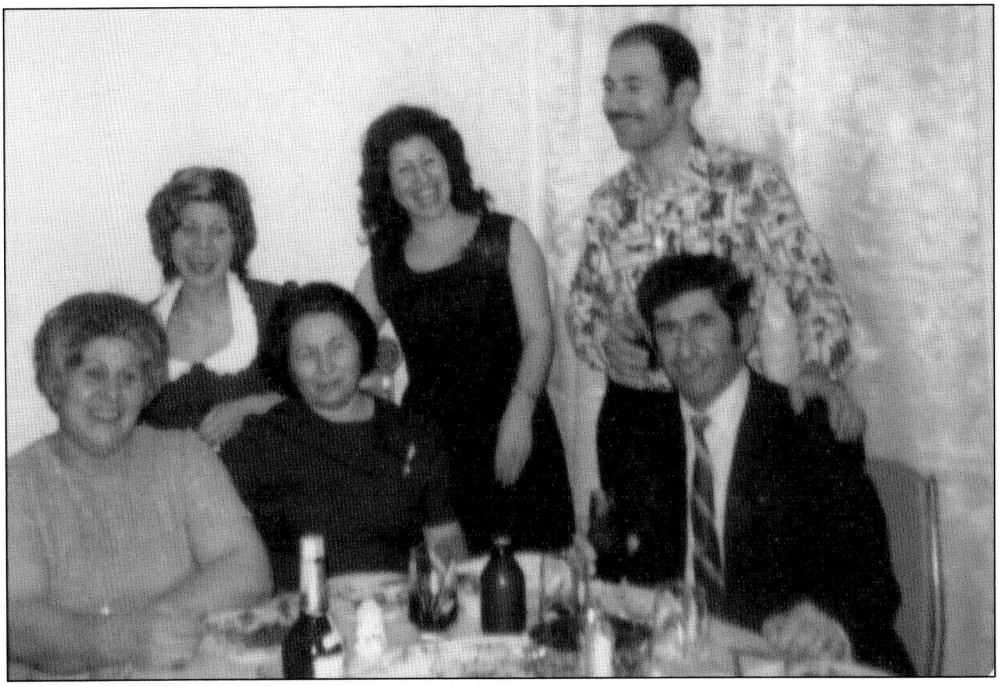

This group poses while visiting Katrina and Shamiran Babazaya for lunch. From left to right are (first row) Katrina, Nancy George, and Albert George; (second row) Shamiran, Nahrin George, and Abraham George.

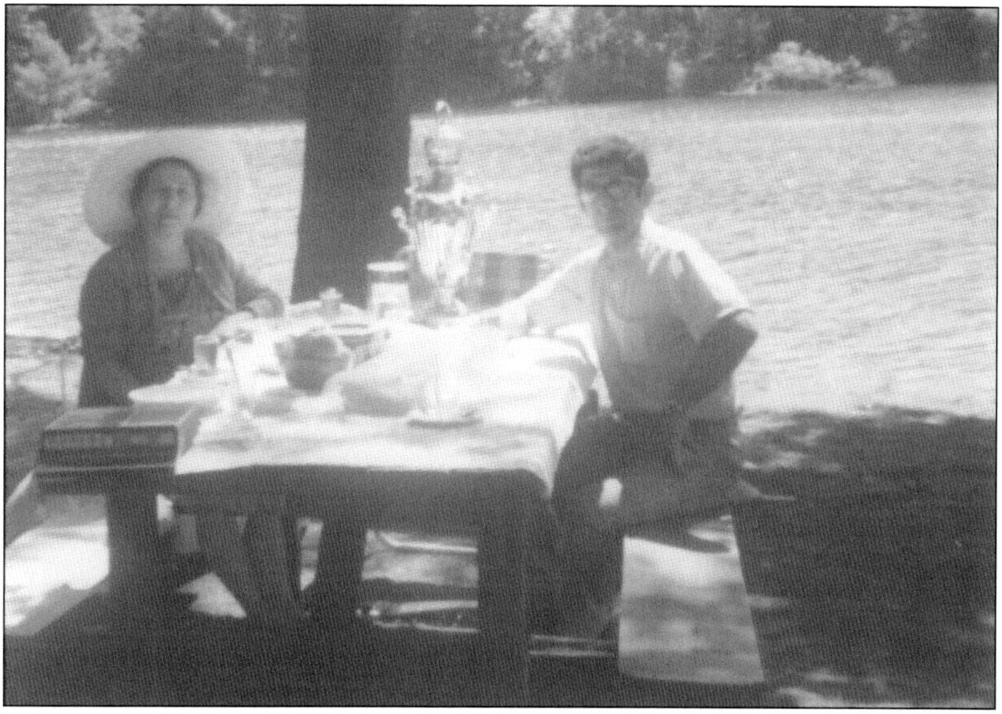

This picnic took place at Connecticut Lake, with samovar ready-to-serve tea on the table. Seated are Nancy and Albert George.

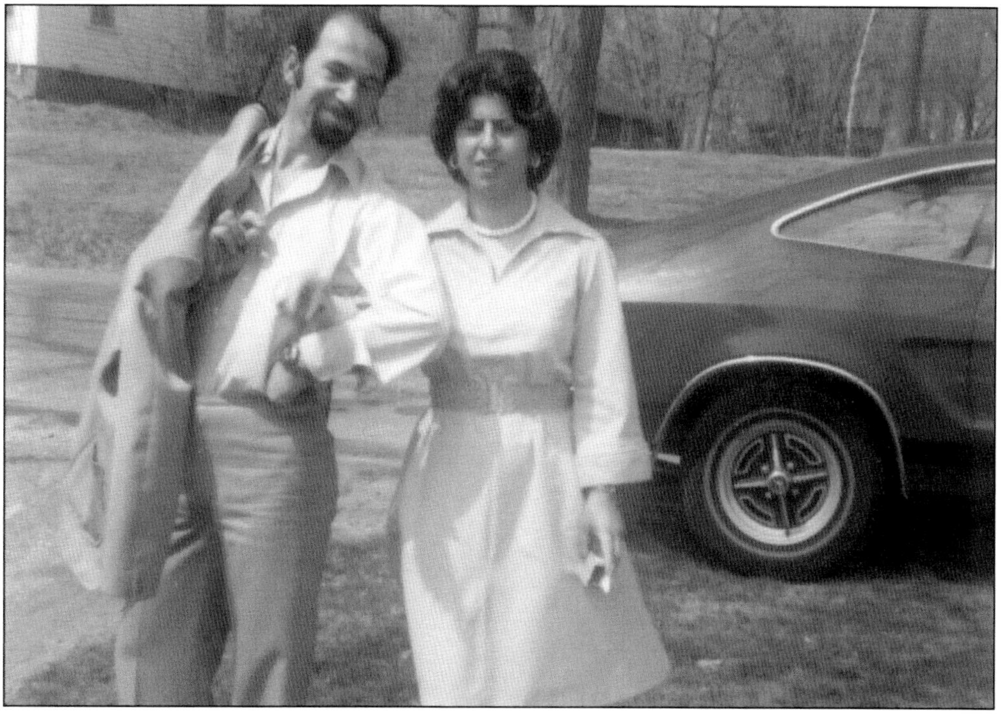

Siblings Nahrin and Abraham Zaya George model near Abraham's car. Abraham was the first of his family to come to the United States.

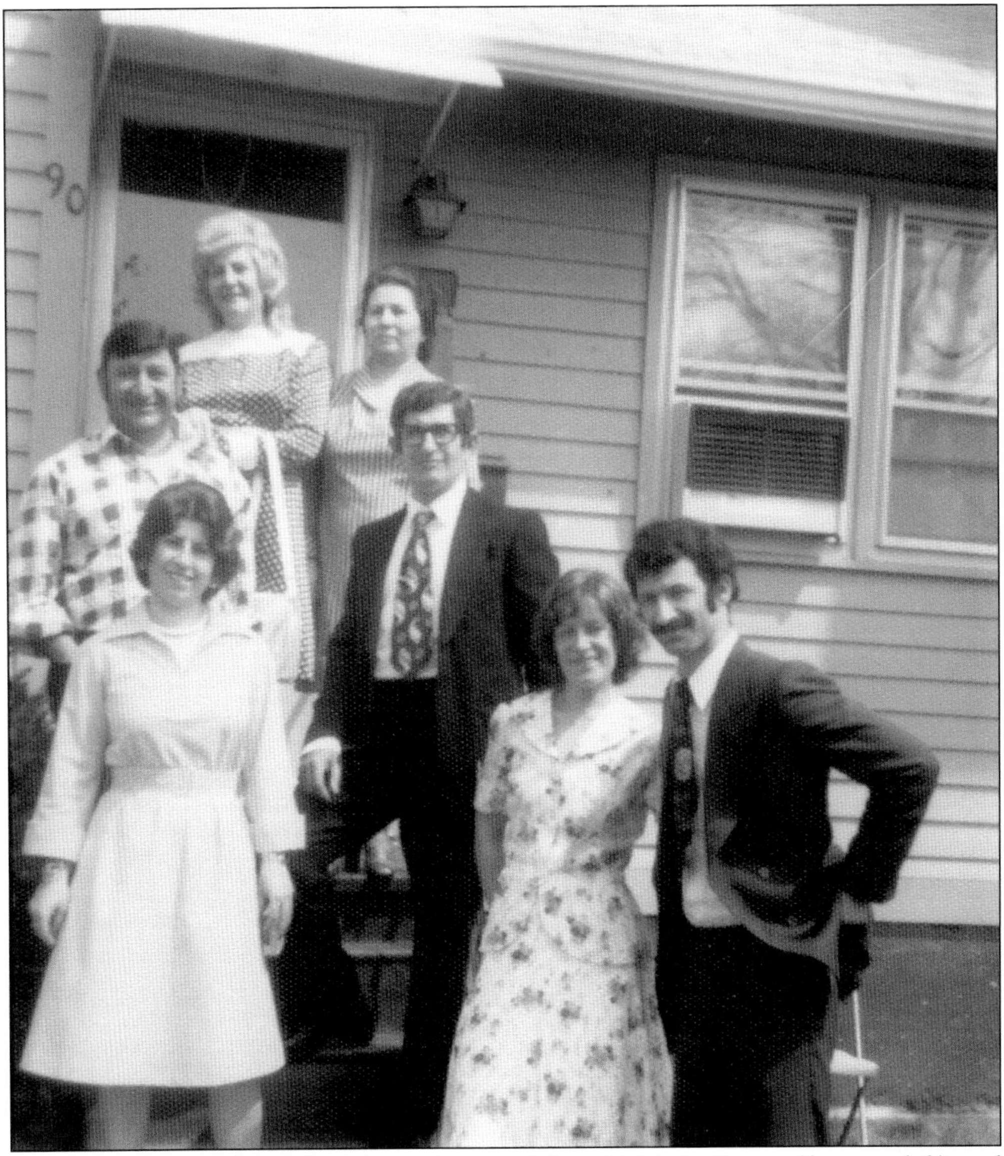

Nancy (third row, right), Albert (second row, right), and Nahrin George (first row, left), and Isaac BetGeorge (first row, right) are shown in this photograph while visiting their neighbors.

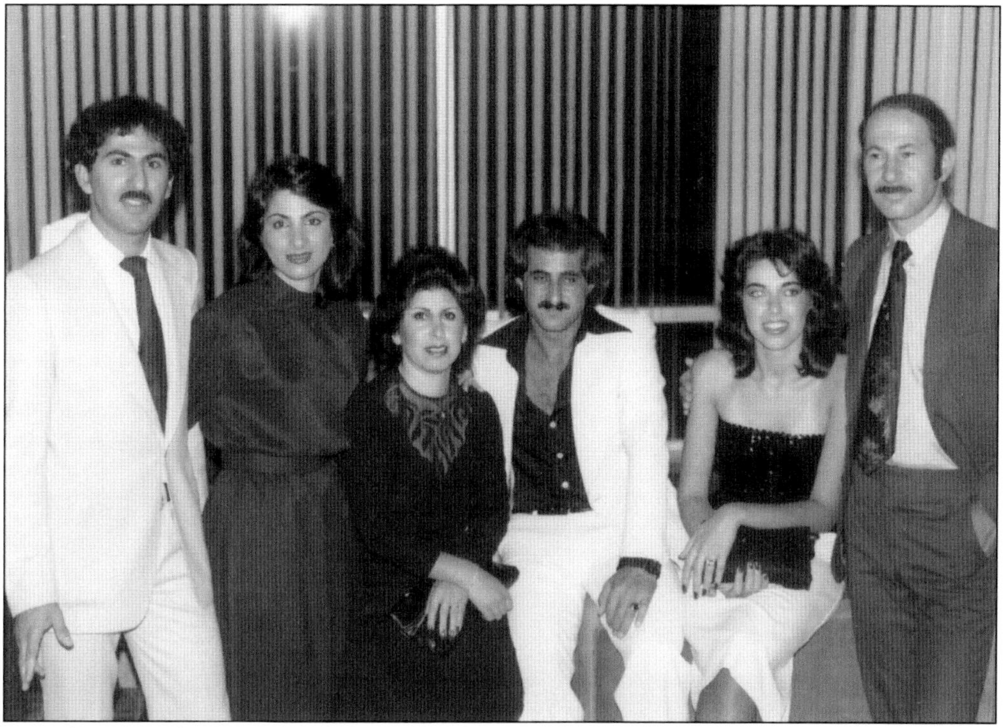

From left to right, Henry George, Helen BetGivargis, Nahrin George, Ninos Yadegar, and Jacqueline and Zaya George are shown in this photograph.

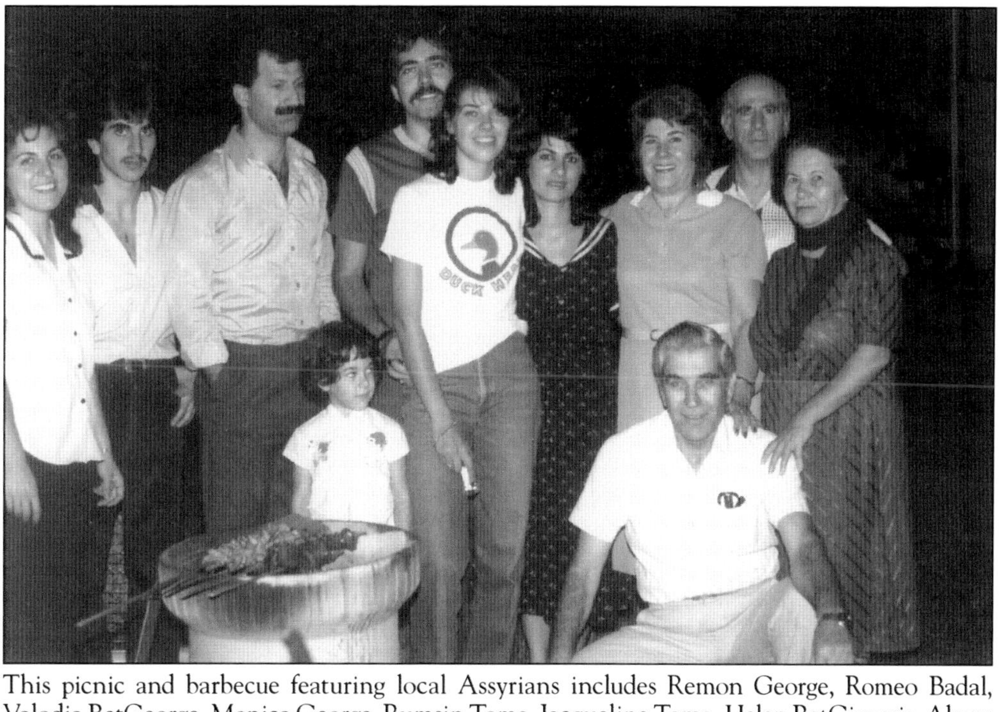

This picnic and barbecue featuring local Assyrians includes Remon George, Romeo Badal, Valodia BetGeorge, Monica George, Rumsin Toma, Jacqueline Toma, Helen BetGivargis, Almas Toma, Yacob Toma, and Nancy George.

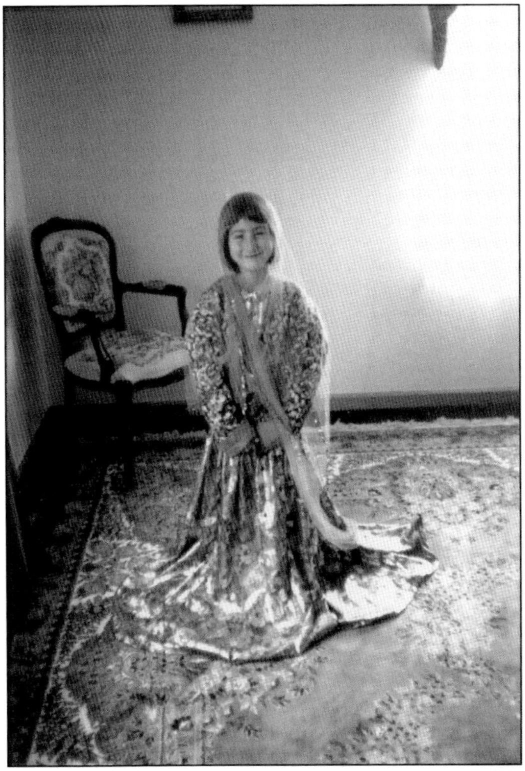

Author Maegan BetGivargis-McDaniel displays a type of traditional Assyrian clothing that was sewn by her grandmother Florence BetGeorge.

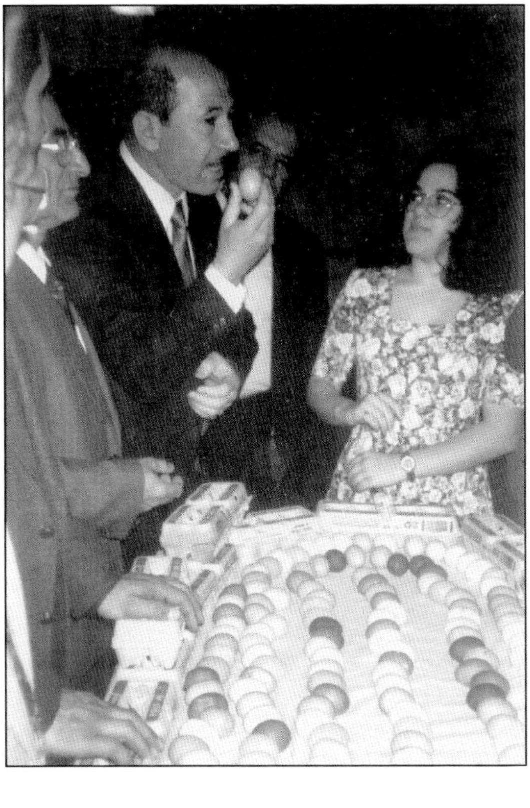

Assyrian Easter celebrations include a game that involves breaking as many rival-dyed Easter eggs with one's own, while trying to escape with as little damage to one's egg as possible. Abraham Zaya George is shown here testing the strength of this egg prior to using it in the game.

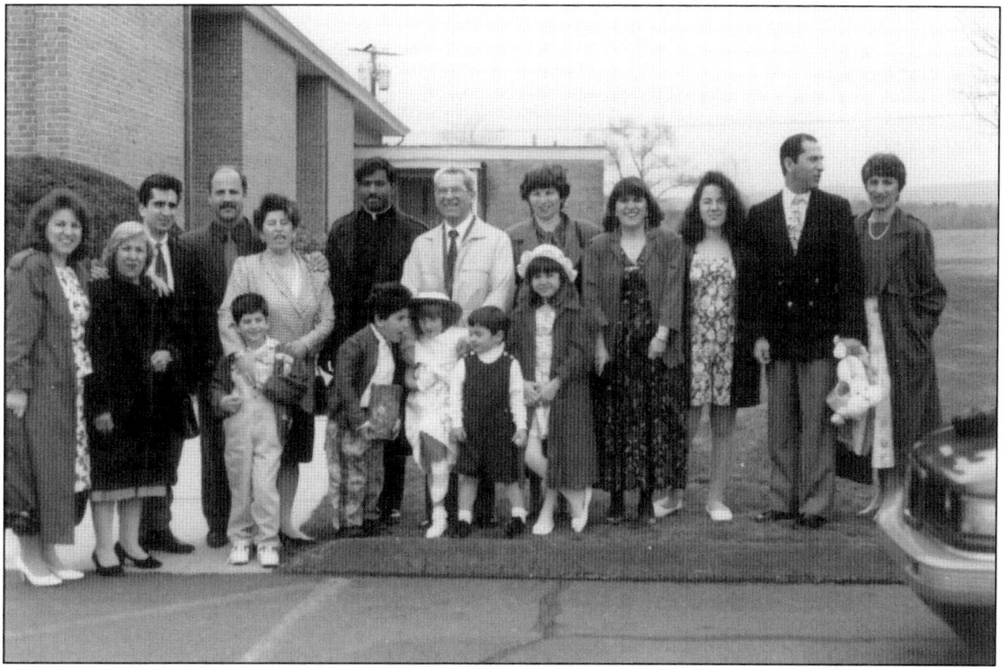

Assyrians belong to a number of different branches of Christianity. The majority of the individuals shown here are Catholic. Extended family poses together on Easter morning at St. Gregory's Church, located in Bristol, including Remon George, Marie, Romeo, Arthur, Nahrin, Rumsin and Jason Givargiznia, Maegan and Ben BetGivargis-McDaniel, George BetGeorge Bianca George, Florence Bet George, Leo, Monica George, Henry George, and Helen BetGivargis.

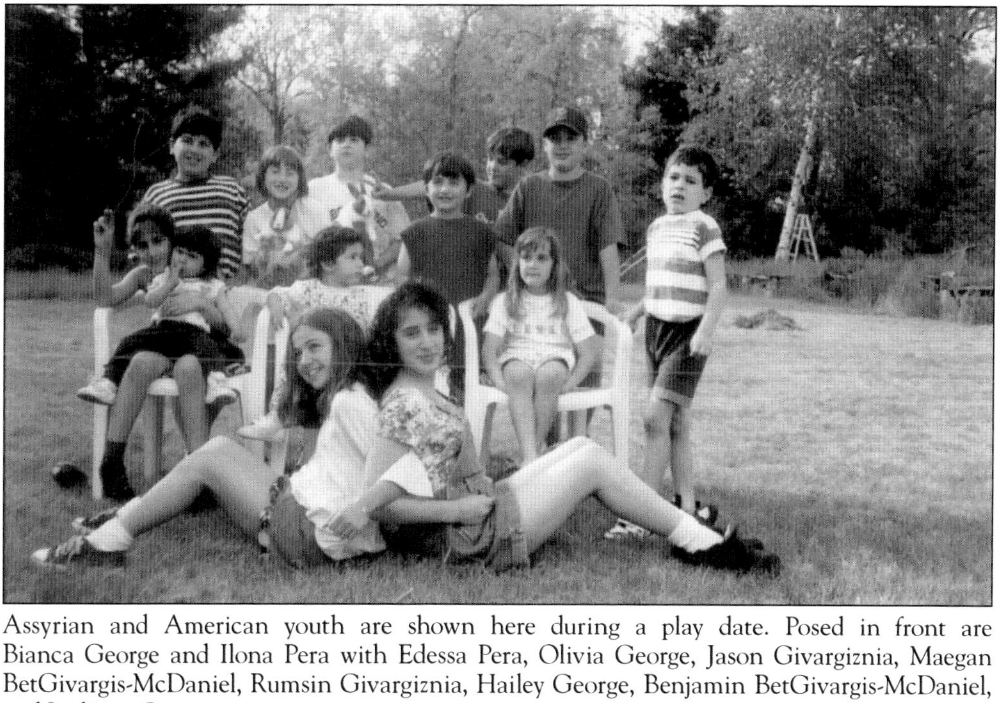

Assyrian and American youth are shown here during a play date. Posed in front are Bianca George and Ilona Pera with Edessa Pera, Olivia George, Jason Givargiznia, Maegan BetGivargis-McDaniel, Rumsin Givargiznia, Hailey George, Benjamin BetGivargis-McDaniel, and Ladimer George.

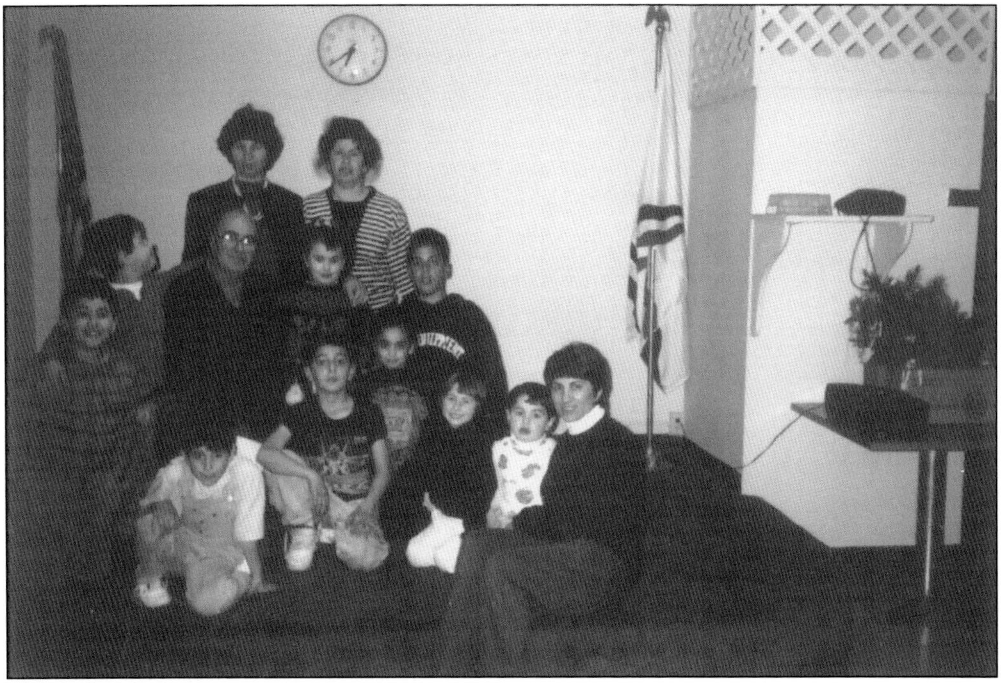

The Assyrian Kid's Club was a group led by Helen BetGivargis, Nahrin George, Yulius Petros, and Florence BetIshoo, focusing on allowing Assyrian youth to socialize while participating in activities that broadened their knowledge of their Assyrian heritage, especially on its history and language.

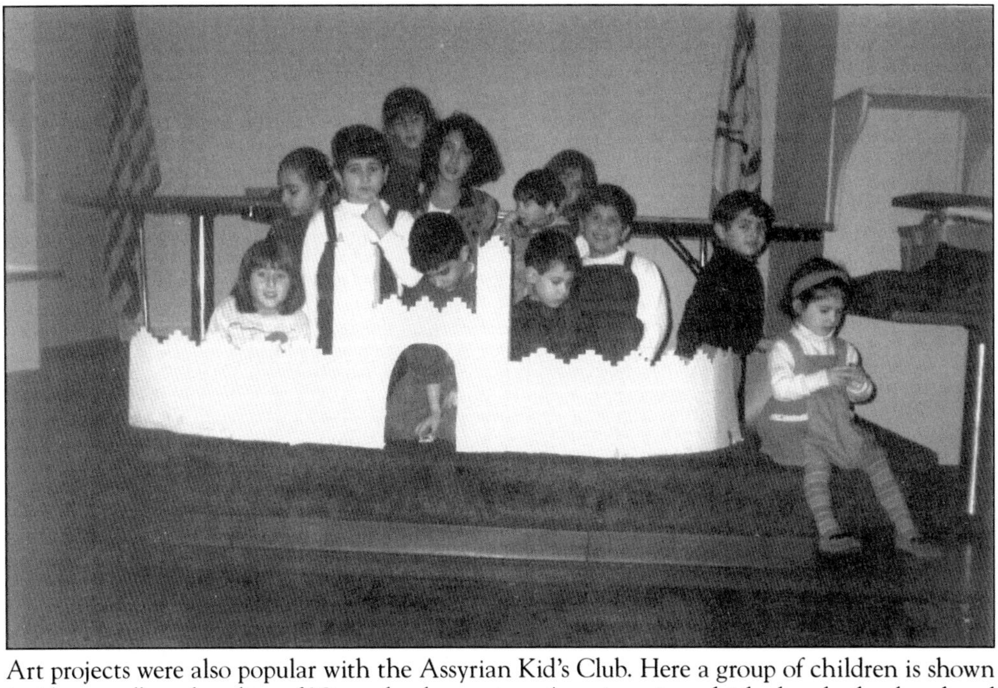

Art projects were also popular with the Assyrian Kid's Club. Here a group of children is shown inside a cardboard replica of Nineveh, the ancient Assyrian city, which they had colored and put together.

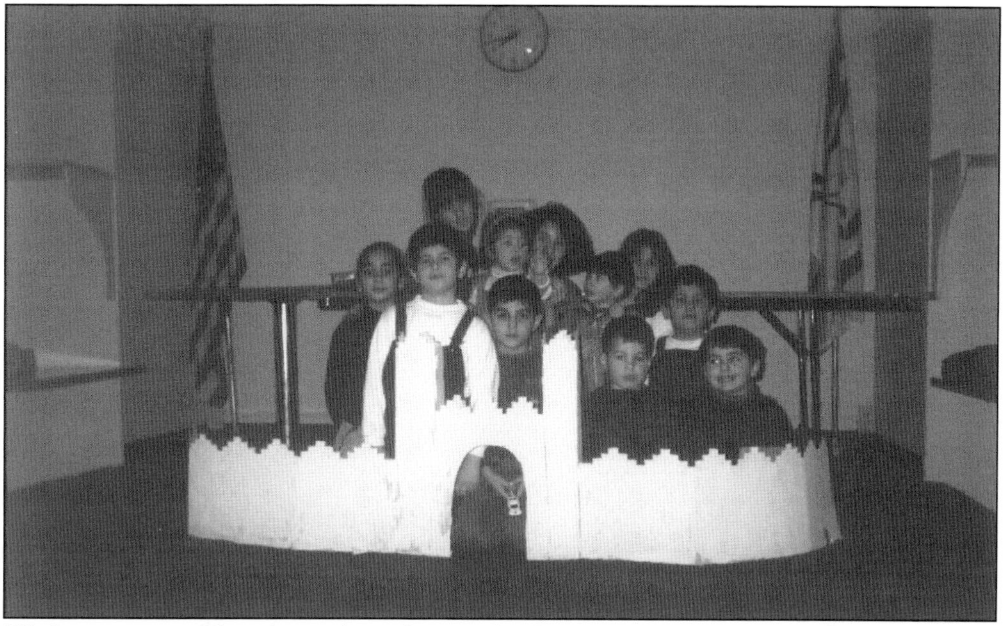

While putting together this replica of Nineveh, the ancient Assyrian city, the children were taught about the history of this city as well as a number of other ancient Assyrian locations in Iraq. Featured in the photograph are Lorissa Ebrahimi, Rumsin Givargiznia, Edessa Pera, Alex BetGeorge, Paul Oshana, Ilona Pera, Max BetGeorge, Bianca George, Jason Givargiznia, Ladimer George, and Benjamin BetGivargis-McDaniel.

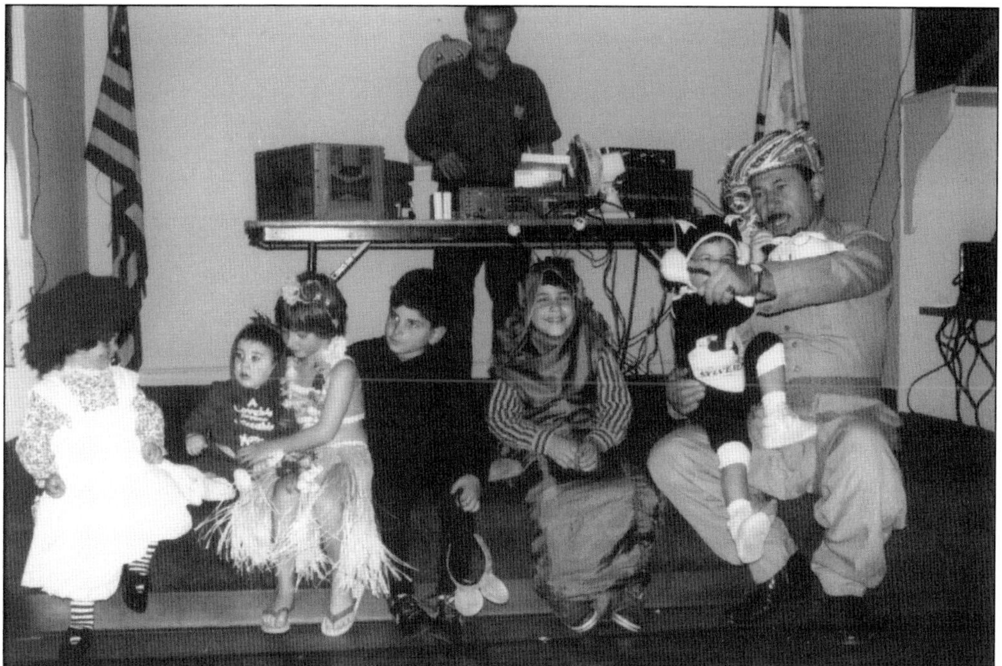

Children are shown here dressed up for Halloween at the Assyrian Cultural Club in New Britain. The individuals in the picture are Alex and Max BetGeorge, author Maegan BetGivargis-McDaniel, Rumsin and Jason Givargiznia, and Ladimer and Abraham George.

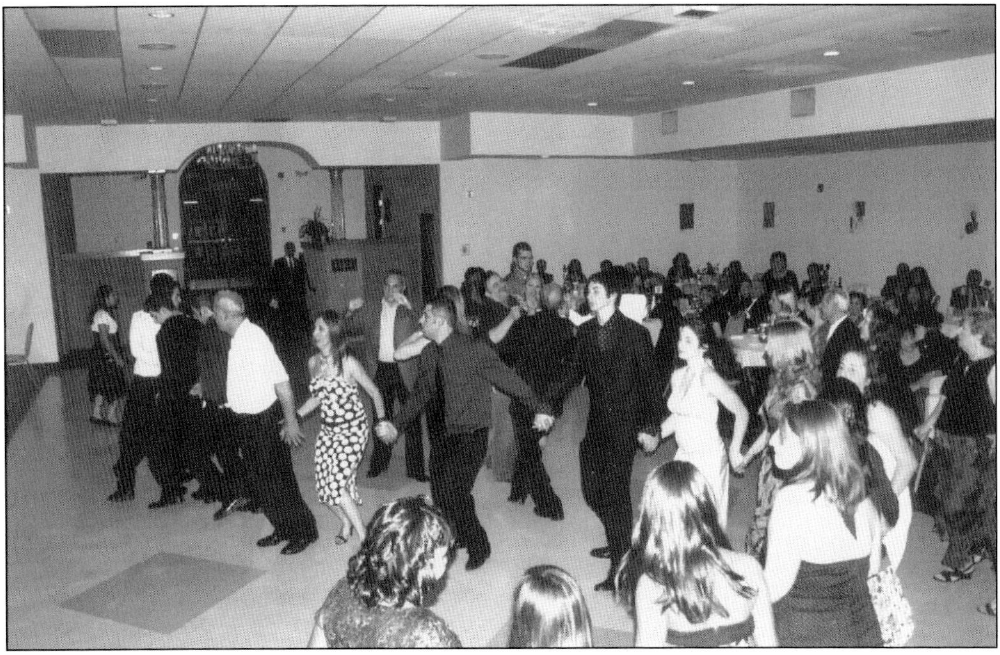

Shown here is an anniversary celebration at the St. Thomas Church of the East ballroom. The people in the picture are performing a traditional Assyrian dance.

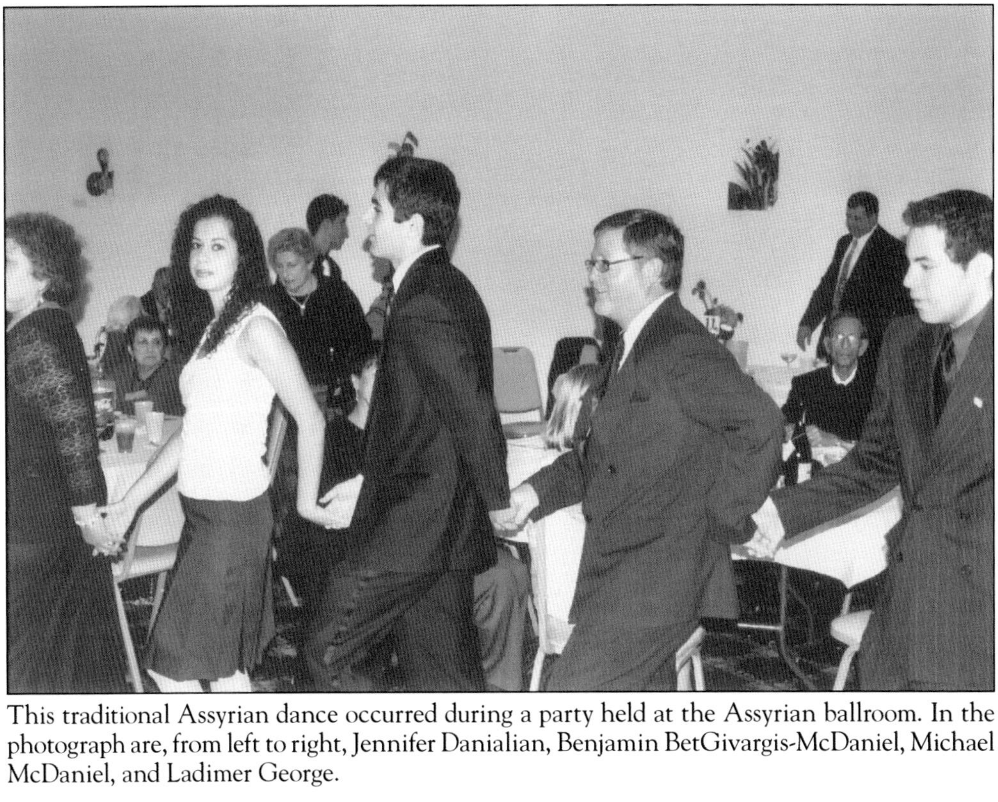

This traditional Assyrian dance occurred during a party held at the Assyrian ballroom. In the photograph are, from left to right, Jennifer Danialian, Benjamin BetGivargis-McDaniel, Michael McDaniel, and Ladimer George.

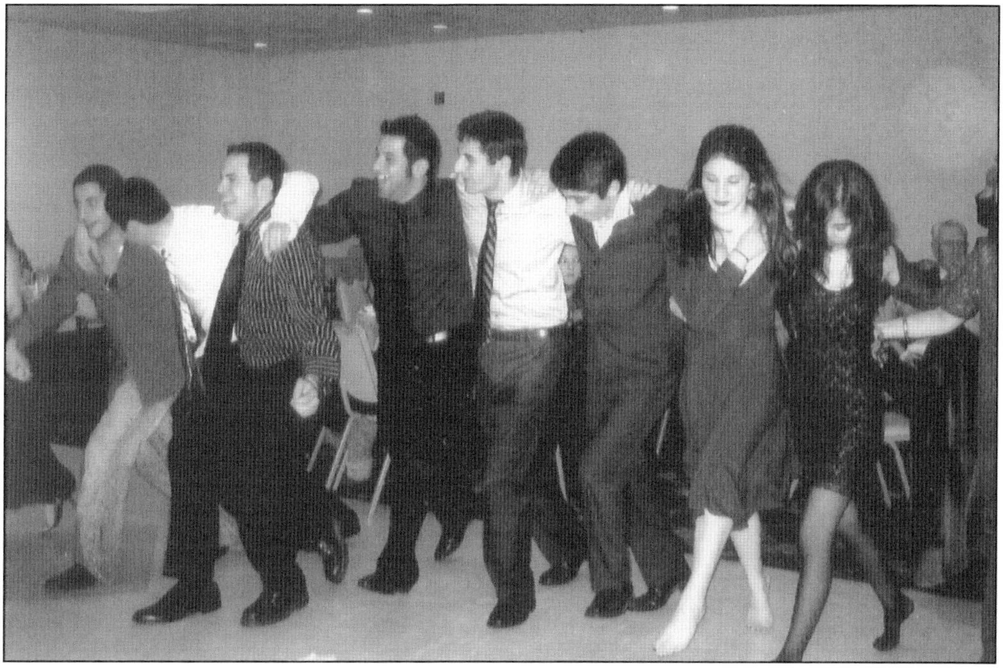

A group of youth is shown dancing during the New Year's party welcoming 2007 at the Assyrian Cultural Club.

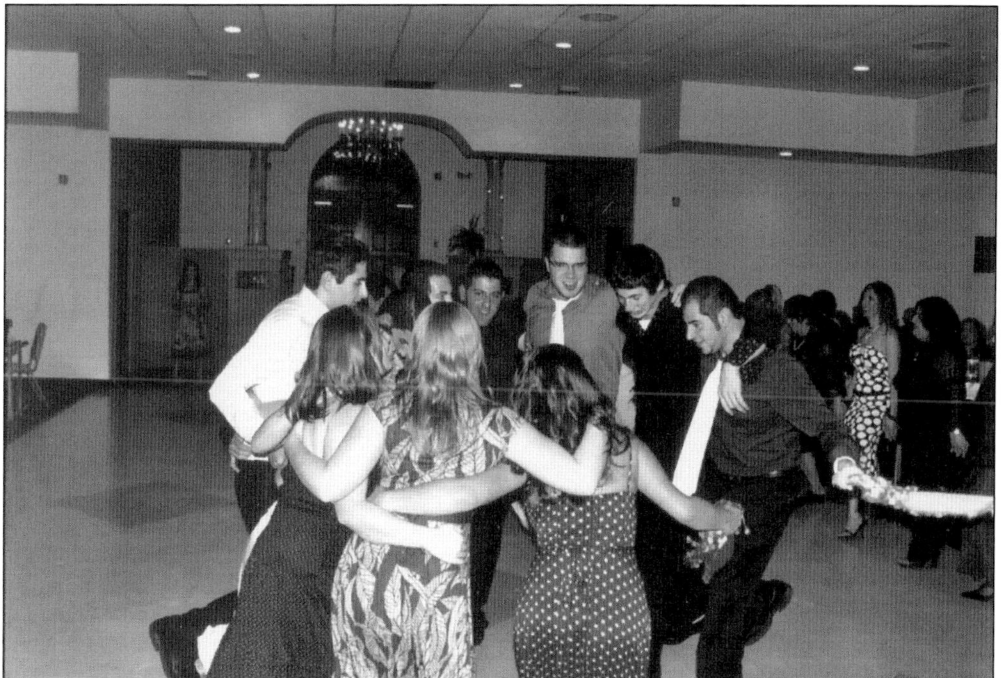

Often when adults join hands in a traditional Assyrian dance, the youth will clasp arms in a fast-paced version of the dance. Here a group of Assyrian and American youth is shown exhibiting this dance.

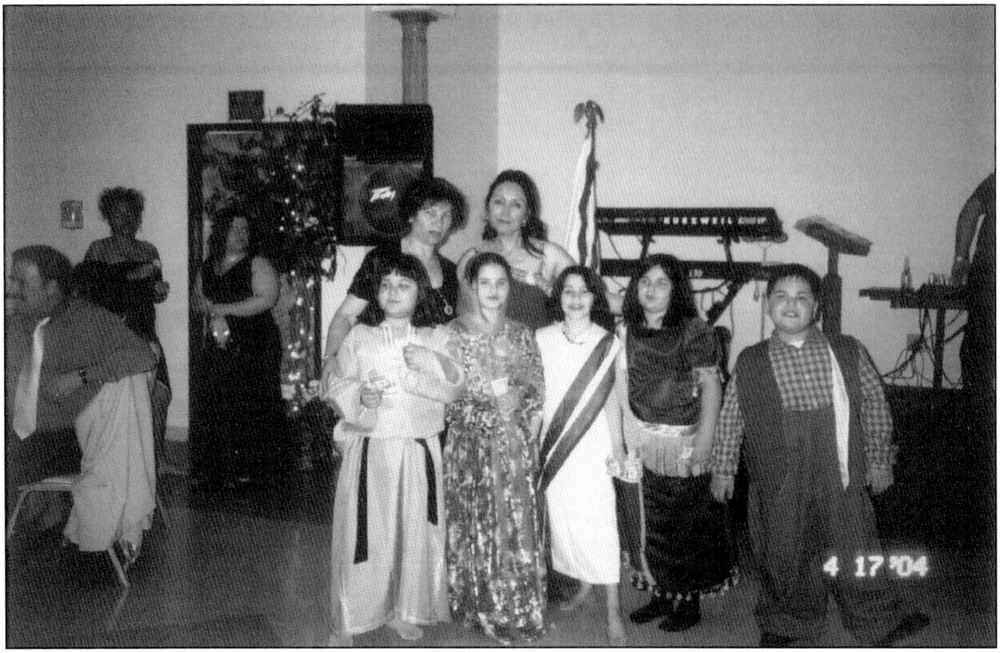

These children wear traditional Assyrian clothing as they perform an Assyrian dance at the Assyrian Cultural center and ballroom. The children are Nadrina Ebrahimi, Akadeena BetGivargis-McDaniel, Gabby BetGeorge, Audrina BetZomaya, and Robert Ebrahimi with their teacher Florence BetIshoo and Assyrian singer Lida Lewando behind them.

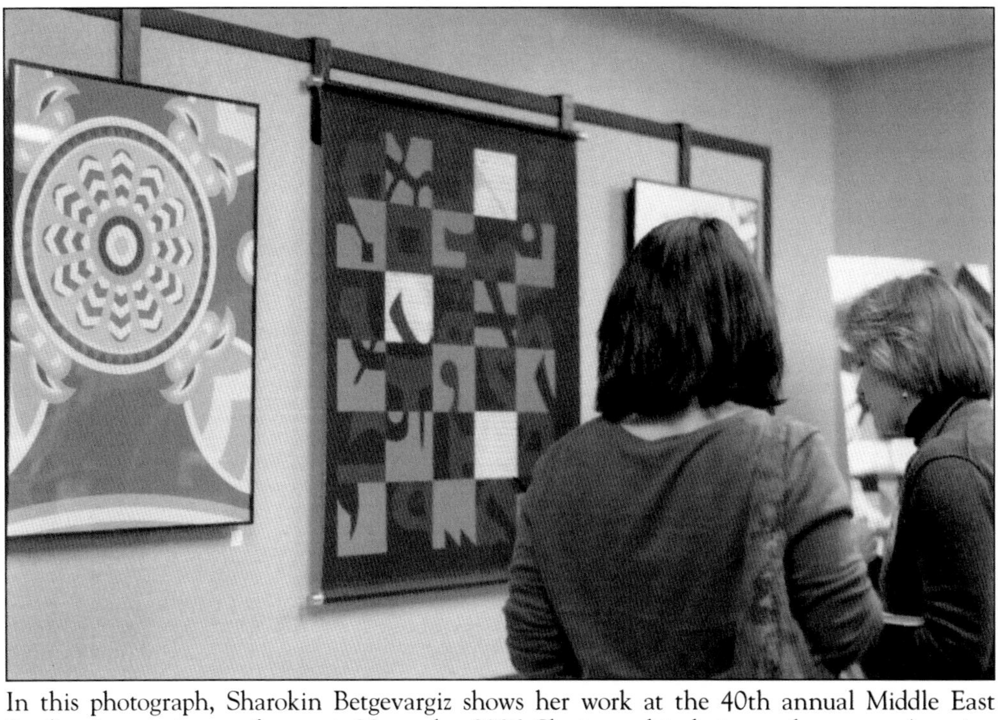

In this photograph, Sharokin Betgevargiz shows her work at the 40th annual Middle East Studies Association conference in November 2006. She is graphic designer who merges Assyrian lettering with politically themed posters that focus on Assyrians.

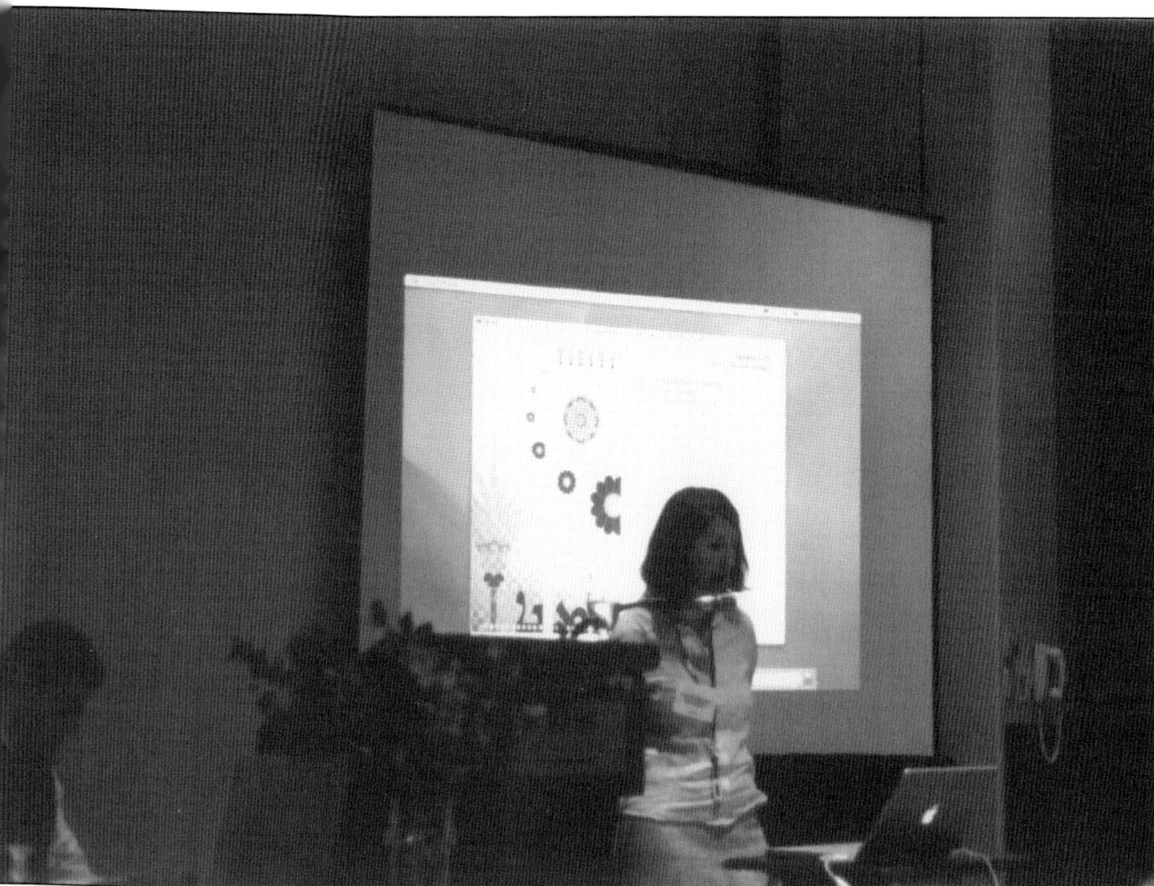

Sharokin Betgevargiz spoke at the 40th annual Middle East Studies Association conference. Here she is shown giving a lecture on "Form Follows Function: A Design of an Assyrian Identity."

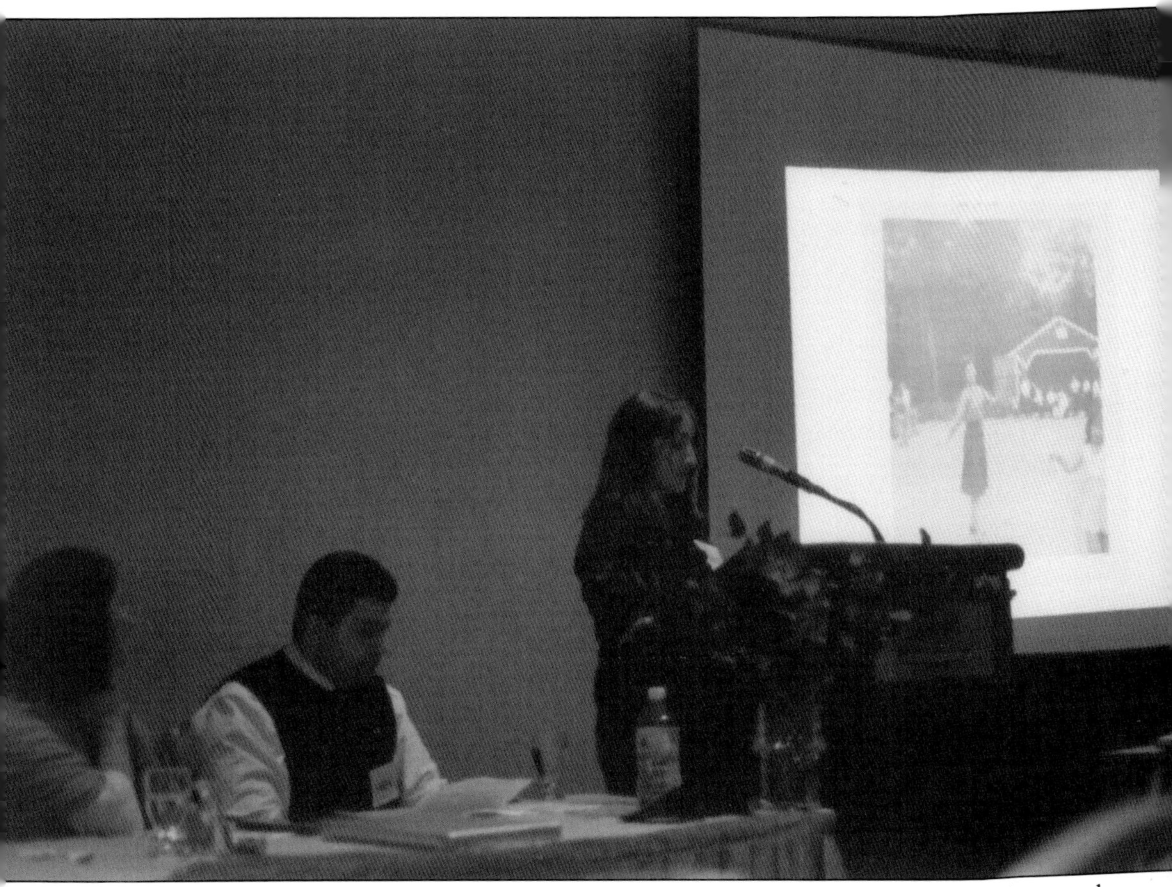

Here, author Maegan BetGivargis-McDaniel is shown giving a presentation at the 40th annual Middle East Studies Association conference in November 2006. The presentation is on the "Establishment of Religious and Cultural Associations in Connecticut."

INDEX